EJB™ Design Patterns

Advanced Patterns, Processes, and Idioms

Floyd Marinescu

Wiley Computer Publishing

John Wiley & Sons, Inc.

NEW YORK • CHICHESTER • WEINHEIM • BRISBANE • SINGAPORE • TORONTO

Publisher: Robert Ipsen
Editor: Robert Elliott
Developmental Editor: Emilie Herman
Managing Editor: John Atkins
Text Design & Composition: John Wiley Composition Services

ISBN: 0-471-20831-0

Printed in the United States of America.

10 9 8 7 6 5 4 3

Advance Praise for
EJB Design Patterns

"Floyd Marinescu has done a great job of documenting and organizing a cornucopia of EJB design strategies into one concise and balanced book. What I like best is that the book takes a very non-pretentious, pragmatic approach to presenting EJB design patterns in an easy-to-understand format. I recommend this book to all EJB developers."

Richard Monson-Haefel
Author of *Enterprise JavaBeans, 3rd Edition* (O'Reilly 2001)

"This book is a vital resource for anyone building EJB systems. Floyd Marinescu describes fundamental techniques proven through hard-earned experience in a manner that is straightforward and easy to understand. You can either read this book or spend a couple of years and maybe figure it out for yourself—it's your choice."

Scott W. Ambler
President, Ronin International
Co-author of *Mastering EJB, Second Edition,*
and author of *Agile Modeling*

"*EJB Design Patterns* is an excellent book for junior and senior EJB developers alike. EJB newbies will find a plethora of best practices in this book that are positioned for use in real design scenarios. Seasoned EJB developers are sure to discover a number of tips and tricks to make their own designs even more efficient. The content applies for all versions of the EJB specification and is a must-have for all EJB developers."

Tyler Jewell
Director, Technical Evangelism

"I have participated in numerous postings and discussions since the release of the first draft of the EJB specification, and I'm thrilled that someone has finally written a book dedicated to EJB patterns. It covers both basic and more complex patterns, and guides you in setting up and deploying projects that use Enterprise JavaBeans. This book answers much-asked questions on how to use and access Enterprise JavaBeans correctly and how to transfer data between the components in your system. An excellent and well-thought-through book."

Kjetil H. Paulsen
Senior Software Architect, Mogul Technology

"Enterprise JavaBeans developers have been long challenged by the degree of freedom that one has when building a distributed business system. *EJB Design Patterns* provides us with the first and only resource of its kind: a comprehensive discussion of the kinds of tradeoffs, variations, and problems that a real-world EJB project has to deal with. It represents years of in-the-trenches expertise, and will be the first book I recommend to improve the productivity of any EJB project."

Stuart Charlton
Senior Architect and Trainer,
Infusion Development Corporation

This book is dedicated to my little sister Jacqueline Marinescu.
Let this book stand as proof that you can achieve anything in life
if you put your heart and mind into it.

Contents

Foreword

Most well-architected EJB projects make use of *design patterns*. Whether or not a developer is actually aware that he's using design patterns is another story. Oftentimes developers conceive of *best practices* during their projects, and aren't aware that these best practices are actually design patterns—reusable approaches to programming—that are beneficial to other developers on their projects as well.

That is the beauty of the EJB design patterns presented in this book—they are practical, real-world patterns extracted from *actual* EJB projects. Members of the J2EE community were encouraged to share their patterns on TheServer-Side.com, a Web site where J2EE developers learn from each other. We've all worked together as a community to flesh out those patterns and bring them to you.

Floyd Marinescu, the world's leading expert in EJB design patterns, led this EJB design patterns project initiative. Floyd and I have been working together for the past several years building The Middleware Company, a training and consulting company that helps developers master Enterprise Java. At The Middleware Company, we've been consulting on real-world projects to enhance the quality of the design patterns. We've also been teaching training courses on EJB design patterns to developers like you, and the feedback from those courses have improved the quality of this book tremendously.

In this book, Floyd will show you a multitude of EJB design patterns that you can harness to enhance your EJB projects *today*. By applying these design patterns with proper judgment, you can improve the quality of your architecture, make your code more reusable and elegant, and architect your systems to be easily understood by developers who are familiar with these patterns.

The best news about this book is that it's very approachable. Floyd has chosen to use an easy-to-understand style of writing patterns, called the Alexandrian form. This makes it easy for anyone who knows how to program with EJB to read and learn from this book. (And if you don't know EJB yet, you may want to read my book, *Mastering Enterprise JavaBeans, Second Edition*, which is available in bookstores and as a complimentary download on TheServerSide.com.) Another choice is for you to take a training course in EJB, such as one of those we offer at The Middleware Company.

When you're ready to read on, you're in for a treat. Floyd has devoted an entire year of his life to tackling the toughest EJB design patterns concepts, and the results benefit the entire EJB community. I'm honored to have worked with Floyd on this project, and I've learned a lot myself along the way. I'm sure you will as well.

Ed Roman
CEO, The Middleware Company
Author, *Mastering Enterprise JavaBeans, Second Edition*

Introduction

It's all about quality of life. Whether you're a developer, architect, or project manager, at the end of the day we all want to feel good about building and deploying well-designed applications, without making costly mistakes, working long hours, and going through months of stress. At the end of the day, we are all human, we all want to see the project proceed on schedule and go home with enough free time to spend on anything we like.

Unfortunately, well-designed applications are not easy to come by when using new and still maturing technologies such as Java 2 Enterprise Edition (J2EE). In relatively new fields such as this, there is always a large deficit of information about designing good systems. Developers are either reinventing the wheel or simply making costly design mistakes on projects every day. With no clear set of best practices to follow, the job of the EJB developer is very difficult. Learning good design is particularly difficult for newcomers to the technology, many of whom have never built distributed systems before and don't understand the fundamental needs that influence distributed systems design.

What makes things worse is that changes in the EJB specification from version to version tend to bring about significant changes to the way that good EJB systems should be designed. Particularly with the introduction of EJB 2.0, many years worth of best practices discussed in even the most recently published books on EJB simply no longer apply or do not have the same purpose, and using such best practices can result in poorly designed systems.

It is with the concern for spreading good design ideas and improving the quality of applications that developers design, and as a result the overall quality of life of the developers themselves, that this book (and The Middleware Company's *EJB for Architects* course—where the patterns in this book are taught) was written. The end result is that we hope to help you learn the top design strategies used in the industry today so that you will be able to quickly design efficient, scalable, and maintainable systems.

The mechanism by which we hope to impart design knowledge to you is the *pattern*.

What Is a Pattern?

I like to think of a pattern as a *best practice solution to a common recurring problem*. That is, a pattern documents and explains an important or challenging problem that can occur when designing or implementing an application, and then discusses a best practice solution to that problem. Over time, patterns begin to embody the collective knowledge and experiences of the industry that spawned it. For example, the patterns in this book represent the collective knowledge of thousands of EJB developers from TheServerSide and in and around the industry, all of whom contributed via ideas or reviews the material in this book.

Benefits of Patterns

Of course there are many uses of patterns, but the following are some of the most important benefits that can help drive the maturity of a new software platform such as J2EE:

Helps provide a high-level language for discussing design issues. EJB developers can use the pattern names in this book to discuss implementation details together efficiently. Imagine how much quicker it is to say that an application was built using the stateless Session Façade pattern than trying to explain all the semantics of how the session beans wrapped entity beans.

Provides much of the design work upfront. A well-written pattern discusses in detail the problem and issues that need to be solved and shows how the problem solves it, with a good discussion of the pros, cons, and other issues to be aware of. By reading a pattern, many challenging and potentially hidden issues can be discussed and considered upfront.

Combinations of patterns lend themselves to reusable architectures. Patterns tend to reference and built upon each other. This connection between patterns serves to create what is called a *pattern language*: a series of interconnected patterns that, as a whole, often suggest an overall architecture for an application. Thus, when reading this book, certain sets of patterns in combination will form a reusable architecture that can be applied across projects again and again.

In this book in particular, we take a very low level, EJB-specific patterns focus. That is, rather than document general abstract patterns that could potentially be applied across technologies, we focus on how to get things done with EJB, discussing EJB-specific problems, and EJB-specific intricacies of implementation. Thus, in this book we part from many other patterns books in often showing exact implementations of a pattern (where the pattern is not-project specific). The goal is to provide you, the EJB developer/architect with all the information you need to readily begin using these patterns in your EJB/J2EE-based applications.

Origins of Patterns

For many people, patterns were first introduced to them via the landmark book, *Design Patterns: Elements of Reusable Object-Oriented Software* (Gamma, et al., 1994). Not the first work on software patterns, this book had the positive effect of bringing the concept and use of patterns for software development into the mainstream.

The actual origin of patterns begins long before *Design Patterns* was published in 1994. Patterns were first described by Christopher Alexander, applied to the construction/architecture of towns and buildings in the 1970s. In *A Pattern Language* (1977), Alexander writes: "Each pattern describes a problem which occurs over and over again in our environment, and then describes the core of the solution to that problem, in such a way that you can use this solution a million times over, without ever doing it the same way twice."

Patterns are a great way of organizing knowledge and solutions in any domain of life, not just civil engineering and software design. What makes patterns well suited for cataloging knowledge is their structure and hands-on nature. Good patterns show ways to solve problems and are structured in a *style* that lends itself well to explaining the aspects of the problem and solution at work.

Pattern Style Used in This Book

The patterns in this book are described with a style very similar to the original style used by Alexander, called *Alexandrian form*. The form I use consists of a pattern written up in a prose-like form, separated by a problem and solution statement as follows:

Context: One or two sentences to describe the *context* in which the pattern applies.

Problem: **A question that illustrates the problem this pattern is solving.**

* * *

Forces: A set of paragraphs explaining the context and problem in greater detail, explaining many of the forces at work that requires a solution. Here the reader will fully understand the need for this pattern.

Solution: **One or two sentences that introduce the pattern as the solution to the problems described above.**

Solution Description: Paragraphs describing the solution, including pros, cons, high-level and low-level explanation of the pattern, and implementation issues in EJB.

Related Patterns

The related patterns may cross-reference other patterns in the book, or else point you toward the same or similar patterns in other sources, which are detailed in the "References" section of this book.

What sets Alexandrian form and the style used in this book apart from most other popular software patterns books is the use of prose over point form for structuring the pattern data. One of the goals of this book is to enable both experienced architects and newcomers to read a pattern and understand it fully. The way that I tried to realize this is by writing a pattern in a fluid, prose format, in which the reader is led through the problem and the solution, with all the necessary points explained step by step, with language as simple as possible. The emphasis is on learning the pattern in a simple and pleasant fashion.

With non-Alexandrian styles, the patterns are broken up into separate sections, using point form descriptions within each section. My own opinion of these styles is that they tend to focus on packing as much info into each point as possible, making it difficult to casually read and learn, as the information tends to be categorized in a manner more suitable for *reference* purposes than for end-to-end reading. Such patterns books are great for reference purposes, but the goal of this book is to teach patterns to the experienced architect as well as inexperienced developer, and so a format that lends itself to learning was chosen, and Alexandrian form seemed best suited for that purpose.

How This Book Is Organized

This book is organized into two parts and a code appendix. Part One, "EJB Pattern Language," is the EJB patterns catalog, detailing 20 patterns. Part Two, "Best Practices for EJB Design and Implementation," provides support chapters that teach best practices in other topics, such as applying the patterns and actually implementing EJB-based systems. The appendix contains larger source code examples from the patterns in Part One; this code is also downloadable from this book's Web site. The goal is to give the reader not just a catalog of patterns, but to give the reader the tools needed to take knowledge of these patterns and *get work done*. Also included in Part Two is a chapter on Alternatives to Entity Beans, which gives an EJB developer's perspective on using Java Data Objects (JDO) to persist an object model, and a chapter on more fine-grained design tips and strategies that were too small to qualify as full patterns.

I would recommend that you read through the patterns in Part One before proceeding to Part Two. If you are more of a hands-on type, you can start reading through the first few chapters of Part Two and refer to the patterns in Part One when they are mentioned.

Who Should Read This Book?

In order for this book to get into difficult and technically in-depth discussions on advanced EJB topics, it was assumed that the reader would have a good understanding of the fundamentals of EJB before reading this book. In particular, I recommend reading Ed Roman's *Mastering Enterprise JavaBeans, Second Edition* (Wiley 2001), which is a great book for learning both the fundamentals and advanced applications of EJB. *EJB Design Patterns* was originally meant to be a chapter in Ed Roman's book, but as the chapter kept growing in size, we decided to promote it into its own book. Another excellent way to gain the background for this book is to take the Mastering EJB class offered by The Middleware Company, or you can learn all the patterns in this book hands-on in The Middleware Company's EJB for Architects course.

Although the book requires an understanding of EJB, it is not only for experienced architects. The tone of the book and the language used in the patterns is intended to be accessible to entry-level developers as well as architects. In particular, the following three mantras were used in this book's development:

1. Someone who has just read Ed Roman's *Mastering EJB* or another EJB book should be able to read through and grasp the concepts without too much difficulty.

2. The content is hardcore and technical enough to make the book a fascinating read even for experts.

3. Each part of the book should answer more questions than it raises.

These three rules were taken to heart in writing this book. Rule 3 is designed to keep us providing the necessary background required to explain a difficult topic, but not so much that there would be duplication with an introductory text on EJB (Rule 1). Rule 2 kept our focus on discussing the most useful and important topics not usually covered in other books of this nature.

What's on the Web Site?

The book's companion Web site, www.theserverside.com/patterns/ejbpatterns, contains the book's running/compiling source code examples, as well as a readers' discussion forum. This Web site will also hopefully be continuously evolving, with more patterns added to it over time from the community.

Summary

This book is a patterns book unlike any other patterns book. Not only will you learn valuable and fundamental patterns that will help you improve the quality of the EJB-based applications you write, but you will also learn how to take the knowledge of these patterns and apply them in a use-case driven manner. You'll also learn many best practices for actually implementing an application once it's designed.

If this book contributes to your career and the quality of the projects you work on, then I will feel happy that it helped. If the book benefits your overall quality of life by streamlining your projects, then its mission will have been accomplished tenfold!

Acknowledgments

I would like to thank Ed Roman and Agnieszka Zdaniuk, for without their confidence and belief in me, this book would not have been possible.

I would like to thank Florin and Carmen Marinescu, for having taught me *what matters* from an early age.

Special thanks to Aravind Krishnaswamy and Mark Turnbull, for allowing me to make more time for the book by helping me deal with some of my other responsibilities in life.

Text Contributors

I would like to thank Randy Stafford for his contribution of Chapter 7 on development process, and Craig Russell for his contribution of material on JDO in the alternatives to entity beans chapter.

Code/Pattern Idea Contributors

Richard Monson-Haefel for the notion of using Rowsets for Data Transfer.

Jonathan Weedon of Borland, for his contribution of a source code example upon which the Sequence Blocks pattern is based.

Doug Bateman for the initial suggestion of using Stored Procedures for Auto-Generated Keys.

Steve Woodcock for the idea and code contribution of the UUID for EJB pattern.

Stuart Charlton for the Generic Attribute Access idea.

Patterns Guidance

I would like to thank Markus Voelter, Ralph Johnson, and especially Bobby Woolf, without whose early suggestions on patterns style this book would have been pretty confusing.

Reviewers

EJB Design Patterns could never have been completed without the reviews, suggestions, corrections, and even questions of all the members of TheServer-Side.com J2EE Community who reviewed my work over a period of eight months:

Alex Tyurin, Alex Wologodzew, Allan Schweitz, Alun R. Butler, Andre Cesta, Andre Winssen, Andreas Krüger, Andy Stevens, Andy Turner, Ankur Kumar, Anthony Catalfano, Anuj Vohra, Anup Kumar Maliyackel, Aparna Walawalkar, Ashim Chakraborty, Babur Begg, Ben Beazley, Bill Ennis, Billy Newport, Blasius Lofi Dewanto, Bob Lee, Boris Melamed, Botnen Trygve, Brian Benton, Brian Dobby, Brian Walsh, Brian Weith, Carmine Scotto d'Antuono, Cecile Saint-Martin, Chad Vawter, Chandra Mora, Charles N. May, Colin He, Constantin Gonciulea, Cristina Belderrain, Curt Smith, Dan Bereczki, Dan Zainea, Daniel F. Burke, Daniel Massey, Darrow Kirkpatrick, Dave Churchville, David E. Jones, David Ezzio, David Ziegler, Dimitri Rakitine, Dimitrios Varsos, Dion Almaer, Doal Miller, Don Schaefer, Donnie Hale, Eduard Skhisov, Emmanuel Valentin, Engström Anders, Erez Nahir, Faisal , aveed, Fernando Bellas Permuy, FM Spruzen Simon, Forslöf Mats, Frank Robbins, Frank Sampson, Frank Stefan, Fried Hoeben, Gabriela Chiribau, Ganesh Ramani, Geert Mergan, Gene McKenna, Geoff Soutter, Gjino Bledar, Gunnar Eikman, Hai Hoang, Heng Ngee Mok, Hildebrando Arguello, Hossein S. Attar, Howard Katz, Huu-An Nguyen, Iain McCorquodale, J.D. Bertron, James Hicks, James Kelly, Janne Nykanen, Jean Safar, Jean-Pierre Belanger, Jeff Anderson, Jérôme Beau, Jesper Andersen, John Ipe, Jonathan Asbell, Jörg Winter, Joseph Sheinis, Juan-Francisco Borras-Correa, Julian Chee, Junaid Bhatra, Justin Leavesley, Justin Walsh, Ken Hoying, Ken Sizer, Krishnan Subramanian, Kristin Love, Kyle Brown, Lance Hankins, Larry Yang, Laura Fang, Laurent Rieu, Leo Shuster, M Heling, Madhu Gopinathan, Mark Buchner, Mark L. Stevens, Martin Squicciarini, Matt Mikulics, Mattias Fagerström, Mohan Radhakrishnan, Mohit Sehgal, Muhammad Farhat Kaleem, Muller Laszlo, Murray Knox, Nakamura Tadashi, Nicholas Jackson, Nick Minutello, Nick Smith, Niklas Eriksson, Oliver Kamps, Olivier Brand, Partha Nageswaran, Patrick Caulfield, Paul Wadmore, Paulo Ferreira de Moura Jr., Paulo Merson, Peter Miller, Pontus Hellgren, Raffaele Spazzoli, Rais Ahmed, Rajesh Jayaprakash, Reg Whitton, Richard Dedeyan, Rick Vogel, Robert McIntosh, Robert Nicholson, Robert O'Leary, Roger Rhoades, Roman Stepanenko, Samuel Santiago, Sashi Guduri, Scot McPhee, Scott Chen, Scott Stirling, Scott W. Ambler, Sébastien Couturiaux, Sergey Oreshko, Shorn Tolley, Simon Brown, Simon Harris, Simone Milani, Stefan Piesche, Stefan Tilkov, Stephan J. Schmidt, Steve Divers, Steve Hill, Steven Sagaert, Sun-Lai Chang, Tarek Hammoud, Taylor Cowan, Terry Griffey, Thanh C. Bryan, Therese Hermansson, Thierry Janaudy, Thomas Bohn, Toby Reyelts, Tom Wood, Tracy Milburn,

Trond Andersen, Tyler Jewell, Udaya Kumar, Vaheesan Selvarajah, Vincent Harcq, Yagiz Erkan, Yi Lin, and Yousef Syed.

And finally, I would like to thank other important people who indirectly contributed to this book being published, by virtue of their positive influence on my life: Nitin Bharti, Sudeep Dutt, Morrissey, Calvin Broadus, George Kecskemeti, Johnny Marr, Geoff McGuire, Andre Young, Katerina Ilievska, Chogyam Trungpa, Siddhartha Gautama, Nadia Staltieri, Dale Carnegie, Lao-Tzu, David Gahan, Bogdan and Andre Cristescu, Umar Sheikh, Robert Smith, Ursula and Suzanna Lipstajn, James McDonald, Jacob Murphy, Olivia Horvath, Peter Coad, Mohandas K. Gandhi, Adib Saikali, Giacomo Casanova, Sasa Nikolic, Deanna Ciampa, Aravind Krishnaswamy, Mikola Michon, Mark Turnull, Laura Ilisie, Gregory Peres, Stuart Charlton, and Carlos Martinez.

About the Author

Floyd Marinescu is one of the world's leading experts on EJB design patterns. He architected, built, and runs TheServerSide.com, the world's leading J2EE community Web site. Floyd has written numerous EJB design patterns and worked heavily with the community to foster EJB best practices. He has written countless articles and is a frequent speaker at major Java conferences. Floyd also works for The Middleware Company (www.middleware-company.com), a training and consulting company specializing in EJB and J2EE. He can be reached at floyd@middleware-company.com.

About the Contributors

Randy Stafford is an accomplished professional in many aspects of software development, with 15 years of Information Technology experience across industries such as financial services, DBMS software, hospitality, telecommunications, transportation, CASE, and aerospace and defense. He has had broad exposure as a consultant or permanent employee of large public companies such as Travelers Express, Oracle, AMS, and Martin Marietta; and of small private companies such as GemStone, SynXis, and Ascent Logic Corporation. As a Smalltalk developer, he has been immersed in object-oriented and distributed-object system development since 1988, and has been involved in Web development and e-commerce projects since 1995.

Currently Chief Architect at IQNavigator, Inc., Mr. Stafford has developed eight production-distributed Java applications since 1997, using various J2EE application servers and Java ORBs. He was the originator and architect of FoodSmart, the example J2EE application from GemStone Systems, Inc. He was also the author of GemStone's pattern language on designing J2EE applications, and of the GemStone Professional Services Foundation Classes, a framework for J2EE application development. He has used Ant to build automation on his last five J2EE applications, dating back to its initial release in the summer of 2000. He has used JUnit since its initial release in early 1998, and its predecessor, SmalltalkUnit, since 1995.

Mr. Stafford is an alumnus of Colorado State University with a Bachelor of Science degree in Applied Mathematics, and graduate coursework in Computer Science. He is published in the object-oriented simulation and systems-engineering literatures.

Craig Russell is Product Architect at Sun Microsystems, where he is responsible for the architecture of Transparent Persistence, an object-to-relational mapping engine. During the past 30 years, he has worked on architecture, design, and support for enterprise-scale distributed-transactional and database systems.

Craig serves as Specification Lead on Java Data Objects, a specification for Java-centric persistence, managed as a Java Specification Request via the Java Community Process.

EJB Pattern Language

EJB Layer Architectural Patterns

When first designing Enterprise JavaBean (EJB) systems, choosing a correct architecture, or partitioning of logic, that satisfies project concerns, such as performance, maintainability, and portability, is one of most difficult tasks faced by developers. This chapter covers some fundamental architectural patterns in use in the industry today, specifically:

Session Façade. The most widely used of all EJB design patterns, the Session Façade shows how to properly partition the business logic in your system to help minimize dependencies between client and server, while forcing use cases to execute in one network call and in one transaction.

Message Façade. The Message Façade pattern discusses when and how to partition logic for use cases that are asynchronous in nature.

EJB Command. The antithesis of the Session Façade pattern, the EJB Command Pattern advocates placing business logic in lightweight, plain Java Command beans. The main benefits of the pattern are the complete decoupling of the client from EJB itself and the execution of use cases in one network call and transaction.

Data Transfer Object Factory. Debunks the old practice of placing DTO creation/consumption logic on the entity bean itself and prescribes centralizing data transfer object creation and consumption logic into a single layer (implemented as session beans or plain java factories).

Generic Attribute Access. This pattern discusses when and how to provide a domain-generic interface to the attributes of an entity bean for maintainability and performance purposes.

Business Interface. This pattern shows how to implement an interface implementation scheme that can provide compile-time checking of the method signatures on the Remote/Local interfaces and the EJB bean class.

Session Façade

An EJB client needs to execute business logic in order to complete a use case.

How can an EJB client execute a use case's business logic in one transaction and one bulk network call?

✳ ✳ ✳

To execute the business logic of a typical use case, multiple server-side objects (such as session or entity beans) usually need to be accessed and possibly modified. The problem is that multiple fine-grained invocations of session/entity beans add the overhead of multiple network calls (and possibly multiple transactions), as well as contributing to less maintainable code, since data access and workflow/business logic is scattered across clients.

Consider an online banking scenario where a servlet receives a request to transfer funds from one account to another, on behalf of a Web client. In this scenario (as depicted in Figure 1.1), a servlet must check to ensure that the user is authorized, withdraw funds from one bank account entity bean, and deposit them to the other bank account entity bean.

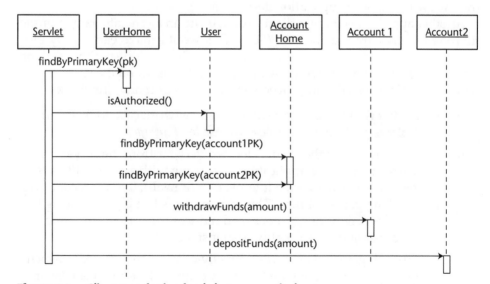

Figure 1.1   Client transferring funds between entity beans.

When executing methods on the entity beans home and remote interface, this approach will not scale under serious loads, because the whole scenario requires at least six network calls: three for finding the appropriate entity beans, and three more for actually transferring the funds. Furthermore, since entity beans are transactional creatures, each method call on an entity will require a separate transaction on the server side, requiring synchronization of the remote entity with its underlying data store and maintenance on behalf of the application server.

What's worse is that this approach won't guarantee the safety of the client's money. If something goes wrong with the deposit, the client's money will have already been withdrawn, and his money will be lost. The user authorization check, the withdrawal, and the deposit all run completely separately, and if the deposit fails, the withdrawal will not be rolled back, resulting in an inconsistent state. The problem here is that when calling an entity bean's methods directly, each method call is a separate unit of work, and a separate transaction.

One solution is to push extra logic into our entity beans to perform many operations on behalf of a single client call. This solution introduces maintenance problems, because our entity bean layer will likely be used in many different ways over time. If we add application logic to our entity beans each time we need a performance enhancement, our entity beans will quickly become very bloated and difficult to understand, maintain, and reuse. We are effectively merging our application logic (verbs) with our persistence logic (nouns), which is poor application design.

Another approach is for our client to demarcate an aggregate, large transaction via the Java Transaction API (JTA). This would make each entity bean method call operate under the same transaction, in an all-or-nothing fashion. If the deposit fails, then the withdrawal will be rolled back and the users' money will be safe. However, this improved solution also has many drawbacks:

- **High network overhead.** We still have six network calls to deal with, which slows performance (unless we use *local interfaces*).

- **Poor concurrency.** If the client is located very far from the server (as in the case of an applet or application interacting with a remote EJB system, perhaps even across the Internet or a firewall), the transaction will last for a long period of time. This causes excess locking, increasing the chances of collisions or deadlock, and reduces concurrency of other clients accessing the same entity bean instances.

- **High coupling.** Our client writes directly to an entity bean API, which tightly couples the client with the entity bean. If the entity bean layer needs changing in the future, then we must also change the client.

- **Poor reusability.** The business logic that executed the "transfer funds" use case was embedded directly in the client. It therefore effectively becomes trapped in that client. Other types of clients (Java applications, applets, servlets, and so on) cannot reuse this business logic. This mixing of presentation logic with business logic is a poor application design for any serious deployment.

- **Poor maintainability.** Usage of the Java Transaction API causes middleware logic for performing transactions to be interlaced with application logic. It is much cleaner to separate the two via declarative transactions, so that we can tweak and tune our middleware without affecting our business rules.

- **Poor separation of development roles.** A common practice on large-scale projects is to separate the development tasks of presentation logic programmers (such as servlet/jsp developers) from the business logic/middleware programmers (EJB developers). If business logic is coded in the client/presentation layer, a clear separation of roles is not possible. Business logic and presentation logic programmers will step on each other's toes if both program in the presentation layer.

The takeaway point from our discussion is that we need a server-side abstraction that serves as an intermediary and buffers calls to entity beans. Session beans are designed just for this.

Therefore:

> **Wrap the entity bean layer in a layer of session beans called the Session Façade. Clients should have access only to session beans not to entity beans.**

The Session Façade pattern applies the benefits of the traditional Façade pattern to EJB by completely hiding the object model on the server from the client layer, by having a layer of session beans be the single point of access to the client. Figure 1.2 illustrates how an architecture can be improved by taking this approach. The Session Façade pattern further adds the benefits of enforcing the execution of a use case in one network call and providing a clean layer in which to encapsulate business and workflow logic used to fulfill use cases. The Session Façade is usually implemented as a layer of stateless session beans (although the pattern can also be implemented with stateful session beans).

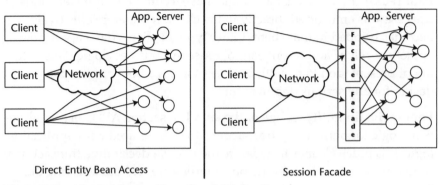

Figure 1.2   The Architectural benefits of Session Façade.

To illustrate how this paradigm works and the benefits of this paradigm, let's take our previous example. Our business logic for the transferring funds use case will now be placed in a session bean, which has a method called *transferFunds(userpk, accountpk, accountpk, amount)*. The Bank Teller session bean thus performs bulk operations on Users and Bank Accounts, as shown in Figure 1.3.

Since the BankTeller session bean is collocated with the User and Account entity beans, it should be hard-coded to communicate with the entity beans through their local interfaces, thus reducing the network overhead required to execute this use case to just one call (the call to the BankTeller from the client). Also, all updates to the entity bean layer should run within the transaction initiated by the BankTeller, defined in its deployment descriptor, almost always, with a setting of TX_REQUIRED. This effectively wraps the entire use case within one transaction, ensuring that all updates to the entity beans run within the transaction initiated upon execution of the *transferFunds* method on the Bank Teller.

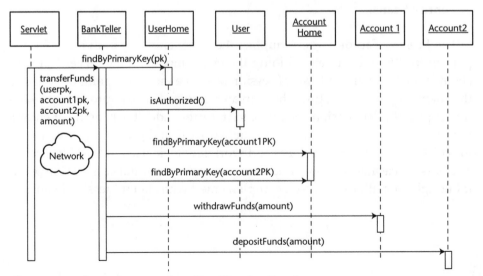

Figure 1.3   The Performance benefits of Session Façade.

The Session Façade pattern is the most fundamental EJB pattern in use today (which is why it is the very first pattern in this book). It not only provides performance benefits, but it also suggests a standard architecture for EJB systems-partitioning your J2EE applications in such a way that the boundary between the client and sever is separated by a layer of session beans, whose methods map to (and contain the business logic of) all the use cases in the application.

Taking the Bank Teller example further, there are obviously more use cases involving a bank application than simply transferring funds. Using the Session Façade pattern, session beans would be created to group use cases with similar functions into one bean. Thus we can add other ancillary banking operations to the Bank Teller (such as *withdrawFunds, depositFunds, getBalance()*). Elsewhere in the banking application, use cases for different purposes would also be grouped into a session bean. For example, every bank has a Loans Department. The use cases required to model the operations of a Loans Department are not that related to the use cases on a Bank Teller; therefore, they would be grouped into a *LoanServices* session bean. Similarly, a banking application would also need a session bean to encapsulate use cases related to investments. Using the Session Façade pattern, the architectural layout of this banking application would look like Figure 1.4.

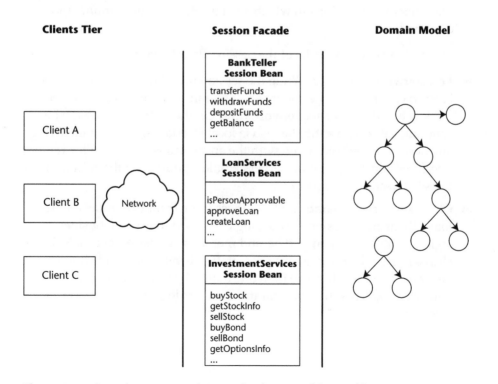

Figure 1.4 Grouping use cases into session beans architectural layout.

The Session Façade pattern works so well, that often it is easy to abuse it. It is common to find projects in which the Session Façade is misused:

- **Creating a session bean God-class.** Often developers put all the use cases in a system in one session bean. This results in a bloated session bean and reduced development productivity, because all the developers need access to this one class. Session beans should be split to house groupings of related use cases.

- **Placing domain logic in session beans.** A well-designed object-oriented domain model should contain all of the business/use case logic in your application (Fowler, 2001). Most Session Façade methods should simply delegate to the appropriate entity bean, *unless* the use case involves workflow logic that needs to operate across different beans that may not be directly related.

- **Duplication of business logic across the façade.** As the project grows, often session bean methods contain duplicate code, such as executing logic to *checkCreditHistory*, which could be part of the workflow for any number of use cases. The solution is to add a layer of services (implemented as session beans or plain Java classes) that encapsulate this reusable, use-case-independent business logic. This services layer is hidden from the client. As projects grow in size, it is useful to have regular refactoring sessions in which such duplicate logic is found and extracted.

The following are the benefits of the Session Façade pattern:

- **Low network overhead.** While the session bean layer does add an extra layer to call through, the client can now transfer funds in just one network call, rather than six network calls. On the server, the session bean communicates with entity beans via local interfaces, thus not incurring any network overhead. Even with the entity beans only used for remote interfaces, most application servers would optimize on the communications between collocated EJBs.

- **Clean and strict separation of business logic from presentation layer logic.** By using a Session Façade, logic required to execute business logic is completely wrapped behind methods on session beans. EJB clients need only worry about presentation layer issues and should never have to execute more than one method on an EJB to get a unit of work done. This strictly separates business logic from presentation layer logic.

- **Transactional Integrity.** Our session bean encapsulates all logic to perform the bank transfer in one transaction. The session bean thus acts as a transactional façade, which localizes transactions to the server side, and keeps them short. Transactions are also demarcated at the session bean method level, configurable via deployment descriptors.

- **Low coupling.** The session bean buffers requests between the client and entity beans. If the entity bean layer needs changing in the future, we may be able to avoid changing the client because of the session bean layer of indirection.

- **Good reusability.** Our bank teller logic is encapsulated into a modular session bean, which can be accessed by any type of client (JSPs, servlets, applications, or applets). The encapsulation of application logic into session beans means that our entity beans can contain data and data access logic only, making them reusable across session beans in the same or even in different applications.

- **Good maintainability.** One should define the transaction declaratively in the Bank Teller session bean's deployment descriptor, rather than programmatically via the JTA. This gives us a clean separation of middleware and application logic, which increases maintainability and reduces the likelihood of errors.

- **A clean verb-noun separation.** The session bean layer models the application specific use cases, the verbs in our application, while the entity bean layer models the business objects, or the "nouns," in our application. This architecture makes it very easy to map use cases from a requirements document to a real EJB architecture.

The Session Façade pattern is a staple in EJB development. It enforces highly efficient and reusable design, as well as clearly separates presentation logic (the client), business logic (the session façade) and data logic (entity beans, and so on). Session Façade describes a useful architecture for implementing any type of use case; however, if a use case is asynchronous in nature, the Message Façade pattern provides a more scalable approach.

Related Patterns

Message Façade
Data Transfer Object
Session Façade (Alur, et al., 2001)
Session Façade (MartinFowler.com)

Message Façade

An enterprise Java bean client wants to invoke the methods of multiple EJBs within the context of one use case, and doesn't require an immediate response from the server.

> **How can an EJB client invoke the methods of multiple session or entity beans within one transaction, without the need to block and wait for responses from each bean?**

* * *

Especially in large-scale systems, scalability dictates that the business logic of a use case execute separately from that of the client, without requiring the client to wait for the execution to complete. This type of behavior, called asynchronous behavior, allows clients to interact with the User Interface (UI) with maximum response times, because they don't need to sit and wait while the use case they initiated executes. This approach allows a large system to scale, because use cases can be queued and operated on in a batch, transparent to the user, who instantly moves on to the next part of a UI. Portions of the system that actually execute the use cases can also be scaled up and go through system upgrades if backlogs of queued use cases begin to develop, all without changing the quality or availability of service for the clients.

Consider a simple Web-based airline registration system in which a servlet receives a request to reserve a seat for a user for a particular flight. In this scenario, a servlet must register a user with an airline, determine if seats are available on a flight, and if so, reserve a seat for a user, as shown in Figure 1.5.

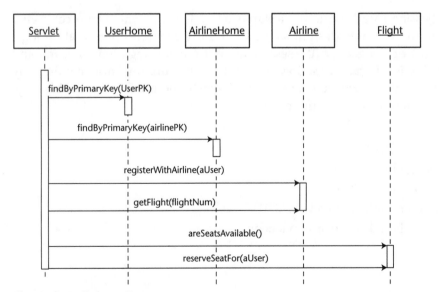

Figure 1.5 Reserve Seat use case.

In this example, we have a client performing multiple synchronous calls to the server to execute a use case. Each step of the process requires a separate network call and blocking on the part of the client. On a system as massive as an airline reservation application, this bottleneck is obviously unacceptable. Furthermore, executing the logic in this fashion reduces the maintainability and reusability of the system and does not provide transaction consistency or isolation for the use case.

The most common solution is to use the Session Façade pattern. With this pattern, an application creates a layer of session beans that contain business logic to fulfill business use cases. Each session bean performs bulk operations on entity beans or other server-side resources on behalf of the clients, in one bulk call, as shown in Figure 1.3 in the *Session Façade* pattern. Unfortunately, even if the entire use case is wrapped in one Session Façade method, the approach still suffers from several drawbacks:

- **Unacceptable Response Time.** A user interacting with a Web site will not stick around for longer than a couple of seconds. The execution of this use case requires a lot of background processing that could span multiple databases on different airline systems. Because the call to the EJB layer is a "synchronous" call, the client would have to block until the entire process has been completed.

- **Unreliable/not fault tolerant.** This use case could potentially involve EJBs that are spread out on as many as three separate EJB Server instances and three separate databases (one for users, one for airlines, one for flights). If any one of those servers were down, the entire process would fail, and the user's reservation request would be lost. Even if the servlet layer were communicating with only one EJB server, the process would fail if the server were down.

Using Session Façade solves the problems of coupling, performance, maintainability, reusability, and consistency, but does not completely solve the problems of response time and reliability. The client still has to block while a complex and time-consuming reservation use case runs. The use case will also fail if the EJB server or any of the systems it relies on is not running at the time the use case is executed.

The takeaway point from our discussion is that we need a fault-tolerant server-side abstraction that serves as an intermediary, executing use cases in one call and one transaction (sheltering clients from the complexities of the server-side object model), which doesn't require a client to block and wait for the use case to complete. Message-driven beans are designed just for this.

Therefore:

> **Use message-driven beans to create a fault-tolerant, asynchronous façade. Clients should have access to message-driven beans only, not to entity beans.**

Using message-driven beans (MDB) as a façade improves upon the Session Façade pattern by adding the capability to execute use cases in an asynchronous, fault-tolerant manner. When we use a message façade, the business logic in each of the use cases of an application maps to its own MDB.

Consider the previous example. Our business logic for reserving a seat on a flight will now be placed in the *onMessage()* method on a *ReserveSeat* message-driven bean. The purpose of this MDB is to encapsulate all business/workflow logic related to reserving a seat on a flight, and to execute asynchronously, as shown in Figure 1.6.

Here we have a servlet client creating a Java Message Service (JMS) message and passing in the necessary parameters. The servlet constructs a message containing all the parameters required (user's primary key, flight number, airline primary key) and sends this message to a JMS destination created for the Reserve Seat use case. Upon receiving the message at the appropriate destination, the client will be free to continue (display the next Web page). At this point, the message-driven bean container will attempt to pass the message to the next available ReserveSeat message-driven bean. If all ReserveSeat MDBs in the pool are being used at the time of message reception, the JMS server should wait until the next one becomes available. Had this use case been executed through a session façade, a fully used session bean pool would have been a single point of failure, and the client would have to manually retry.

Once a MDB becomes available, the container will execute the *onMessage()* method. At this point, the ReserveSeat message-driven bean will linearly go through the process of executing the use case: register the user with the airline, check if seats are available, and reserve a seat. While this time-consuming process is occurring, the end user is free to surf around the site and go about his or her business.

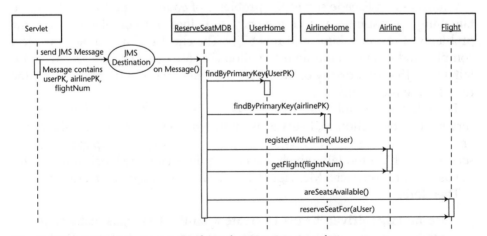

Figure 1.6   Reserve Seat use case through a Message Façade.

One important advantage that the Message Façade pattern has over the Session Façade pattern is that asychrononously executed use cases can be guaranteed. That is, if the transaction fails at any point (perhaps the airlines's systems go down or some other system failure occurs), the transaction will be rolled back and the JMS message will be put back in the queue. The transaction will then be retried later, without the knowledge of the client.

This *behind-the-scenes* behavior also presents a problem. How is the client to be notified if the use case fails or succeeds? For example, if a seat cannot be reserved because the plane is fully booked, the client needs to be notified. In a synchronous model (using a session façade), the client would know immediately. In the asynchronous model, the client is no longer waiting to see if the use case succeeded, and needs to be alerted in some application-specific form. The most common solution is email. If the use case succeeds/fails then the system will notify the user by email. Some companies might implement a system in such a way that a human being would make a phone call, and so on. If the application requirements allow it, some applications could use a polling model. That is, an end user will be assigned a particular place they can go to check the status of their request, similar to a tracking number used by modern courier services.

The takeaway point here is that when using the Message Façade pattern, developers must devise novel ways to communicate the results of a use case to the client.

One disadvantage of using the Message Façade pattern is that now business logic is distributed across both message-driven beans (for the message façade) and session beans (for the session façade). This may not be a major concern for most, but it would be nice to keep business logic in one place in the application. A clever way to solve this problem is to implement all the use cases on the session façade itself, and use the message façade to delegate to the session façade. This way, all the benefits of using an asynchronous, fault-tolerant construct such as a message-driven bean is maintained, while keeping logic localized to the session bean layer.

The advantages of the Message Façade pattern include all those outlined in the *Session Façade* pattern, as well as:

- **Instant response time/asynchronous communication.** When a client sends a JMS message, it is free to continue processing without waiting for the server to complete the use case and respond. A lengthy, complex use case can thus be initiated while control flow instantly returns to the user.

- **Eliminates single points of failure.** Using messaging will ensure that your application continues functioning even if the EJB server or some other subsystem it relies upon is down. For example, if the database is

down, the MDB's transaction will not complete, and the *reserve seat*
message will remain on the queue and be retried later. If the EJB container is down, the message will again be stored. Such fail-over capabilities would not be possible if we used a synchronous model. Of course
if your JMS server is not clustered and it goes down, this still represents
a single point of failure, but at least the number of potential show stop-
pers is reduced.

However, as a by-product of using message-driven beans, the Message
Façade pattern also has some drawbacks:

- **Message-driven beans have weakly-typed input parameters.** The role
  of a message-driven bean is to consume JMS messages, all of which
  appear identical at compile time. This is in contrast to session/entity
  beans, which leverage Java's built-in strong typing of the methods and
  parameters of the remote and local interfaces to catch common errors at
  compile time. Extra care must be taken by the developer to load a JMS
  message with the appropriate contents required by its destined MDB.
  One solution to this problem is to encapsulate all the data from the JMS
  message into a custom data transfer object, and serialize this object into
  the JMS Message.

- **Message-driven beans do not have any return values.** Since MDB
  invocations are asynchronous, Message Façade cannot be used for use
  cases that require a return value after execution. Using Message Façade
  is thus superficially similar to using Session Façade, in which all session
  bean methods simply return *void*. However, it is possible to get a
  response from a message-driven bean back to the message creator
  by using JMS as the transport mechanism, please refer to the book
  Mastering Enterprise Java Beans, Second Edition for a discussion of this
  mechanism.

- **Message-driven beans do not propagate exceptions back to clients.**
  Unlike session/entity beans, message-driven beans cannot throw application exceptions or *RemoteException* from any of their methods. MDBs
  must therefore handle all the exceptions presented in some application-
  specific format (that is, emailing the user if something went wrong,
  logging errors to an admin log, and so on).

Message Façade is a very powerful pattern for building decoupled, highly
scalable applications. A typical EJB system would likely use a combination of
the Session Façade and Message Façade patterns. Session Façade is the clear
choice for "read" type operations, where a client requires some data from the
server, or when a client needs to explicitly wait for a use case to complete. Message Façade is clear choice for update operations, where the client does not
need to instantly see the results of the update.

The scalability and fault-tolerance benefits that the Message Façade pattern has over the Session Façade pattern are significant. In terms of performance, a message-based system will scale better than a clustered session bean approach because message beans pull work rather than have work pushed to them. The pull approach scales better when we cluster boxes together because it makes optimal use of system resources.

Developers should evaluate each use case in their designs carefully, asking themselves if the use case is of a synchronous or asynchronous nature. This will be a decisive factor in choosing one pattern over the other.

Related Patterns

Session Façade

EJB Command

An EJB client needs to execute business logic in order to complete a use case.

How can a developer implement a use case's business logic in a lightweight manner, decoupling the client from EJB and executing the use case in one transaction and one network call?

* * *

A critical architectural decision when designing an EJB system is where to put the business logic. The business logic of a use case is the logic that either delegates to the appropriate method on your domain model or executes logic that operates across multiple other entity beans and/or session beans (work-flow logic).

Placing business logic on the client (servlets, applets, and so on) has serious negative consequences, affecting performance and maintainability, as explained in the *Session Façade Pattern*. These problems can be corrected by using the Session Façade pattern, which requires that business logic be placed in session bean methods, where each method on a session bean maps to a particular unit of work, or use case. In doing so, the client is shielded from the object model on the server and use cases are executed in one transaction and in one network round trip.

The Session Façade pattern itself is a staple in EJB development, but also comes with its own shortcomings. Calling the session façade directly from the client can cause dependencies between the client and the server teams on a large project and complicate client code because of tight coupling to EJB, as discussed in the *Business Delegate Pattern*. These problems can be alleviated by using business delegates, which add a layer of objects that encapsulate all access in the EJB layer. Business Delegates can help keep client code simple, minimizing dependencies between client and server.

Then Session Façade pattern in combination with the Business Delegate pattern provides a best practice for writing business logic in a format that decouples the client from the implementation details of the server and allows the execution of use cases in one network call and in one transaction. As always, there are trade-offs:

- **Slower development process.** Because use case logic (which frequently can change) runs in a session bean, whenever a use case needs to be changed (that is, to add a parameter to a method or return an extra attribute), the session bean method that implements that use case may need to be changed. The process of changing a session bean is not trivial—a change often requires editing three different files (interface, bean class, deployment descriptor) as well as redeployment into the EJB server and possible restarting of the server. Additionally, the business delegate that encapsulates the changed session bean on the client will usually also need to be changed.

- **Division of labor in a large project is more difficult.** Depending on the strategies used to partition work across developers on a project, the session façade is often a bottleneck which different teams or developers will fight over, since it can be the subject of frequent change as a project progresses.

- **Server resources often controlled by just one team in a large corporation.** For large corporations with established and working sets of deployed EJBs, it can be difficult for teams working on other projects to effect any changes on existing classes.

In short, developing with a session façade and business delegates can result in long change-deploy-test round trips, which can become a bottleneck in a large project. The crux of the problem is that the business logic is being placed in a layer of session EJBs, which can be pretty heavyweight to develop with. Therefore:

> **Use the Command pattern to wrap business logic in lightweight command beans that decouple the client from EJB, execute in one network call, and act as a façade for the EJB layer.**

A command bean is just a plain Java class with gets, sets, and an execute method, as described in the original Command pattern (Gamma, et al., 1995). Applied to EJB, the Command pattern provides a lightweight solution for achieving the same benefits as the Session Façade and Business Delegate patterns: a façade that hides the object model on the EJB layer, execution of a use case in one transaction and one network call, and complete decoupling of the client from EJB. The Command pattern achieves these by providing clients with classes that they interact with locally, but which actually execute within a remote EJB server, transparent to the client.

Commands are used to encapsulate individual units of work in an application. A use case such as *placeOrder, transferFunds,* and so on, would have its business/workflow logic encapsulated in a special command made just for that use case, as shown in Figure 1.7.

TransferFunds
withdrawAccountID
depositAccountID
transferAmount
withdrawAccountBalance
depositAccountBalance
setTransferAmount(double)
setWithdrawAccountID(int)
set DepositAccountID(int)
execute()
getWithdrawAccountBalance()
getDepositAccountBalance()

Figure 1.7   Transfer Funds Command client view.

The client interaction with a command is very simple. Once a client gets a command (either by creating one or getting it from a factory, depending upon implementation), it simply *sets* attributes onto the command, until the command contains all the data required to execute a use case. At this point the client can call the command's execute method, then simply executes *gets* on the command until it has retrieved all the data resulting from the execution of the command/use case.

When the client executes the command, interesting things happen behind the scenes. Instead of executing locally, the command is actually transferred to a remote EJB server and executed within the EJB server's JVM. All the EJBs called by the command during the execution of its use case thus occurs within the EJB server itself. When the command has completed executing, it is returned to the client, which can then call *get* methods to retrieve data. By having the command execute within the EJB server, a use case can execute within just one transaction. The implementation mechanics of this behavior will be explained later in the discussion of this pattern.

Using the transferFunds example, a client would set the IDs of the account from which to withdraw money, the account to which to deposit money, and the amount to transfer. After calling *execute* on the transferFunds command, the client can get the final balances of the accounts, as shown in Figure 1.8.

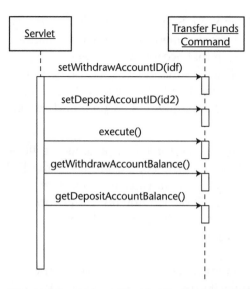

Figure 1.8   Using a Transfer Funds command.

Probably one of the most comprehensive implementations of the Command pattern is IBM's Command framework, which ships with Websphere, part of IBM's patterns for e-business. For illustration purposes, a basic command framework implementation is provided in the *EJB Command Pattern* section in the appendix, which is partially based on concepts from IBM's framework. There are many different ways to implement the EJB Command pattern, but all of them have the same three elements:

- **Command Beans.** A simple Java bean class with gets, sets, and an execute method that contains the business logic required to execute a use case. See the appendix for a code example of the Transfer Funds use case implemented as a command. The command beans are the only part of the Command pattern that need to be written by application developers, the other components explained below are reusable across projects.

- **Client-side routing logic.** Usually a framework of classes that is responsible for taking a Command and sending it to the remote EJB server. This routing logic is usually not visible to the client, and is triggered by calling a command's *execute* method. The routing logic/framework is a generic set of classes that can be reused across projects. In the appendix code example, the routing logic takes form as the CommandExecutor and EJBCommandTarget classes, which take a command and send it to the EJB server for consumption, all transparent to the client.

■ **Remote Command Server.** The Command Server is a service that simply accepts commands and executes them. Applied to EJB, the Command-Server class is a stateless session bean that accepts a command as a parameter and executes it locally. The CommandServer is also generic and completely reusable across projects. The *EJB Command Pattern* section of the appendix contains an implementation of a Command Server stateless session bean.

The interactions between the client and these three components are illustrated in Figure 1.9. In this example (based on the code example in the *EJB Command Pattern* section in the appendix), the client calls an *executeCommand* method on the routing logic component. In IBM's Command framework, the client only needs to call *execute* on the command itself, since the method call will actually be received by the superclass of the command, which is part of the routing logic framework.

Behind the scenes, the CommandExecutor delegates the call to an EJBCommandTarget (not shown in Figure 1.9 since it is part of the routing logic), which is encoded with knowledge of EJB and knows how to send the command to the CommandServer stateless session bean. Upon receiving the command, the CommandServer simply calls the execute method on the command, which then goes about its business logic.

The benefits of the Command pattern are:

■ **Facilitates Rapid Application Development (RAD) due to lightweight dev/deploy process.** Writing a use case as a command bean makes it considerably easier and quicker to deploy and test than writing it as a session bean method. Frequent changes can be done on a plain Java class, as opposed to a full EJB.

■ **Separation of business logic from presentation logic.** Commands act as a façade to the object model on the server by encapsulating business logic inside commands, exposing only a simple command interface for clients to use. This separation allows the client and server to evolve separately.

■ **Forces execution of use cases in single round trip.** Since the command actually executes in the EJB server, only one network call (and transaction) is required to complete a complicated use case.

■ **Decouples the client from EJB.** Clients are completely decoupled from the implementation details of the server—all they see is the command bean, which appears to be a local class.

■ **Commands can execute locally or produce dummy data.** Empty or bogus commands can be created at the beginning of a project, allowing the presentation layer developers to write, compile, and test their code independently of the business logic/EJB team.

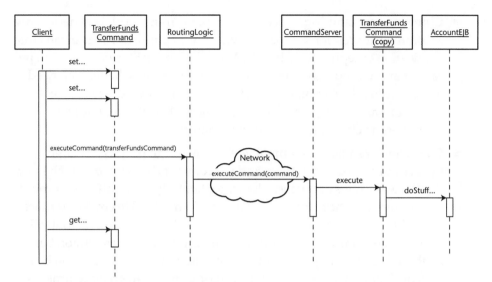

Figure 1.9 Command pattern interactions.

In many ways the Command pattern sounds like the ultimate solution, combining the benefits of the Session Façade and Business Delegate patterns, with a lighter-weight infrastructure, however the benefits are as usual, balanced by important trade-offs:

- **Very coarse-grained transaction control.** Since commands are just plain Java beans, there is no automatic way to mark a command to run under a particular transaction setting or isolation level, as you can session bean methods. Commands can only run under the transaction settings of the CommandServer that executes them. The workaround for this is to deploy multiple command server session beans with different jndi names and transaction settings (configured in the deployment descriptors). The routing logic component needs to be configured to send certain commands to certain command servers. That is, one may wish to send all read-only commands to session beans that run with without transactions, whereas update commands could execute in a command server running with tx_requires and isolation level serializable.

- **Commands are stateless.** The Command object cannot store any state in the session bean that executes it. Storing state in the EJB layer is thus not possible with the Command pattern.

- **Clumsy error handling.** Since the command framework is generic, only a CommandException can be thrown from a command. This means that application exceptions, such as *NoMoneyInAccountException*, need to be caught and wrapped within a CommandException. Clients then need to look inside the command object for particular exceptions. Since exceptions are not explicitly declared, clients lose the benefit of compile-time checking for exception handling.

- **Commands can become unmanageable on large projects.** A large project can explode with thousands of commands, many of which have duplicate portions of business logic, particularly when different project teams are using the same back-end domain model. This makes it much more difficult to maintain the business logic layer, in contrast to the Session Façade pattern, where use cases are implemented as session bean methods, nicely grouped together into a small number of Session beans. This proliferation of classes can be a serious problem on large projects.

- **CommandServer ejb-jar tightly coupled to command beans and other EJBs.** Since command beans execute within environment of the CommandServer session beans, the command bean classes need to be deployed with the CommandServer session bean (in the same ejb-jar or EAR) in order for the command beans to be deserialized and executed. This means that whenever a command bean is changed, the CommandServer session bean EAR or ejb-jar will need to be redeployed (so that the CommandServers classloader can read the new versions of all included commands) in order to test the changes, or completely restarted if your application server doesn't support hot deployment. Furthermore, command beans need to have visibility of any home, remote, local home, or local interfaces they may use in their business logic. This requires that either the CommandServer be deployed in the same EAR as the other EJBs accessed by any of its command beans, or the interfaces of the accessed EJBs be packaged with the command server's ejb-jar.

The Command pattern and the Session Façade pattern both provide two important benefits: they act as a façade and they execute in one network round trip. The other major advantage that the Command pattern has over the Session Façade pattern is that it decouples the client from the EJB, which can also be achieved by applying the Business Delegate pattern, in conjunction with the Session Façade pattern. So how can a developer choose between one and the other? It is helpful to think of commands as *cheaper* session beans. They are more lightweight, resulting in a quicker initial development process, at the expense of possibly less maintainability over time.

Related Patterns

Command (Gamma, et al., 1995)

Data Transfer HashMap

Data Transfer Object Factory

A J2EE system using data transfer objects (DTOs) finds that its DTO layer tends to change very often.

How should data transfer object creation and consumption logic be implemented, in order to minimize the impact of frequent changes in the DTO layer on the rest of the system?

* * *

Data transfer objects have a tendency to change often. Domain DTOs change whenever the domain objects change (adding a new attribute to an entity bean, and so on). Custom DTOs are just use case-specific data holders for transporting data across a network; they can change as frequently as your application's presentation view. A medium to large application could potentially have tens, or even hundreds, of different data transfer objects, each of which would require custom logic to create it. A critical question then becomes: how and where should this logic be implemented, in order to decouple and protect the rest of this system from data transfer object changes?

A common solution employed in EJB 1.X applications is to place *getXXXDTO/setXXXDTO* methods directly on entity beans. In this scenario, the entity bean would be responsible for populating this data transfer object, and for updating itself based on the attributes of the *set* DTO. The problem with this approach is that it tightly couples the data transfer object layer to the entity bean layer. That is, placing use-case-specific data transfer object creation code on an entity bean could cause serious dependencies between your entity beans and your clients in medium to large applications. Every time a Web page changed and a different view of the data model was required, you would have to add a new method to an entity bean, recompile your entity bean, and redistribute your remote interfaces to any client using them.

Entity beans are supposed to be reusable business components, which can be separately assembled to create an application. In order to build truly reusable business components, it is important to maintain strict separation between your application logic and your business logic, allowing the two to evolve separately. Some other solution is required for creating and consuming entity beans, one that can decouple DTO-related logic from other components in the system.

Therefore:

Place the responsibility for creating and consuming data transfer objects in a *data transfer object factory*.

A data transfer object factory separates the logic related to data transfer objects (part of the application domain) from other components in your system such as entity beans (part of the business domain). When new views or different subsets of server-side data become necessary, new DTO creation methods can be added to a *DTOFactory*, instead of being placed onto an entity bean. These new methods will interact with the entity bean layer (or any other source of data such as connectors, straight JDBC, and so forth), calling getters and traversing relationships as required to generate domain or custom data tranfer objects. The advantage to this approach is that the entity beans themselves do not need to know about these different views of their data, in fact, no code on an entity bean needs to be changed at all.

For example, consider an automotive application that allows users to browse for information on cars and their manufacturers. The application thus has a domain model that consists of (among others) a Car and a Manufacturer entity bean. Such an application will have a UI with many different pages that allows users to browse different properties of cars and their manufacturers, including different subsets of a Car's attributes (engine properties, body properties, chassis, and so on) and data that spans multiple entity beans (info about a car and its manufacturer, and so forth). These different sets of data should be transferred to the client using custom DTOs, however, instead of placing the Java methods required to create these different DTOs on a Car or Manufacturer entity bean, they would be placed on a DTOFactory such as the one in Figure 1.10.

The CarDTOFactory now becomes a single point where use-case-specific DTO logic resides, helping to decouple the clients from the domain model. Entity beans on the domain model are now free to be domain objects, exposing only business methods to the clients, not ugly DTO get/set logic, which really have nothing to do with the *business concept* embodied by the particular domain model.

CarDTOFactory

//domain value objects
getCarDTOt(CarPK aCarPK)
getManufacturerDTOForCar(CarPK, aCarPK)
 	
//custom value objects
getCarEngineDTO(CarPK aCarPK)
getCarBodyDTO(CarPK aCarPK)
getCarChassisDTO(CarPK aCarPK)
getCarAndManufacturerDTO(CarPK aCarPK)
getCarAndDealersDTO(CarPK aCarPK)

Figure 1.10   CarDTOFactory.

There are two fundamental ways to implement the DTO Factory pattern, depending on whether the client of the factory is a session bean or a non-ejb client such as a servlet. When used behind a session bean façade, the DTO factory can be implemented as a plain Java class that simply stores creation/consumption logic for different data transfer objects in its methods. This type of Factory lends itself well to reuse because the data transfer objects it generates can be reused across different session beans and/or in different projects.

When used from a non-ejb client, the DTO factory should be implemented as a stateless session bean. A typical interaction between this client and the data transfer object is outlined in Figure 1.11. Here, a servlet client wants to get a Custom DTO called CarAndManufacturerDTO, so it queries a CarDTO-Factory for this object. The CarDTOFactory then creates and populates the DTO by calling *get* methods on the Car entity bean and its related Manufacturer entity bean through their *local interfaces*.

Data transfer object factories can be used to easily create any type of DTO. Even complex hierarchies of Aggregate DTOs (domain DTOs that contain other domain DTOs) can be created that map to different *slices* of the server-side entity bean object model. Complex data transfer object hierarchies can be created by explicitly writing logic that knows how to navigate (and copy) a use-case-specific *slice* of a hierarchy of entity beans. These DTO hierarchies can all be created up front on the server, and passed to the client in one network call.

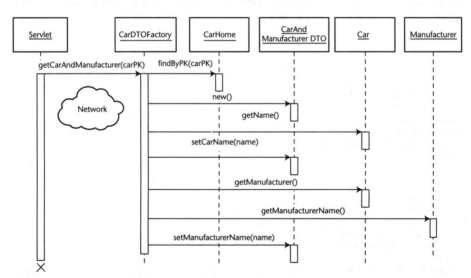

Figure 1.11   Using a Car DTO factory as a session bean.

One important benefit that results from this practice is that the entity beans in our application are now fully reusable. For example, imagine two separate development teams in a corporation working on separate applications. These two teams can reuse the same entity bean business components (a beautiful example of EJB reuse in action by the way) by using separate data transfer object factories. The teams could achieve complete reuse by each maintaining its own separate DTO factory that passed out use-case-specific DTO "slices" of entity bean state—independently of the other team. By maintaining their own DTO factory, they could also develop and deploy their own applications completely independently from each other. This concept is illustrated in Figure 1.12.

Note that the Data Transfer Object Factory pattern does *not* imply creating one DTO factory for each entity bean class. For example you don't necessarily need to create a CarDTOFactory for a Car entity bean. This would result in explosion of VO factories. Where requirements permit, it can be more straightforward to create a DTO factory for a whole set of entity beans and/or other sources of server-side data.

DTO factories provide a way to read data from the server, but what about updating data? Techniques similar to those used for reading server-side data can be used for updating data. That is, clients can pass either a domain DTO or a custom DTO to the server, where it can, in turn, perform Create, Read, Update, Delete (CRUD) operations on entity beans or other data stores on the server side.

For domain DTOs (which are typically made mutable), a client will perform its updates onto a DTO locally, and then update the server by passing a domain DTO to an *updateXXXEntity* method on a DTO factory, which would copy the attributes of the DTO into the appropriate entity bean, using fine-grained *set* methods on the entity bean's local interface. Clients can similarly create entity beans by populating a domain DTO locally and passing it to a *createXXXEntity* method on the factory.

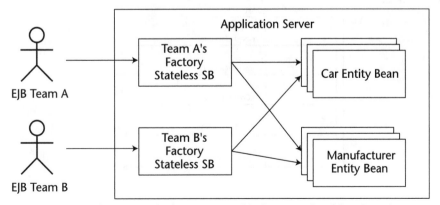

Figure 1.12   Achieving entity bean reuse with data transfer object factories.

Using the previous example, if the application administrator wanted to update a particular car or manufacturer, these updates would be done with separate UI displays (one for the car, and one for the manufacturer). Updates would be performed, and either a Car or a Manufacturer domain DTO would be sent back to the server for updating in a single transaction, as shown in Figure 1.13.

For performing any sort of update above and beyond CRUD updating of domain objects, the server should be updated by passing custom DTOs to the session/message façade. Remember that the façade is supposed to contain all the business logic required to execute use cases in an application, such as placing an order on Amazon, or transferring funds at a bank. For these types of operations, a client will typically create a custom DTO that contains all the data required to perform the update, pass this DTO to the façade, which will in turn create, update, or delete any number of server-side resources.

The advantages to the data transfer object factory approach are numerous:

- **Better maintainability.** Separating your application logic (use cases) and your data object model (entity beans), so the two can evolve separately. Entity beans no longer need to be changed and recompiled when the needs of the client change.

- **Encourages entity bean reuse.** Entity beans can be reused across projects, since different DTO factories can be written to suit the needs of different applications.

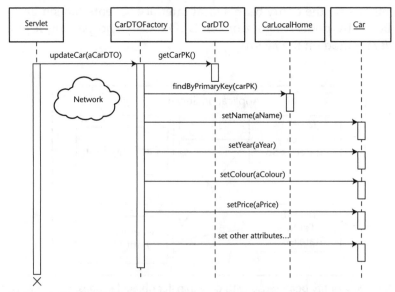

Figure 1.13   Updating data by using a data transfer object factory.

- **Allow for creating complex graphs of DTOs.** By writing DTO creation logic up front, developers can create complex graphs/hierarchies of DTOs that can be used to transfer the data from complex entity bean hierarchies containing one-to-one, one-to-many, many-to-many, and cyclic relationships, and combinations of such relationships. This provides clients with fine-grained control over what parts of entity bean data they need to display. For non-Web clients such as Java applications and applets, the ability to get non-tabular data is particularly important.

- **Increases performance.** When the DTO factory is used as a session façade, attributes from multiple entity beans can be passed to the client with just one network call.

The Data Transfer Object Factory pattern can build maintainable and flexible systems, providing a simple and consistent method for creating arbitrarily complex data transfer objects and passing them to the client in one bulk network call, without causing dependencies between data transfer objects and other components in a J2EE system.

Related Patterns

Session Façade
Data Transfer Object
Value Object Assembler (Alur, et al., 2001)

Generic Attribute Access

An entity bean client needs to access the attributes of an entity bean.

> **How can an entity bean client efficiently access and manipulate the attributes of an entity bean in a bulk, generic fashion?**

* * *

In usual practice, entity beans are accessed through either local interface *get/set* methods (for entity beans written for EJB 2.X and up) or via bulk data transfer objects off the remote interface (for EJB 1.X entity beans). With the former, methods on the session façade or data transfer object factory interact with the entity bean by calling multiple fine-grained getters and setters, in order to access and manipulate attributes, as required by the particular use case. Through the latter, data transfer objects are used to access and manipulate the entity bean state in bulk, in order to minimize network calls associated with communication with the remote interface. The use of DTOs as a mechanism to manipulate entity beans is a common pattern for optimizing communications with EJB 1.X entity beans.

The trade-off for using DTOs to access EJB 1.X entity beans is reduced maintainability of the entity bean layer (see the DTO Factory pattern). With the advent of EJB 2.0, local interfaces allow the extraction of DTO creation and consumption logic into a data transfer object factory; here the DTO factory interacts with an entity bean via fine-grained get/sets on the local interface, alleviating some of the problems with using DTOs.

Unfortunately, EJB 1.X entity beans do not have local interfaces. The consequence of this is that DTO creation/consumption logic cannot be extracted from an entity bean into a DTO factory (because it is bad for performance for a DTO factory to make multiple fine-grained calls on an entity bean's remote interface). Some other mechanism is needed, one that will allow bulk access to entity bean data through the remote interface, without cluttering it up with DTO creation/consumption logic.

Even for local interfaces, there are cases in which exposing multiple fine-grained *get/set* methods is not a good idea:

- **Does not scale well from small to large entity beans.** Imagine a stock/bonds entity bean for a financial application. Such an entity bean could have well over 200 attributes. To write and expose getters/setters for all of those attributes could result in a nightmare of tedious coding and an explosion in interface size.

- **Results in tightly coupled, hard-coded clients.** Entity bean clients (such as the session façade) need to be tightly coupled to the interface of the entity bean, making it sensitive to even minute changes that can frequently occur—such as the adding or removing of an attribute.

The takeaway point is that some other mechanism is needed to access entity bean data, one that that can allow a DTO factory to use the remote interface to dynamically grab different subsets of the entity bean state in one bulk network call, and also help decouple entity bean clients from an entity bean's attribute accessors, when using a local interface.

Therefore:

> **Abstract entity bean attribute access logic into a generic attribute access interface, using HashMaps to pass key-value attributes in and out of entity beans.**

The attribute access interface is implemented by entity beans on the remote or local interface, and looks like this:

```
public interface AttributeAccess {
        public Map getAttributes(Collection keysOfAttributes);
        public Map getAllAttributes();
        public void setAttributes(Map keyAndValuePairs);
}
```

Attribute Access provides a generic interface that allows arbitrary sets of data to be *get* or *set* from an entity bean dynamically. The interface allows EJB 1.X entity beans to use a DTO factory to extract DTO creation logic and optimize on remote calls, as well as allowing EJB 2.X entity beans to simplify their local interfaces by removing the need for fine-grained *get/set* methods. The only dependency been client and entity bean code is the naming conventions placed on the *keys* used to identify attributes, described later in this pattern.

The session façade or DTO factory can access an entity bean's attributes through the attribute access interface. Figure 1.14 illustrates a typical case. Here, a client is interested in gathering a subset of the data of a "Car" entity bean relating to its engine. A client calls the *getCarEngineData* method on the session façade, which in turn asks an entity bean for the exact attributes that are part of the car engine, by first creating a collection that includes the *key* values of the attributes of interest (horsepower, volume, and so on), then passing this collection to the *getAttributes(collection)* method on the entity bean, which will return a HashMap with this exact subset.

After receiving the populated HashMap from the Car entity bean, the session bean can:

1. **Return the HashMap to a remote client**. Here the session bean uses the HashMap as serializable container for transferring data across the network (as described in the *Data Transfer HashMap pattern* in Chapter 2).

2. **Convert HashMap into a DTO and return it.** As a DTO factory, the session bean can extract the values of the HashMap and add them to a data transfer object, returning the DTO to the client.

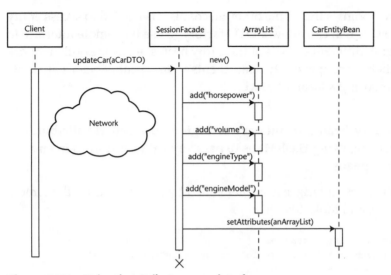

Figure 1.14   Using the attribute access interface.

Which option to choose, is up to the developer. As a mechanism for data transfer, HashMaps provide many advantages over data transfer objects (as described in the *Data Transfer HashMap* pattern), but also come at the expense of significant additional complexity. If the attribute access interface is used behind a DTO factory, dependencies between key/value names can be kept localized to the server, where the session beans need to be aware of the entity beans anyway.

Using the attribute access interface, a session bean can thus dynamically decide which subsets of entity bean data it requires at run time, eliminating the need for manual, design time programming of data transfer objects.

Like the interface itself, the implementation of the attribute access interface is generic. Under Bean-Managed Persistence (BMP), an entity bean can be further simplified by storing all of its attributes in a private, internal HashMap, rather than the relying on the obvious hard-coding of attributes that usually takes place. For large entity beans, this optimization can simplify an entity bean's code greatly. Using this internal HashMap, the implementation of the methods on AttributeAccess thus become completely generic and reusable across BMP entity beans:

```
private java.util.HashMap attributes;

/**
 * Returns key/value pairs of entity bean attributes
 * @return java.util.Map
 */
```

```java
public Map getAllAttributes()
{
    return(HashMap)attributes.clone();
}


/**
 * Used by clients to specify the attributes they are interested in
 * @return java.util.Map
 * @param keysofAttributes the name of the attributes the client is
 * interested in
 */
public Map getAttributes(Collection keysofAttributes)
{
    Iterator keys = keysofAttributes.iterator();
    Object aKey = null;
    HashMap aMap = new HashMap();

    while ( keys.hasNext() )
    {
    aKey = keys.next();
        aMap.put( aKey, this.attributes.get(aKey));
    }

    //map now has all requested data
    return aMap;
}



/**
 * Used by clients to update particular attributes in the entity bean
 * @param keyValuePairs java.util.Map
 */
public void setAttributes(Map keyValuePairs)
{
    Iterator entries = keyValuePairs.entrySet().iterator();
    Map.Entry anEntry = null;

    while ( entries.hasNext() )
    {
        anEntry = (Map.Entry)entries.next();
        this.attributes.put(anEntry.getKey(), anEntry.getValue());
    }
}
```

In Container-Managed Persistence (CMP), using an internal map of attributes is not possible, since the implementation of an entity bean's classes is abstracted behind container generated *get* and *set* methods. When using an internal map is not possible, the attribute access interface can be implemented generically using the Java Reflection API. That is, in *setAttributes*, reflection can be performed on the key-value of the attribute a client wants to set. Specifically, if the key-value is *XXX* the *setAttribute* implementation will attempt to call *setXXX(...)* on the entity bean. Similarly, in the *getAttributes* method, reflection can be used to find all *get* methods on an entity bean, invoke them and populate a map for the client. If a developer would prefer not to use the Reflection API, then implementing the Attribute Access method cannot be done generically for CMP. The developer will need to interlace his Attribute Access implementation with IF statements that call hard-coded *get/set* methods on the entity bean, depending on the key-value string.

In order to make the Attribute Access implementation code reusable across all entity beans, a superclass can be used to implement the interface methods, which are completely generic, whether we use the reflection method or the internal map of attributes style of implementation. All entity beans wanting to make use of the Attribute Access services need only to subclass the superclass implementation, thus automatically exposing this unified interface to their attributes with no extra coding required.

The final piece of the puzzle is how to name the keys, which identify the attributes of an entity bean. Not only do the attributes need to be identified by key, but both the logic that accesses an entity bean via the attribute access interface and the entity bean itself need to agree on the naming conventions. Some sort of "contract" is required between client and server. Several possibilities are discussed:

- **Establish a consistent, well-documented naming convention.** The client and the entity bean can agree upon a well-documented, consistent naming convention for attributes. For an Account entity bean, *"com.bank.Account.accountName,"* or simply *"accountName"* would be an example of a consistent convention. The drawback with this approach is that the contract exists in the minds of developers and on paper only. When developing, it is easy to misspell the attribute name, resulting in costly development errors that are hard to track down.

- **Define static final member variables in the entity bean remote or local interface.** An entity bean client can make calls to the entity bean using references to static final variables containing the correct key-string required to get an attribute. For example, in order to retrieve the attributes from an *Employee* entity bean; a session bean could use the following code:

```
//Ask employee for personal attributes
Collection aCollection = new ArrayList();
aCollection.add(Employee.NAME);
aCollection.add(Employee.EMAIL);
aCollection.add(Employee.SEX);
```

```
aCollection.add(Employee.SSN);

Map aMap = employee.getAttributes(aCollection);
```

Where the entity beans local interface contains the following definitions:

```
public interface Employee extends EJBLocalObject, AttributeAccess
{

    //Since attributes are stored in a hashmap in the entity bean,
    //we need a central place to store the 'keys' used to reference
    //attributes, so that the clients and the entity bean won't need
    //need to be hard-coded with knowledge of the attribute key strings
    public final static String ID = "EMPLOYEEID";
    public final static String NAME = "NAME";
    public final static String EMAIL = "EMAIL";
    public final static String AGE = "AGE";
    public final static String SSN = "SSN";
    public final static String SEX = "SEX";
...
}
```

This approach works great for the DTO factory approach, where a session bean is querying the entity bean directly for its attributes, with the intention of returning a hard-coded data transfer object to the client, instead of a HashMap. Here, only the session bean and the entity bean need to agree on the names of the attribute keys, making the local/remote interface a good place to localize names of the attributes. This approach breaks down when using the Data Transfer Hashmap pattern, since the client also needs to know the names of the key-values, but the client does not have access to the entity bean's remote/local interface.

- **Shared class with static final member variables.** Here we can create a class that is shared by both the client classes and the server classes, which is used to encapsulate the actual strings used to populate and read strings from a HashMap behind a hard-coded final static variable, accessible by both client and server. For example, a client would query a hashmap for an attribute as follows:

```
accountMap.get(Names.ACCOUNTBALANCE)
```

Where the shared class called Names would look like:

```
public class Names {

    public final static String ACCOUNTBALANCE = "BALANCE";
...
}
```

One disadvantage to this method is that should the key mappings need to be updated or added to, the new class would need to be redistributed to the client and the server (and their JVM would thus need to be restarted).

- **Place the Attribute contract in a JNDI tree.** In this approach, a single-ton of sorts is maintained by placing a class containing the keys in a JNDI tree, accessible by client and server. Client and server code would not need to be recompiled or rebooted, when keys were changed/updated, since a central object in a JNDI tree would always contain the freshest copy of keys. The trade-off with this solution is the overhead incurred in grabbing the contract from the JNDI tree whenever key-values are required.

The Generic Attribute Access pattern has many advantages:

- **One interface across all entity beans.** Entity bean clients can manipulate entity beans consistently via the attribute access interface, simplifying client code. Entity beans are also simplified, because the attribute access can be encapsulated in a superclass.

- **Scales well to large entity beans.** Whether an entity bean has 20 or 2000 attributes, attribute access logic is simplified to just a few lines.

- **Low cost of maintenance over time.** New views of server-side data can be created that do not require any server-side programming. Clients can dynamically decide which attributes to display.

- **Allows for dynamic addition of attributes at run time.** When using BMP, this pattern can easily be extended to allow for the ability to add and remove attributes from an entity bean dynamically. This can be achieved by adding an *addAttribute* and *removeAttribute* method to the interface, which simply performs operations on the attribute HashMap.

Like all patterns, using Generic Attribute Access has its trade-offs:

- **Additional overhead per method call.** For each attribute call, clients must use an attribute key to identify attributes. Finally, attributes need to be *cast* to their appropriate type after being extracted from the HashMap object.

- **Need to maintain a contract for attribute keys.** Since attributes are requested by string, clients need to remember the key-strings used to identify attributes. Defining a key-attribute contract (discussed earlier in this pattern), can alleviate these dependencies.

- **Loss of strong typing/compile-time checking.** When we use DTOs, values passed by *gets* or *sets* are always of the correct type; any errors would be passed at compile time. When we use Generic Attribute

Access, attribute access must be managed by the client at run time by casting objects to their correct type and associating the correct attribute type with the correct key.

Overall, the Generic Attribute Access pattern provides a generic method of managing the state of entity beans, eliminating the bulky repetitive code associated with domain-specific entity bean data access.

Related Patterns

Property Container (Carey, et al., 2000)
Data Transfer HashMap

Business Interface

The EJB specification mandates that the enterprise bean class provide an implementation of all methods declared in the remote or local interface, but the bean cannot directly implement these interfaces.

How can inconsistencies between remote/local interface methods and the enterprise bean implementation be discovered at compile time?

* * *

One of the most common errors experienced during the EJB development process is the lack of consistency between the business method definitions in the remote or local interfaces and implementations in the enterprise bean class. The EJB specification requires that the enterprise bean properly implement all the business method signatures defined in the remote/local interface, but does not provide for an automatic way to detect problems with this at compile time. Many types of errors can arise from this *decoupling* of interface definition and implementation, including mistyping of method names, parameter types, exceptions, inconsistent parameters, and so on. As a result, these types of errors cannot be detected at compile time, the EJB developer must manually maintain consistency between interface definition and bean implementation.

The errors can only be detected when using your EJB server vendor's proprietary postcompilation tool. These tools are typically used to take compiled Java classes and test them for compliance to the EJB spec, before packaging and deploying them. These postcompilation tools are typically slow and arduous to use, and are less viable for incremental compilation practices that developers often use to catch errors early. The end result is that development errors are caught later on in the development process.

One solution would be to have the enterprise bean directly implement the remote or local interface in the bean class. This would enforce consistency between method definition and implementation, using any standard Java compiler. Unfortunately, the EJB specification advises against this practice, and with good reason. The remote interface extends javax.ejb.EJBObject interface, and the local interface implements the javax.ejb.EJBLocalObject interface, as shown in Figure 1.15. These interfaces define extra methods (*isIdentical, getPrimaryKey, remove, etc*), which are meant to be implemented by the EJBObject and EJBLocalObject stubs, not by the enterprise bean class.

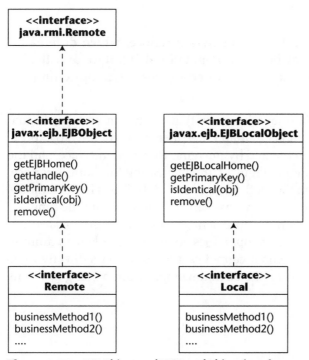

Figure 1.15   EJBObject and EJBLocalObject interfaces.

In order to make your bean compile, you would have to clutter your enterprise bean class by writing dummy implementations of these extra methods. Furthermore, if the enterprise bean class directly implemented the remote or local interface, the bean could be directly cast to one of these interfaces, allowing a developer to pass an instance of *this* to a client. This behavior is not allowed by the EJB specification. To pass a reference to oneself, a bean needs to first get a reference to itself by calling *getEJBObject* or *getEJBLocalObject* from the *SessionContext* or *EntityContext* interface.

EJB developers should not implement the remote or local interfaces directly in their enterprise bean class, but developers need a mechanism that would allow compile-time confirmation of consistency between remote/local interface method definitions and implementations in the bean class.

Therefore:

Create a superinterface called a business interface, which defines all business methods. Let both the remote/local interface and the enterprise bean class implement this interface, forcing compile-time consistency checks.

A *business interface* is a plain Java interface that defines the method signatures for all the business methods that an enterprise bean chooses to expose. The business interface is implemented by the remote or local interface, and the enterprise bean class, as shown in Figure 1.16. By creating this superinterface, errors in consistency between the method signature definitions in the remote/local interface and the enterprise bean class can be caught at compile time.

The business interface does not implement *javax.ejb.EjbObject* or *javax.ejb.EJBLocalObject*, so the bean class developer does not have to implement dummy methods. Furthermore, the developer cannot cast the bean class directly to its remote or local interfaces, keeping the bean developer from passing *this* to its clients.

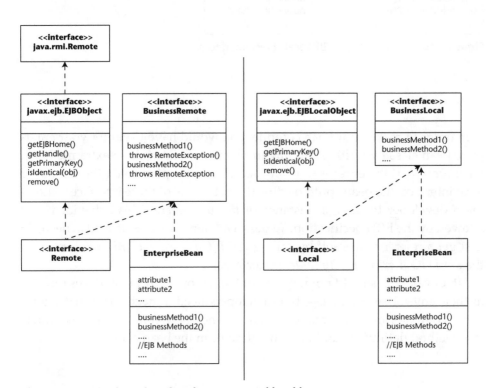

Figure 1.16   Business interface for remote and local beans.

The business interface pattern differs slightly, depending on whether the enterprise bean exposes its business methods on the local interface or the remote interface. If the entity bean exposes the remote interface, all method signatures on the business interface need to throw *java.rmi.RemoteException* (but do not need to extend java.rmi.Remote). Note that the method implementations in the enterprise bean class should not throw *RemoteException*, this has been deprecated by the EJB specification. Instead, business methods can throw *EJBException* from within the body of a method, without declaring it in the throws clause, since *EJBException* is a subclass of *RuntimeException*.

When using the business interface with a local interface, the business interface need not implement any other interface, and the business method signatures can be written without any special rules.

There is one dangerous side effect of using the Business Interface pattern. For methods whose return values are the remote/local interface of the bean itself, implementing the business interface allows the bean developer to return *this* without any compile-time problems being detected. This is possible because both the bean class and the remote/local interface implement the business interface. Returning *this* is always caught at compile time when the Business Interface pattern is not used (since the bean class doesn't implement the remote/local interface). Thus, special care must be taken by bean developers using a business interface pattern to not return *this*, or unpredictable errors can occur at run time.

The Business Interface pattern is a common pattern in EJB development. It allows developers to catch common programming errors at compile time, ensuring consistency between business method definition and implementation.

Inter-Tier Data
Transfer Patterns

Inter-tier data transfer patterns answer the fundamental question: How can you get data from the server to the client and back? The notion of transferring copies of server-side data across tiers can be very confusing for first-time developers of distributed systems, because there isn't really a similar paradigm in non-distributed Java application development world.

This chapter covers the following patterns:

Data Transfer Object. The essential design pattern. Discusses why, how, and when to marshal data across the network in bulk bundles called data transfer objects (DTOs). The two follow-up patterns (Domain and Custom DTO) provide guidance about how DTOs should be designed.

Domain Data Transfer Object. Interacting with the domain model is an intuitive practice that is unfortunately a performance killer in the EJB world (see the Session Façade pattern for explanation). The Domain DTO pattern describes how DTOs can be used to marshal domain model copies to the client in place of the domain objects themselves.

Custom Data Transfer Object. The opposite approach to domain DTOs, custom DTOs do not represent any server-side domain object, rather, they are structured according to the needs of the client.

Data Transfer HashMap. Discusses how HashMaps can be used as methods of inter-tier communication, eliminating the need to write a layer of DTOs.

Data Transfer RowSet. When the data being passed to the client is read-only and tabular, the RowSet interface provides an excellent abstraction for passing tabular data to the client straight out of a ResultSet.

Data Transfer Object

The client tier in an EJB system needs a way to transfer bulk data to and from the server.

How can a client exchange bulk data with the server without making multiple fine-grained network calls?

✲ ✲ ✲

In any distributed application there are generally two reasons why a client may interact with a server. The first is to read some data from the server for display purposes; the second is to change some data on the server by creating, updating, or removing data. In an EJB context, these types of operations typically involve the exchange of data between the client (servlet, applet, and so on), and a session bean, entity bean, or message-driven bean.

When large amounts of data need to be exchanged, this can be achieved by loading many parameters into a method call (when updating data on the server), or by making multiple fine-grained calls to the server to retrieve data (when a client needs to read data from the server). The former option can quickly get out of hand when dealing with large amounts of parameters, and the latter option can be a performance killer.

Imagine the scenario where a client UI needs to display a set of attributes that live on the server; these attributes could live in an entity bean or be accessible through a session bean. One way that the client could get the data it needs is by executing multiple fine-grained calls to the server, as shown in Figure 2.1.

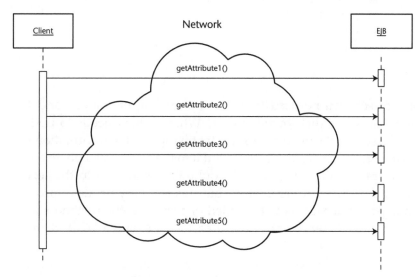

Figure 2.1 An inefficient way to get data from the server.

The problem with this approach is that each call to the server is a network call, requiring the serialization and deserialization of return values, blocking on the client while the EJB server intercepts the call to the server and performs transaction and security checks, and of course the retrieval of the attribute in question. Furthermore, each method call might actually execute in its own separate transaction if the client is not using Java Transaction API client-demarcated transactions.

Executing multiple network calls in this fashion will contribute to significant degradation in performance. A better alternative is required, one that would allow the client to get all the data it required in one bulk call.

Therefore:

Create plain Java classes called data transfer objects, which contain and encapsulate bulk data in one network transportable bundle.

A data transfer object is a plain serializable Java class that represents a snapshot of some server-side data, as in the following example:

```java
import java.io.Serializable;

public class SomeDTO implements Serializable {

    private long    attribute1;
    private String attribute2;
    private String attribute3;

    ...

    public long    getAttribute1();
    public String getAttribute2();
    public String getAttribute3();
    ...


}//SomeSTO
```

Data transfer objects can be used both for the reading operations and the updating operations in a distributed system. When a client needs to update some data in the server, it can create a DTO that wraps all the information the server needs to perform the updates, and send it to the server (usually to a session façade) for processing. Of course, it could also send data to the server using zillions of fine-grained parameters, but this is a very brittle approach. Whenever one parameter needs to be added or removed, the method signature needs to change. By wrapping method parameters with a DTO, changes are isolated to the DTO itself.

Where data transfer objects are clearly needed is for reading operations. When a client needs to read some server-side data (usually for the purpose of populating a client-side UI), the client can get all the data it needs in one bulk network call by wrapping the data in data transfer object form.

Using the previous example, the server-side EJB would create a DTO (as shown in Figure 2.2) and populate it with the attributes that the client required. This data would then be returned to the client in one bulk return value—the data transfer object. Data transfer objects are basically "envelopes," used to transport any kind of data between the tiers in a J2EE system.

A common problem that developers face when using data transfer objects is choosing what granularity to design into them. That is, how do you choose how much data to wrap with a DTO? At what point do you decide that a DTO is necessary? As the primary method of exchange between client and server, data transfer objects form part of the interface that separates client developers and server developers. At the beginning of a project, client and server developers need to agree on the data transfer object design at about the same time they need to decide upon what EJB interfaces to use. Despite this need, designing data transfer objects at the beginning of a project can be difficult since developers often don't completely understand exactly what units of data should be transferred between the client and server.

An easy way to start in designing data transfer objects is as copies of server-side entity beans (or domain objects), as described in the Domain Data Transfer Object pattern. Designing domain data transfer objects is easy, because project teams usually have a good idea of the domain model that a project will utilize early on, since these requirements are established in the initial design phases of a project. Thus, making Domain DTOs the unit of exchange between client and server can help get a team up and running more quickly.

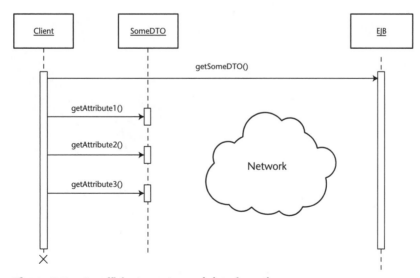

Figure 2.2   An efficient way to read data from the server.

Ultimately, data exchanged between the client and server should be designed to fit the client's needs. Thus, as the project progresses and the needs of the clients become finalized, domain data transfer objects often become cumbersome as units of exchange, too coarse-grained to be useful to the fine-grained needs of the client. A client may need access to data that simply isn't encapsulated in any domain data transfer objects. At this point, developers can design *custom data transfer objects*, that is, data transfer objects that wrap arbitrary sets of data, completely driven on the particular needs of the client.

The differences between these two design paradigms can have significant impact on the design of the application as a whole. Although they represent contradictory approaches, they can and usually do coexist in any J2EE application.

When deciding where to put the logic to create and consume data transfer objects, the Data Transfer Object Factory pattern illustrates a proven and maintainable solution. One major issue that occurs with any sort of data transfer across tiers (be it with DTOs, HashMaps, or RowSets), is that as soon as the data reaches the client, it has the potential of being stale. The Version Number pattern (see Chapter 3) can help protect against problems with staleness.

Related Patterns

State Holder

Value Object (Alur, et al., 2001)

Details Object

Domain Data Transfer Object

A client wants to access and manipulate data from the server-side domain object model.

How can a client access and manipulate the server-side domain (entity bean) object model without the performance overhead of remote calls?

* * *

A domain model, or domain object model refers to the layer of objects in your system that map to real-world concepts, such as a person, a bank account, or a car. In an EJB setting, the most common example of a domain model is your application-specific layer of entity beans. A domain object in this sense is a particular entity bean, such as a Car entity bean. Other technologies for creating domain models can also be used in an EJB setting, such as Java data objects, data access objects, or the proprietary domain object layer provided by an object-relational mapping tool.

In a distributed scenario, domain object models live completely on the server. However, depending on the implementation technology chosen (entity beans, JDO, and so forth), a domain object model can manifest itself into two types: one that can be accessed by clients remotely across a network (entity beans), and one that cannot be accessed by clients remotely (JDO, proprietary frameworks, and so on). For the latter, only other business components living on the server can access the domain model.

Entity beans are remotely accessible. A client can access an EJBObject stub that maintains a direct connection to a particular entity bean living on the EJB server across a network. However, as explained in the Session Façade pattern, accessing entity beans remotely is a very poor practice. The most powerful way to optimize on entity bean access is not to access entity beans from the client at all. Instead, a client would execute a method on a session façade, which would directly interact with entity beans through their local interfaces, allowing complex operations to be completed in one network call. When we use the Session Façade pattern, entity beans are thus no longer accessible by a client across a network.

This addresses the performance problems associated with using entity beans directly from clients, but puts the client in a difficult situation: If the client cannot access entity beans (or any type of domain object), how can it work with the same data object abstractions (the same domain model) on the client side as are being used on the server side? How is a client to read and display the attributes of a particular domain object that lives on the server side, and work with this data using the same object-oriented semantics on the client side?

For example, consider a car dealership application, in which the business requirements of the system define the notion of a Car and a Manufacturer, implemented as entity beans on the server side. For the client-side portion of this application, the most intuitive thing to do would be to also display and update similar Car and Manufacturer abstractions on the client side. A client would like to read data from Car and Manufacturer, update values on Car and Manufacturer, and naturally traverse relationships to other related entity beans if it needed data from them.

Performance concerns require that the client not have direct access to the entity bean domain object model, and other types of object domain models cannot even be accessed remotely. However, to be able to work with an applications domain model on the client side is desirable. Thus, a mechanism is needed to allow clients to traverse and manipulate the same data object abstractions as exist on the server.

Therefore:

> **Design data transfer object copies of the server-side domain objects (entity beans). Clients may operate on local DTO copies of domain object data, performing bulk reads and updates.**

Domain data transfer objects are a special application of the Data Transfer Object pattern. Whereas the Data Transfer Object pattern simply says to use DTOs to exchange *data* between client and server, the Domain Data Transfer Object pattern says that data transfer objects can be used to provide clients with optimized local access to data transfer object copies of server-side domain objects. Thus, domain data transfer objects have one-to-one correspondence with domain objects on the server side. If you have an Account entity bean, then you will have an Account DTO, as shown in Figure 2.3.

AccountBean	**AccountDTO**
accountNumber name password balance	accountNumber name password balance

//ejb methods
ejbLoad()
ejbStore()
...
	getAccountNumber()
	getName()
	getPassword()
	getBalance()
	setAccountNumber()
	setName()
	setPassword()
	setBalance()

Figure 2.3   Account EJB and Account domain DTO.

Using domain data transfer objects provides a simple way for clients to interact with the entity bean object model in a distributed application:

- **Displaying entity bean data.** When a client wants to display the data from an Account entity bean, it could call a *getDTO* method on Account, which would retrieve an AccountDTO, containing a copy of all the attributes of the account entity bean. The client could then perform multiple *get* calls on this local data transfer object, without the burden of network calls.

- **Modifying entity bean data.** If a client wants to modify the contents of the Account entity bean, it would perform its update by calling *set* methods on its local copy of the AccountDTO, then pass this updated data transfer object to the server for merging with the Account entity bean.

- **Displaying data from that spans related entity beans.** Entity beans can contain references to other entity beans in a one-to-one, one-to-many, or many-to-many fashion. Often a client will be interested in getting data from multiple related entity beans, but manually traversing the entity bean objects to get separate data transfer object copies would involve significant network call overhead. A better solution would be to assemble a data transfer object copy of these related entity beans on the server side, and pass it to the client in one network call. This can be achieved by using special data transfer objects called *aggregate data transfer objects* (domain data transfer objects that contain references to other domain data transfer objects). Aggregate data transfer objects can be created that contain data transfer object copies of hierarchies of related entity beans. The client would navigate this *local* hierarchy of data transfer objects just as it would navigate the remote entity beans themselves.

- **Creating entity beans.** To create a new Account, a client could locally create and populate an AccountDTO, and pass this object to the session façade, which would use it in the *ejbCreate* method on AccountHome. The less maintainable alternative would be to pass all the attributes of Account as method parameters to the session façade and then to ejb-Create(). For example, which looks more maintainable: *ejbCreate(attrib1, attrib2, attrib3, attrib4, attrib5, ...)*, or *ejbCreate(aDTO)*?

Much debate has arisen as to whether domain data transfer objects should be *mutable* or *immutable*. That is, should a client be allowed to modify a domain DTO (by calling *set* methods on it), or should domain DTOs be read-only, without *set* methods. When using domain DTOs, it makes sense to make them mutable. The client knows it is interacting with a client-side copy of an entity bean, it can read and update the data transfer object as though it were doing so on the entity bean itself. Since the client knows the data transfer object came from the server, it is reasonable to give it the responsibility of *knowing to send* the DTO back to the server once modifications have been made. Where immutable data transfer objects make sense is when data transfer objects don't represent server-side entity beans, as in the Custom Data Transfer Object pattern. Here, data transfer objects simply represent arbitrary collections of read-only data.

Designing domain data transfer objects as copies of server-side entity beans has the following benefits:

- **Domain model data structures are replicated to client in one network call.** Copies of entity beans and even multiple entity beans can be assembled on the server and passed to the client in one network call. The client can then traverse the local data transfer objects, reading and updating them without incurring network call overhead. A client can then update the server by passing the data transfer object back.

- **It is easy to quickly build a functional site.** Early in the development process, the specific data access needs of the client are unclear and always changing. Whereas the needs of the client UIs are unclear, the application's entity bean's object model has usually already been built. A functional application can quickly be built using the entity bean data transfer objects as the medium of exchange between client and server.

- **Client-side attribute validation.** Syntactic validation of entity bean attributes can be performed on the client side by embedding this validation logic in domain data transfer object *set* methods. This allows errors with entity bean editing and creation to be caught on the client side instead of using up a network call only to have exceptions be thrown from the server. Of course, the semantic/business validation of attributes still needs to occur, and this generally can only be done on the server.

The process also has the following trade-offs:

- **Couples the client to the server-side domain object model.** With the Domain Data Transfer Object pattern, a client is working with a direct copy of a server-side domain object (entity bean). Thus, session façade or not, the client is effectively coupled to object model that lives on the server. If an entity bean is changed, its corresponding data transfer object must be changed, thus any clients using that data transfer object must be recompiled.

- **Does not always map well to the needs of clients.** The entity bean object model used on the server side often does not map well to the client's needs. Different UIs may require different sets of data that simply don't map to "bundles of data" that entity bean data transfer objects provide. A client may want one or two attributes of an entity bean that has 20 attributes. To use a domain DTO to transfer 20 attributes to the client when only two are needed is a waste of network resources.

- **Results in a parallel hierarchy.** Domain DTOs duplicate objects in the domain model, resulting in duplicate attributes and methods.

- **Cumbersome for updating domain objects.** Merging changes from an aggregate data transfer object (a domain object that contains other domain objects) is difficult and cumbersome. What if only one domain data transfer object deep in the tree was changed? Ugly code needs to be written to detect this.

The reader may have noted that the above examples have implied that domain data transfer objects could be created and consumed by the entity beans themselves. Back in the EJB 1.X days (before entity beans had local interfaces), it was common to see entity beans expose a *getDTO* and a *setDTO* method, instead of fine-grained *getAttribute/setAttribute* methods. Every entity bean in an application housed logic that created a data transfer object copy of itself (*getDTO)* and logic that updated itself based on changed values in a data transfer object (*setDTO*). The reason was that all calls to an entity bean were potentially remote calls, even if they came from session beans or other entity beans collocated in the same server. The Data Transfer Object pattern arose out of this need to optimize calls to entity beans, be they from non-ejb clients or from other session and entity beans. With the introduction of EJB 2.0 local interfaces, session beans and other entity beans no longer need to use data transfer objects to optimize entity bean data access. Instead, they can simply use fine-grained *getAttribute/setAttribute* methods on the entity bean, now data transfer objects can be used properly: to exchange domain object copies between client and server.

Since domain data transfer objects should not be created and consumed on the domain objects themselves, this raises the question: Where should data transfer objects be created and consumed? The Data Transfer Object Factory pattern provides a best practice for this type of code. Another related pattern is the Custom Data Transfer Object pattern, which takes the opposite perspective to the Entity Bean Data Transfer Object pattern: Data transfer objects should be immutable and map to the specific needs of the client, not the domain model.

Custom Data Transfer Objects

A client finds that the domain object model and associated domain data transfer objects don't map well to its needs.

> **How can data transfer objects be designed when domain data transfer objects don't fit?**

* * *

The Data Transfer Object pattern introduced the notion of using a data transfer object to pass bulk data between the client and server. The Data Transfer Object pattern described a common method of designing data transfer objects—by mapping directly to the object model used on the server side. Although this method of designing data transfer objects works well early on in a project, EJB clients often have much more fine-grained data access needs.

For example, consider a Car entity bean. A car could potentially be described by hundreds of attributes (color, weight, model, length, width, height, year, etc.). In most typical scenarios, a client is only interested in a small subset of those attributes. For example, consider a Web page that lists a car's model, year, and type. To populate this page, it would be extremely wasteful to transfer a CarValueObject (with all its attributes) to the client, when it only wants to list three simple attributes from the car.

A client may have even more complicated needs. Imagine a client that required just one or two attributes from five different related entity beans. In order to optimize network calls, a data transfer object representation could be constructed on the server side that wraps all the required data into one network transportable bundle. One solution would be to create a data transfer object that contains links to other domain data transfer objects. Thus the hierarchy of entity beans on the server side would be copied into a symmetric hierarchy of domain data transfer objects. This approach is terrible for performance and cumbersome in practice. If a client only needs one or two attributes from each server-side entity bean, transferring the complete domain object model as data transfer objects to the client would waste time and network bandwidth.

Another problem is that often a client may be require data that comes from a variety of data sources other than the domain objects on the server. Data sources such as straight JDBC calls and Java Connector Architecture (JCA) adapters, also need to be wrapped in data transfer objects and returned to the client.

Therefore:

> **Design custom data transfer objects that wrap arbitrary sets of data as needed by the client, completely decoupled from the layout of the domain model on the server.**

Custom data transfer objects are just like normal data transfer objects, except that they are typically immutable and don't map to any specific data structures on the server (in contrast to mutable domain data transfer objects). Custom data transfer objects advocate a use-case-driven approach, in which data transfer objects are designed around the needs of the client.

From the Car example, imagine that a client only wanted to display the attributes of a car that related to its engine. In this case, a data transfer object that wraps those particular attributes should be created and passed to the client. This custom data transfer object would contain a subset of the car's attributes, as shown in Figure 2.4.

In general, if an EJB client requires attributes X,Y, and Z, then a data transfer object that wraps X,Y, and Z, and *only* those attributes would be created. With this approach, a data transfer object acts as contract that provides the client with the data it needs, while encapsulating the data that the server has. Custom data transfer object design works perfectly with the Session Façade pattern, in which the details of the entity bean object model are hidden behind a set of session beans. The correct way to think of data transfer objects in this respect is merely as data and not as representing any server-side business abstraction such as an entity bean. If all of the data happens to come from one entity bean, fine, but if not, it's the server's problem how to populate the data transfer object and this doesn't concern the client.

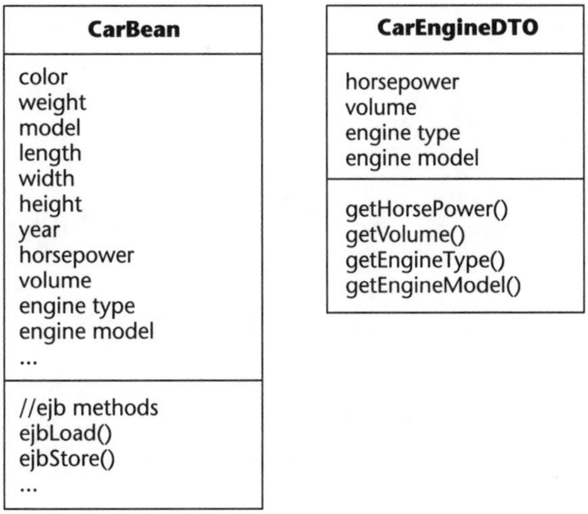

CarBean
color weight model length width height year horsepower volume engine type engine model ...

//ejb methods
ejbLoad()
ejbStore()
...

CarEngineDTO
horsepower volume engine type engine model
getHorsePower() getVolume() getEngineType() getEngineModel()

Figure 2.4 A Custom data transfer object wrapping a subset of data.

A typical J2EE application will have a proliferation of custom DTOs, so many so that often developers may be willing to accept slightly more coarse-grained DTOs (that may contain more attributes than needed) rather than writing new custom DTOs from scratch. As long as there is not too much redundant data being returned, this practical approach is fine. As with any pattern, it is up to the developers to balance the concerns of maintenance versus performance in deciding how far to go in its use.

Custom data transfer objects are typically used for UI-specific read-only operations, and are made immutable. That is, custom DTOs cannot be changed; they are only for display purposes. Since a custom data transfer object is merely a grouping of data, and not really related to any server-side business object, it doesn't make sense to update it. Typically, updates are done via entity bean data transfer objects (since they represent real business objects and can encapsulate validation logic) or through use-case-specific methods on session façades.

Custom DTOs are almost always created via a DTOFactory (see the Data Transfer Object Factory pattern), and are tied to the specific needs of the client.

Data Transfer HashMap

A client needs to exchange bulk data with the server in a generic fashion.

How can arbitrary amounts of data be efficiently transferred across tiers in a generic fashion?

✳ ✳ ✳

As discussed in the Data Transfer Object and Session Façade patterns, performance in an EJB system is realized by minimizing the number of network calls required to execute a given use case. In particular, data transfer objects provide a way to transfer data across a network in bulk, keeping the client from executing more than one network call to an EJB in order to send or receive some data.

The most common way to use DTOs is to use custom DTOs with a DTO-Factory. Here, a new DTO is written for every new use case in the system, providing the client with an object-based wrapper that acts as an envelope to transfer whatever data the use case requires. Despite the simplicity of this approach, using DTOs in this manner also suffers from several drawbacks:

- **High cost of change over time.** The use cases in an application change over time. Different clients may need to access different views or subsets of server-side data than were initially programmed. When we use the custom data transfer object approach (even with DTOFactories), server-side code (such as new DTOs and associated creation logic) must be written to satisfy the changing data access needs of the client. Once an EJB project has been launched, access to server-side programmers tends to be expensive, as is the EJB redeployment process.

- **Need to create a data transfer object layer.** Data transfer objects create a new layer, which can explode to thousands of objects in a large application. Imagine a distributed system with 30 entity beans. Each of those 30 entity beans would likely have a domain DTO to marshal their state to and from the client tier. The application's use cases may also require that data from those entity beans be used in several custom DTOs. Thus, a medium-sized system could require hundreds of DTOs, each with a particular Factory method to create it. Since the DTO layer generally represents attributes in the entity bean layer, changes in entity bean attributes will cause ripples that could require changes in multiple DTOs as well. In large applications, the DTO layer can prove to be very difficult to maintain.

- **Client UIs tightly coupled to the server.** When using custom DTOs, each client UI is tightly coupled to the DTO it uses to populate itself. When the DTO changes, the client needs to be recompiled, even if the changes don't necessarily affect that particular client. On a typical system with tons of different UIs (imagine a large Web site with many JSPs), that represents a lot of dependencies that need to be maintained.

If the domain of an application is relatively simple, data transfer objects are a great way to get the job done. If your domain requirements are more complex, an alternative to data transfer objects may be needed; one that decouples the data being transferred from the object that contains the data, but still allows bulk access and transport of data across tiers.

Therefore:

Use HashMaps to marshal arbitrary sets of data between the client and the EJB tier.

Plain JDK HashMaps (available since JDK 1.2) provide a generic, serializable container for arbitrary sets of data, that can replace an entire layer of data transfer objects. The only dependency in client and server-side code is the naming conventions placed on the *keys* used to identify attributes, described later in this pattern.

Clients request HashMaps by going through the session façade. For example, for the use case of getting all data in an account, a client would call a *getAccountData* method on the session façade, which would return a HashMap populated with all the data in an account, as shown in Figure 2.5. Updates can be made on the same HashMap locally. Once updates are complete, the client simply passes the updated HashMap back to the session façade for updating.

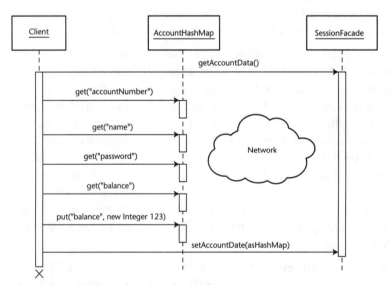

Figure 2.5   Using a data transfer HashMap.

Instead of implementing custom data transfer objects for every use case, a client can simply be passed a HashMap that contains different sets of data, as needed by the particular use case. For example, if a client needs a smaller sub-set of data than a HashMap with all the Account attributes, the session façade can simply be coded to return a HashMap with fewer attributes.

Using a HashMap instead of a data transfer object comes at the cost of addi-tional implementation complexity, since the client now needs to explicitly know the strings used as *keys* to query the HashMap for the attributes of inter-est. Furthermore, both the session façade and the client need to agree on the strings to be used to populate and read from a HashMap. For a discussion of common solutions to this problem, see the Generic Attribute Access Pattern.

The advantages of using HashMaps for data transfer are:

- **Excellent maintainability—eliminates the data transfer object layer.** The extra layer of domain-specific data transfer objects and all that repetitive data transfer object creation logic is now eliminated in favor of the generic reusable map and attribute access interfaces. This repre-sents a potential reduction of thousands of lines of code, particularly when used in conjunction with the Generic Attribute Access pattern.

- **One data object (map) across all clients.** A map of attributes is reusable from the session façade down to the JSPs. In particular, using a map as a data container significantly reduces the complexity of the JSP code, because pages don't need to be written with use-case-specific data transfer objects that are tightly coupled to the entity bean layer.

- **Low cost of maintenance over time.** New views of server-side data can be created that do not require any server-side programming. Clients can dynamically decide which attributes to display.

The trade-offs of using HashMaps for transferring data across the network are:

- **Need to maintain a contract for attribute keys.** Whereas attribute names are hard-coded in the *get* methods of a DTO, clients need to remember the key-values of attributes when using a HashMap. Further-more, the client and server need to agree on the keys, creating an extra dependency between client and server. Good and thorough documenta-tion can also help alleviate these problems.

- **Loss of strong typing/compile-time checking.** When we use data trans-fer objects, values passed by *gets* or *sets* are always of the correct type; any errors are passed at compile time. When we use HashMaps, attribute access must be managed by the client at run time by casting objects to their correct type and associating the correct attribute type with the correct key.

- **Primitives need to be wrapped.** Primitive attributes such as int, double, and long cannot be stored in a map, since they aren't a subclass of Object. Primitives need to be manually wrapped with the appropriate object (Integer for ints, Long for long, Double for double, and so on) before being placed into a map.

- **Casting required for every read.** Whenever data is read from a HashMap, it needs to be cast from Object to the appropriate type. This can complicate client code and reduce performance.

Using HashMaps for genericising a DTO layer comes with some very pyrotechnic advantages as well as disadvantages. Most developers find themselves most comfortable using proper data transfer objects. They have well-understood usage patterns, and it is very difficult for client-side developers to make mistakes when using them. Data transfer HashMaps are a double-edged sword that solve many maintenance problems but also add others. The decision on which method to use is a judgment that should be made based on your own project needs.

Data Transfer RowSet

When using JDBC for Reading, relational data needs to be transferred across the network tier from the session façade to the client.

How can relational data be transferred to the client in a generic, tabular format?

* * *

The JDBC for Reading pattern advocates the practice of using session beans to perform straight JDBC calls to the database (instead of querying through the entity bean layer) when performing a common read-only listing of tabular data, such as populating tables on HTML pages or applets. This practice can improve performance if you are using BMP, or if your CMP engine does not support the bulk loading of entity bean data, or if you cannot make use of entity bean caching (see the JDBC for Reading pattern for more info).

With the session façade performing JDBC calls, the question then becomes: What is the best way to marshal this data across to the client? The most common solution is to use data transfer objects. For example, consider the Employee/Department example used in the JDBC for Reading pattern. Here we want to populate a table that lists all employees in a company with their department, as shown in Figure 2.6.

Data transfer objects can be used to populate this table by creating a custom EmployeeDepartmentDTO, which looks like the following:

```
public class EmployeeDepartmentDTO {
    public String employeeName;
    public String employeeTitle;
    ...
    public String departmentName;
    public String departmentLocation;
    ...
}
```

Employee	Department
Adam Berman	Development
Eileen Sauer	Training
Ed Roman	Management
Clay Roach	Architecture

Figure 2.6 HTML table of employees.

Here, the session bean will perform a JDBC call to get a ResultSet that contains information about an employee and his or her department. The session bean will then manually extract fields from the ResultSet and call the necessary *setters* to populate the DTO. Each row in the ResultSet will be transferred into a DTO, which will be added to a collection. This collection of DTOs now forms a network-transportable bundle, which can be transferred to the client for consumption.

As explained in the Data Transfer HashMap pattern, using DTOs as a data transport mechanism causes maintainability problems because of the often very large DTO layer that needs to be created, as well as the fact that client UIs are tightly coupled to the DTO layer. When using JDBC for Reading, DTOs suffer an additional problem:

- **Performance: tabular to Object Oriented (OO) and back to tabular is redundant.** With the data already represented in rows in tables in a result set, the transferring of the data into a collection of objects and then back into a table (on the client UI) consisting of rows and columns is redundant.

When using JDBC for Reading, ideally a data transfer mechanism should be used that can preserve the tabular nature of the data being transferred in a generic fashion, allowing for simpler clients and simpler parsing into the client UI.

Therefore:

Use RowSets for marshalling raw relational data directly from a ResultSet in the EJB tier to the client tier.

Introduced in as an optional API in JDBC 2.0, javax.sql.RowSet is an interface, a subinterface of *java.sql.ResultSet* (RowSet joined the core JDBC API as of JDBC 3.0). What makes RowSets relevant to EJB developers is that particular implementations the RowSet interface allow you to wrap ResultSet data and marshal it off to the client tier, where a client can operate directly on the rows and fields in a RowSet as they might on a Result Set. This allows developers to take tabular data directly out of the database and have them easily converted into tables on the client tier, without having to manually map the data from the ResultSet into some other form (like data transfer objects) and then back into a table on a UI, such as a JSP.

The type of RowSet implementation that can be used to pass data to the client tier is must be a *disconnected RowSet*, that is, a RowSet that does not keep a live connection to the database. One such implementation provided by Sun is called the CachedRowSet. A CachedRowSet allows you to copy in ResultSet data and bring this data down to the client tier, because a CachedRowSet is *disconnected* from the database. Alternately, you could create your own custom, disconnected implementations of the RowSet or ResultSet interfaces and use them to marshal tabular data to the client.

In our Employee and Department example, using RowSets would allow us to retrieve an entire table of Employee and Department data in one object and pass that on to the client tier. Figure 2.7 illustrates how the RowSet approach differs from the Data Transfer Object approach.

To create this RowSet, the method on the session façade that performs the direct JDBC call would be written as follows:

```
...
ps = conn.prepareStatement("select * from ...");
ps.execute();
ResultSet rs = ps.getResultSet();

RowSet cs = new CachedRowSet();
cs.populate(rs);

return cs;
...
```

On the client tier, the data from the RowSet can now be directly mapped to the columns and rows of a table.

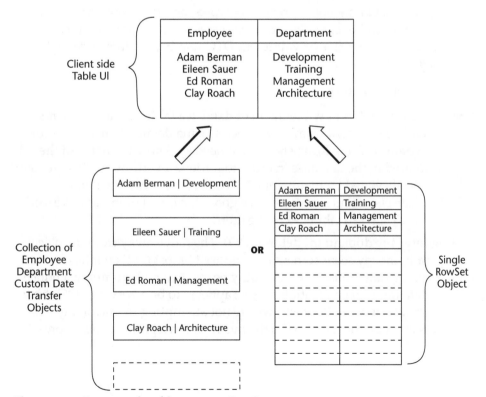

Figure 2.7   Data transfer objects versus RowSets.

RowSets offer a clean and practical way to marshal tabular data from a JDBC ResultSet, straight down to the client-side UI, without the usual overhead of converting data to data transfer objects and then back to tabular client-side lists.

Using RowSets as a method of marshalling data across tiers brings many advantages:

- **RowSet provides a common interface for all query operations.** By using a RowSet, all the clients can use the same interface for all data-querying needs. No matter what the use case is or what data is being returned, the interface a client operates on stays the same. This is in contrast to having hundreds of client UIs tightly coupled to use-case-specific Custom DTOs. Whereas data transfer objects need to be changed when the client's data access needs change, the RowSet interface remains the same.

- **Eliminates the redundant data translation.** RowSets can be created directly from JDBC ResultSets, eliminating the translation step from ResultSet to DTO and then back to a table on the client side.

- **Allows for automation.** Since the RowSet interface never changes, it is possible to create graphical user interface (GUI) builders, such as taglibs, that know how to render RowSets, and then reuse these same tools over and over again across use cases. Contrast this with the DTO approach, in which every different DTO requires custom code to display itself.

Here are the trade-offs:

- **Clients need to know the name of database table columns.** Clients should be insulated from persistence schema details such as table column names. Using RowSets, a client needs to know the name of the column used in the database in order to retrieve an attribute. This problem can be alleviated by maintaining a "contract" of attribute names between client and server (or very good documentation), as described in the Generic Attribute Access pattern.

- **Ignores the domain model (not OO).** The move away from the object paradigm may seem somewhat contrary to most J2EE architectures based on data transfer object/entity beans. After all, dumping a bunch of data into a generic tabular object appears to be a very non-OO thing to do. When using RowSets, we are not attempting to mirror any business concept, the data *itself* is the business concept that is being presented to the user, and not any relationships between the data.

■ **No compile-time checking of query results.** Rather than calling *getXXX()* on a data transfer object, a client must now call *getString("XXX")* on the RowSet. This opens up client-side development to errors that cannot be caught at compile time, such as the mistyping of the attribute name a client wants to retrieve from the RowSet.

One important point to remember is that although some implementations of the RowSet interface are updateable and can synchronize their changes with the database, a developer should never use this facility to perform updates in an application. Updates should be performed by passing parameters to methods on the session façade or using data transfer objects.

Another item to consider is that there is nothing magic about the javax.sql. RowSet interface in particular, other than that it is part of the official JDBC spec, and working implementations of it exist. Developers can write their own RowSet-like classes (or simply wrap a CachedRowSet) and derive all the same benefits. One reason for creating a custom implementation that does not extend the RowSet interface is to hide all the mutator (insert/update/delete) methods the RowSet interface exposes, since these should never be used by the client tier.

Data transfer RowSets are only used for read-only data, in conjunction with the JDBC for Reading pattern.

CHAPTER 3

Transaction and Persistence Patterns

This chapter contains a set of diverse patterns that solves problems involving transaction control, persistence, and performance. The chapter includes:

Version Number. Used to program your entity beans with optimistic concurrency checks that can protect the consistency of your database, when dealing with use cases that span transactions and user think time.

JDBC for Reading. The section on this performance-enhancing pattern discusses when to disregard the entity bean layer and opt for straight JDBC access to the database, for performance reasons, and discusses all the semantics involved with doing so.

Data Access Command Bean. Provides a standard way to decouple an enterprise bean from the persistence logic and details of the persistence store. Makes it really easy to write persistence logic.

Dual Persistent Entity Bean. A pattern for component developers, the Dual Persistent Entity Bean pattern shows how to write entity beans that can be compiled once and then deployed in either a CMP or a BMP engine-simply by editing the deployment descriptors.

Version Number

When a client initiates an update on the server side, based on data that it has read in a previous transaction, the update may be based on stale data.

How can you determine if the data used to update the server is stale?

* * *

Transactions allow developers to make certain assumptions about the data they handle. One of these assumptions is that transactions will operate in isolation from other transactions, allowing developers to simplify their code by assuming that the data being read and written in a transaction is fresh and consistent.

In an EJB context, this means that when a use case is executed (usually as a method on the session façade running under a declarative transaction), the code can update a set of entity beans with the assumption that no other transactions can modify the same entity beans it is currently modifying.

While transaction isolation works well when a use case can be executed in just one transaction, it breaks down for use cases that span multiple transactions. Such use cases typically occur when a user needs to manually process a piece of data before performing an update on the server. Such a use case requires an interval of *user think time* (that is, a user entering updates into a form). The problem with user think time is that it is too long, which makes it infeasible (and impossible in EJB) to wrap the entire process of reading from the server, thinking by the user, and updating of the server in one transaction. Instead, data is usually read from the server in one transaction, processed by the user, and then updated on the server in a second transaction.

The problem with this approach is that we no longer have guarantees of isolation from changes by other transactions, since the entire use case is not wrapped in a single transaction. For example, consider a message board administrative system, in which multiple individuals have moderator access on a forum of messages. A common use case is to edit the contents of a user-posted message for broken links or improper content. At the code level, this involves getting a message's data in one transaction, modifying it during user think time, and then updating it in a second transaction. Now consider what can happen when two moderators A and B try to edit the same message at the same time:

1. Moderator A reads Message X in a transaction.
2. Moderator B reads Message X in a transaction.
3. Moderator A performs local updates on his copy of the Message.
4. Moderator B performs local updates on her copy of the Message.

5. Moderator A updates Message X in one transaction.

6. Moderator B updates Message X in one transaction.

Once Step 6 occurs, all updates executed by Moderator A will be overwritten by those changes made by Moderator B. In Step 5, Moderator A successfully updated Message X. At this point, any copies of the message held by other clients is said to be stale, since it no longer reflects the current state of the Message entity bean. Thus, Moderator B updated the message on the basis on stale data.

In a message board system, such issues may not be much cause for concern, but imagine the ramifications of similar events happening in a medical or a banking system—they could be disastrous. The crux of the problem here is that the Moderator A's and Moderator B's actions were not isolated from each other. Because separate transactions were used for the read and update steps, there was no way to automatically check when the data used to update the server was based on a read that had become stale.

Therefore:

Use version numbers to implement your own staleness checks in entity beans.

A version number is simply an integer that is added to an entity bean (and its underlying table) as a member attribute. The purpose of this integer is to identify the state of an entity bean at any point in time. This can be achieved by incrementing the bean's version number whenever an entity bean is updated. This incrementing of versions allows the detection of updates based on stale data, using the following procedure:

1. **Carry the version number along with any other data read from an entity bean during read transactions.** This is usually done by adding an entity bean's version number to any data transfer objects used to copy its data to the client.

2. **Send the version number back to the entity bean along with any updated data.** When it comes time to perform the update, carry the original version number back with the newly updated data, and compare it with the entity bean's *current version* before performing any updates.

3. **Increment the entity bean's version number when performing an update.** If the current version of the entity bean is equal to that of the updated data from the client, then update the entity bean and increment its version.

4. **Reject the update if the version numbers do not match.** An update carrying an older version number than currently in the entity bean means that the update is based on stale data, so throw an exception.

Using version numbers in this manner will protect against the isolation problems that can occur when a use case spans multiple transactions. Consider the forum moderator example. If, before Step 1, the version number of message X was 4, then both Moderator A and Moderator B will retrieve this version number in their local copy of the message. At Step 5, Moderator A's update will succeed, since the version he is carrying (4) matches that in Message X. At this point, Message X's version number will be incremented from 4 to 5. At Step 6, Moderator B's update will fail, since the version number this moderator is carrying (4) does not match the current version of Message entity bean X, which is currently 5.

When a stale update is detected, the usual recovery procedure is to notify the end user that someone has beat them to the update, and ask them to reapply their changes on the latest copy of server-side data.

The implementation of the Version Number pattern differs slightly, depending on the mechanisms used to access the entity beans. If we use data transfer objects to get and set data in bulk on the entity beans directly (as done with EJB 1.X applications), then the version number is added to the DTO in the entity bean's *getXXXDTO* method, and the version number is checked with the current version in the entity bean's *setXXXDTO* method, as in the following code block:

```
public void setMessageDTO(MessageDTO aMessageDTO)
throws NoSuchMessageException
{
    if (aMessageDTO.getVersion() != this.getVersion())
        throw new NoSuchMessageException();

    this.setSubject(aMessageDTO.getSubject());
    this.setBody(aMessageDTO.getBody());

}
```

However, as discussed in the DTOFactory pattern, using DTOs as a mechanism for accessing entity beans directly is a deprecated practice as of EJB 2.0. Instead, the DTOFactory/session façade is responsible for getting data from an entity bean and updating the entity bean by directly calling *get/set* methods via the entity bean's local interface.

Using this paradigm, a session bean is responsible for updating an entity bean directly via its *set* methods; thus the entity bean can no longer automatically check the version of a set of data before it updates itself. Instead, developers must adopt a programming convention and always remember to pass the version of a set of data they are about to update before beginning the update procedure, as in the following session bean method:

```
public void updateMessage( MessageDTO aMessageDTO)
{
    Message aMessage;
```

```
try //to update the desired message
{
    aMessage = this.messageHome.findByPrimaryKey(
                aMessageDTO.getMessageID() );

    aMessage.checkAndUpdateVersion(aMessageDTO.getVersion());

    //update the message
    aMessage.setBody(    aMessageDTO.getBody()    );
    aMessage.setSubject( aMessageDTO.getSubject() );
}
catch(IncorrectVersionException e)
{
    this.ctx.setRollbackOnly();
    throw new StaleUpdateException();
}
catch (...)
   ...
}
```

Upon the call to *checkAndUpdateVersion*, the Message entity bean will check the version with its own internal version number and throw an *IncorrectVersionException* if the versions do not match. If the versions *do* match, then the entity bean will increment its own internal counter, as in the following code block:

```
public void checkAndUpdateVersion(long version)
throws IncorrectVersionException
{
    int currentVersion = this.getVersion();
    if( version != currentVersion)
       throw new IncorrectVersionException();
    else
       this.setVersion( ++currentVersion );
}
```

The version numbering scheme described here can also be thought of as implementing your own optimistic concurrency. Instead of having entity beans being used by a long-running use case be locked from concurrent access, we allow multiple users to access the data, and only reject an update when we detect that stale data was used as a basis for the update. Databases that implement optimistic concurrency use a similar scheme to allow multiple clients to read data, only rejecting writes when collisions are detected.

Similar implementations can be found that use timestamps instead of version numbers. These two implementations are basically identical, although using version numbers is simpler and protects against possible problems that can occur in the unlikely event that the server's clock is rolled back, or if the database date and time come down to a small enough interval to eliminate the possibility of invalid staleness checks.

The Version Number pattern guarantees that use cases executed across transactions will be properly isolated from each other's changes, in the same way that use cases that execute within a single transaction are guaranteed to be isolated from the operations of other transactions. However, what happens in the *infrequent* event that both moderators attempt to update the server (Steps 5 and 6) at the exact same time? In this example, two instances of the Message entity bean could be loaded into memory with both containing the same version number. The call to *checkAndUpdateVersion* will thus succeed in both instances. Once the first transaction commits, the question then becomes: what happens when the second transaction attempts to commit?

The answer is that the second transaction will be correctly rolled back. Since both transactions are happening at the same time, the same transaction isolation level semantics that protect use cases that execute within one transaction will protect this particular operation from conflicts. The way it achieves this depends on how your database/application server handles concurrency:

- **Isolation of READ_COMMITTED with application server CMP verified updates.** Here the application server will compare the changed attributes in the Message entity bean (including the version number) with that in the database before committing. If the contents do not match (because a previous transaction incremented the version number and other attributes), then the application server will roll back the transaction. This is an optimistic concurrency check implemented at the application server level, allowing you to use a transaction isolation level of just READ_COMMITTED, since the application server guarantees consistency.

- **Isolation of READ_COMMITTED with verified updates implemented in BMP.** BMP developers can manually implement verified updates by comparing the version number in the current bean to that in the database in *ejbStore*. This can be achieved by modifying the SQL UPDATE statement to include a *where version=X* clause. Even if Moderator A's transaction updated the database milliseconds before, this where clause will fail and the developer can manually roll back the exception.

- **Isolation of SERIALIZABLE with Database (DB) that supports optimistic concurrency.** If optimistic concurrency is not implemented at the application server level, then a transaction isolation level of SERIALIZABLE must be used to ensure consistency. If the database itself implements optimistic concurrency checks, then it will automatically roll back the transaction of Moderator B's when it detects that *ejbStore* is trying to overwrite the data inserted by the first transaction.

- **Isolation of SERIALIZABLE with a DB that uses pessimistic concurrency.** Again, SERIALIZABLE must be used since the application server won't enforce consistency. However, since the database is using a pessimistic concurrency strategy, it will lock Message X's row in the database, forcing the MessageEntity.*ejbLoad()* of the second transaction to *wait* until the MessageEntity.*ejbStore()* from the first transaction completes and commits. This means that when Moderators B's transaction calls *checkAndUpdateVersion* this check will correctly fail, since the message X was not *ejbLoad()*'ed until after Moderator A's transaction had committed.

- **Isolation of SERIALIZABLE with a SELECT FOR UPDATE.** Some application servers allow the CMP engine to be configured to issue a *SELECT FOR UPDATE* during ejbLoad, by editing a deployment descriptor setting. The purpose of this is to force a database that uses optimistic concurrency to actually lock the underlying row. This will cause the transactions to execute as in the previous option.

The takeaway point here is that, in the rare instance where the updates are happening at the same time, consistency is maintained, and either the second transaction will be detected at *checkAndUpdateVersion* time or the application server or database will detect the collision and roll back the transaction—either way, consistency is maintained.

Another important point to consider when using the Version Number pattern is that it can cause problems when you have legacy or non-Java applications updating the same data as your EJB application. Legacy applications will probably be using version numbers, resulting in consistency problems between the EJB application and the legacy application. If it is under your control, ensure that other non-Java or legacy applications also properly update the version number when performing updates. If changing the legacy applications is completely beyond your control, then another solution is to implement triggers in the database that will update the version numbers in the database automatically. If you take this approach, don't forget to remove the version number incrementing code from your entity bean.

The Version Number pattern is most often used as a way to protect against stale updates that occur when using data transfer objects. Once a DTO is used to copy some data off of the server, this data could potentially be stale. Version numbers help us detect the stale data at update time.

JDBC for Reading

In an EJB system that uses a relational database in the back end, an EJB client needs to populate a tabular user interface with server-side data, for display purposes.

When should a session façade perform direct database access instead of going through the entity bean layer?

* * *

Perhaps the most common use case encountered in distributed applications is the need to present static server-side data to a client in tabular form. Examples of tabular UIs constitute the majority of Web pages, where data is listed in tables or rows, such as a list of items in a catalog (as opposed to nontabular UIs such as the rare treelike or circular UI). Furthermore, this tabular data is usually read-only; clients tend to do a lot more browsing than updating of the pages they surf.

One common scenario is an application that requires the presentation of a large amount of *read-only* data to the user, perhaps in the form of an HTML table. The table may represent line items in a large order, information on all employees in a company, or the characteristics of all products a company produces.

In Figure 3.1, each row in the table corresponds to one employee in the system and his/her department. On the server side, we would model this with an Employee and a Department entity bean. One way to populate the table would be to call a *getEmployees()* method on a session façade/data transfer object factory, which would call a finder method on an EmployeeHome object, return all employee's, find each employee's related Department entity bean, and create a custom data transfer object with the combined data from these two entity beans. The session bean would then return a collection of EmployeeDepartmentDTOs to the client.

Employee	Department
Adam Berman Eileen Sauer Ed Roman Clay Roach	Development Training Management Architecture

Figure 3.1   HTML table of employees.

Depending on the EJB Server and applications, there are numerous problems with this approach:

- **The $n + 1$ entity bean database calls problem.** With BMP and certain implementations of CMP, retrieving data from N entity beans will require $N + 1$ database calls. Although a good CMP implementation will allow bulk loading, developers should be aware of this dire problem. The $N + 1$ calls problem is as follows: In order to read data from N entity beans, one must first call a finder method (one database call). The container will then execute ejbLoad() individually on each entity bean returned by the finder method, either directly after the finder invocation or just before a business method invocation. This means that ejbLoad() (which will execute a database call) will need to be called for each entity bean. Thus, a simple database query operation requires $N + 1$ database calls when going through the entity bean layer! Each such database call will temporarily lock a database connection from the pool, open and close connections, open and close result sets, and so on. Since most distributed systems have a separate box for the database, each of these database round trips would require a network call, slowing down the speed of each round trip and locking valuable database resources from the rest of the system. For our Employee and Departments example, running this use case will actually require $2N + 1$ database calls (one finder, N Emlpoyee ejbLoads(), and N Department ejbLoads()).

- **Remote call overhead.** If it goes through the entity bean remote interface (as opposed to the local interface), this method would also require $3N$ remote calls for N rows of employee and department data. The remote calls break down as follows:

  - N calls to getValueObject() for each Employee.
  - N calls to getDepartment() on each Employee.
  - N calls to getValueObject() on each Department.

  After grabbing each set of value objects, the session bean would then combine the value objects into the EmployeeProjectViewObjects.

- **Cumbersome for simple join operations.** Whether we use BMP or CMP, this typical use case requires the instantiation of multiple entity beans and traversal of their relationships. Imagine a slightly more complex scenario in which the table needed to list data from an Employee and a related Department, Project, and Company. This would not only require tens of lines of spaghetti code, but would significantly slow down a system because of the database calls, remote calls, and all the application server overhead incurred when traversing multiple entity bean relationships.

When the client side mainly requires tabular data for read-only *listing* purposes, the benefits of querying through the entity bean layer are less clear. Using local interfaces and a good CMP implementation will definitely reduce the performance problems with listing data via entity beans, but BMP developers are not so lucky. In BMP, these problems can only be alleviated by turning on entity bean caching, a luxury usually only available for single EJB server (or nonclustered) deployments in which the database is never modified outside of the EJB application The remaining BMP developers are faced with a serious performance problem. Querying through the entity bean layer simply to list read-only data causes unacceptable performance problems

Therefore:

In BMP, perform listing operations on relational databases using JDBC. Use entity beans for update operations.

If the data that the client UI requires is mainly used for listing purposes, then using JDBC to directly read the rows and columns required by the client can be far faster and more efficient then going through the entity bean layer. Using the previous example, the entire table of employees and departments could be read in bulk from the database in just one JDBC call, as opposed to the potentially required $3N$ remote calls and $N + 1$ database calls required if it is read through the entity bean layer.

After reading in the ResultSet, the data could then be added to Employee-DepartmentDTOs just as in the previous example, or it could be marshaled to the client by using HashMaps (as in the Data Transfer HashMap pattern) or in tabular form using RowSets, as in the Data Transfer Rowset pattern.

The decision to use straight JDBC instead of entity beans for reading data is a tough one for most developers, and has been the subject of raging debates ever since the advent of entity beans. After all, entity beans provide a nice encapsulation of data and data logic, they hide the persistence details such as the type of database being used, they model the business concepts in your system, and they make use of many container features such as pooling, concurrency, transactions, and so on. To go to a non-OO method of data access seems like a step back. Like all design patterns, there are trade-offs.

Using JDBC for reading purposes has the following advantages:

- **No transactional overhead for simple query operations.** Read-only operations do not need to use transactions. Querying the database from a stateless session bean with transactions turned off is more lightweight than querying entity beans. Often it is impossible to query an entity bean without a transaction.

- **Takes advantage of DB built-in caching.** Databases have sophisticated and powerful caches. By using JDBC for these operations we can make better use of the DB's built-in cache. This becomes important when executing queries that span tables, because the database can cache the results of this one bulk query, rather than cache individual table queries generated by entity bean *ejbLoads* calls. The next time a query is run, the one bulk JDBC query will come directly from the database cache.

- **Retrieve the exact data your use case requires.** Using JDBC, you can select the exact columns required across any number of tables. This stands in contrast to using an entity bean layer, in which the client may only need a couple of attributes from a variety of related entity beans. Those entity beans will need to load all of their attributes from the database even if a client only needs one attribute.

- **Perform queries in ONE BULK READ.** All the data a client requires is grabbed in one bulk database call. This is in direct contrast to the $N+1$ database calls problem associated with entity beans.

Here are the trade-offs:

- **Tight coupling between business and persistence logic.** When working with an entity bean, a developer doesn't know what the underlying persistence mechanism is. With this pattern, session bean data querying logic is now coupled to the JDBC APIs and is thus coupled to a relational database. However, other design patterns such as the Data Access Object pattern (not covered in this book) can be used to alleviate this problem.

- **Bug prone and less maintainable.** Bug-prone JDBC code is now mixed around the session bean layer, instead of nicely encapsulated behind entity beans. Changes to the database schema will require changes to multiple code fragments across the session façade. Again, the Data Access Object pattern can help here.

Finally, this pattern does not imply that entity beans should not be used at all, only that there are more efficient alternatives when the client needs to temporarily list data. In this pattern, JDBC is used for listing behavior, and the entity bean layer is used for updating behavior in an application.

Whereas the integrity of business/data objects and their relationships with other business objects are not that important when listing tables of data on a client, these concepts are critical when performing updates. Entity beans (or any other data object framework) encapsulate both data and *rules* for changing that data. When updating an attribute on an entity bean, the entity bean may need to perform validation logic on its changes and institute updates on other entity beans in an application.

For example, consider an application with Book and Chapter entity beans. When modifying the title of a Chapter entity bean, the Chapter will need to perform validation on the new title, and internally call and modify its Book bean to notify it to change its table of contents. The Book entity bean may then need to modify other entity beans, and so on.

Performing updates via JDBC from the session façade forces a developer to write spaghetti code that mixes business logic with the complexities of data logic. All the rules, relationships, and validations required by particular *business concepts* would have to be hacked in the form of updates on rows and tables. The system would become very brittle to changes in the business requirements of the application.

Thus, where the client UI requires read-only tabular data and entity bean caching is not possible, use JDBC to read in data from the database, instead of going through the entity bean layer. All updates should still go through the domain object (entity bean) layer.

The JDBC for Reading pattern occurs behind a session façade or a data transfer object factory. Depending on what type of object is used to transfer the ResultSets contents to the client. (DTOFactory implies that DTOs will be returned to the client, whereas HashMaps or RowSets can be returned from the session façade).

Related Patterns

Fast Lane Reader (J2EE Blueprints)

Data Access Command Beans

An enterprise bean needs to access a persistent data store.

How can persistence logic and persistent store details be decoupled and encapsulated away from enterprise bean business logic?

* * *

When programming with a session bean layer that directly accesses the database (no entity beans), or when writing bean-managed persistent entity beans, a common practice is to mix the persistence logic in with the session bean or entity bean. For session beans, this usually entails writing data-store-specific access code (such as JDBC) mixed in with business logic. For entity beans, the standard practice is to write JDBC in the *ejbCreate()*, *ejbLoad()*, *ejb-Store()* and *ejbRemove()* methods.

Although this gets the job done, this approach suffers from several drawbacks:

- **Data logic mixed in with business logic.** Mixing persistence logic in with business logic has terrible consequences for maintainability. Business logic becomes harder to distinguish among spaghetti persistence code, and persistence code becomes spread across the business layer instead of localized to one layer.

- **Tight coupling to a particular persistent data store (database) type.** By coding a particular persistence API into your business logic (such as JDBC), you tightly couple your application to one particular data store type (OODBMS, RDBMS, LEGACY). This makes it difficult to switch between data store types. Furthermore, on projects that include a legacy integration as well as a more modern data store, two different persistence APIs would be mixed in with business logic, making the code even more convoluted.

- **Vulnerable to data schema changes.** Minor schema changes in the database will require modification and recompilation of the persistence logic and also the business logic, since the two are tightly coupled.

- **Replication of logic.** JDBC programming requires repetitive coding (finding data sources, getting the connection, declaring prepared statements, parsing the results of a ResultSet, closing statements and connections, and so on) that needs to be replicated across all the EJBs that access the database.

The problems with coupling and maintainability described above make it difficult to write truly reusable business components. In many cases, reusability across data store types is not that important. Only projects whose requirements dictate the use of multiple types of data stores (RDBMS, ODBMS, LDAP, and so on), now or in the future, need to be concerned with the coupling of the persistence logic to the details of the database implementation. However, coupling or not, the mixing of persistence logic with enterprise beans still poses significant maintainability problems.

Therefore:

Encapsulate persistence logic into data access command beans, which decouple enterprise beans from all persistence logic.

A data access command bean (DACB) is a plain Java bean style object that exposes a simple get/set/execute interface to the enterprise bean clients. Data access command beans encapsulate persistence logic and all details about the persistent data store, forming a separate, decoupled persistence layer that exists beneath the EJB layers.

A Data Access Command Bean pattern is similar to the original Command pattern (Gamma, et al., 1994), in that it exposes a very simple interface to its clients (see Figure 3.2). All a client needs to do is create a data access command bean, *set* any information it needs to perform its task, call *execute*, and then call *getters* to retrieve the data from the command, as well as a *next* method if the command returns multiple rows of values.

For example, consider an EmployeeServices session bean that handles all the management of employees for a company. EmployeeServices exposes (among others) methods to create and to search for employees within an organization. An example of the session façade, this bean doesn't use a domain model, instead it interacts directly with the database.

To decouple the EmployeeServices bean from persistence logic, two data access command beans would be created, one that handles the creation of an employee, and one that handles finding all employees with the same name. The class diagrams for these DACBs are listed in Figure 3.3.

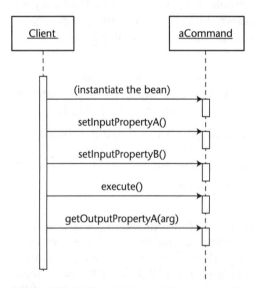

Figure 3.2   Using a data access command bean.

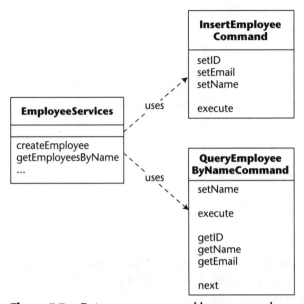

Figure 3.3   Data access command beans example.

By using these data access command beans, the code in EmployeeServices is greatly simplified. The following code shows how the EmployeeServices session bean interacts with the InsertEmployeeCommand:

```
InsertEmployeeCommand insEmp = null;
try
{
    insEmp = new InsertEmployeeCommand();
    insEmp.setEmail("me@home.com");
    insEmp.setId(id);
    insEmp.setName("Ed");
} catch (DataCommandException e)
{
    this.ctx.setRollbackOnly();
    throw new EJBException(e.getMessage());
}
```

Using the QueryEmployeeByName command is slightly different, since the command could potentially return multiple employees by the same name:

```
try
{
    QueryEmployeeByNameCommand query =
        new QueryEmployeeByNameCommand();
    query.setName(name);
    query.execute();
```

```
                    Vector employees;
                    EmployeeDTO anEmployee;
                    while (query.next())
                    {
                        anEmployee = new EmployeeDTO(query.getId(),
                                                    query.getName(),
                                                    query.getEmail());
                    }

                    return employees;

                } catch (DataCommandException e)
                {
                    this.ctx.setRollbackOnly();
                    throw new EJBException(e.getMessage());
                }
```

Note that the data access commands throw a DataCommandException, a generic exception that serves to completely decouple the session bean client from the fact the details of the database type.

Data access command beans are implemented in an inheritance hierarchy as illustrated in Figure 3.4. Every data access command inherits from one of two abstract classes: the BaseReadCommand and the BaseUpdateCommand. (Full source code is provided in the appendix.) These two reusable classes centralize all the setup, database execution and cleanup code common in persistence logic.

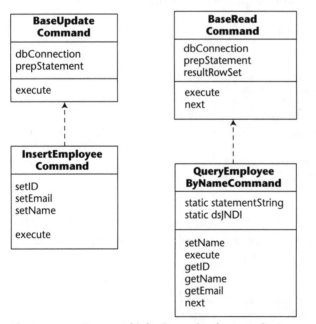

Figure 3.4   Command inheritance implementation.

Implementing data access command beans is simple. If you are implementing an insert, update, or delete, then the class must extend from BaseUpdateCommand. If you are implementing a query, then extend from BaseReadCommand. The abstract superclasses remove most of the details of persistence logic even from the data access command bean developer, who only needs to code in the JNDI name of the data source used, the actual use cases specific SQL string to be executed, and all the use-case-specific gets/sets:

```
public class InsertEmployeeCommand extends BaseUpdateCommand
{

    static String statement =
     "insert into Employees (EMPLOYEEID,NAME,EMAIL) values (?,?,?)";
    static final String dataSourceJNDI = "bookPool";

    protected InsertEmployeeCommand() throws DataCommandException
    {

        super(dataSourceJNDI, statement);
    }

    public void setEmail(String anEmail) throws DataCommandException
    {
        try{
            pstmt.setString(3, anEmail);
        } catch (SQLException e) {
            throw new DataCommandException(e.getMessage());
        }
    }

... //more sets
}
```

The advantages to the Data Access Command Bean pattern are:

- **Decouples business logic from persistence logic.** All the tedious and repetitive persistence logic is encapsulated behind a simple Java bean/command style interface. Business logic no longer needs to worry about ResultSet parsing, driver/statement tracking, and so on.

- **Creates a persistence layer.** Extracting all persistence logic to a layer of data access command beans (beneath the EJB layers) helps both layers to change independently of each other, helping to minimize the effects of changes to one layer on the other.

- **Data source independent.** DACBs can access relational database management systems (RDBMSs), object-oriented database management systems (OODBMSs), legacy adaptors, or any persistence store, all transparently to the client. In fact, migrations between databases are easier since persistence logic is localized to one layer.

- **Useable on any tier.** Although this chapter illustrates the pattern in an EJB context, data access command beans can provides a clean, robust persistence mechanism in any scenario (EJB, Servlets, JSPs, Taglibs, and so on).

- **Consistent interface.** The command style interface remains consistent for all DACBs. Even multiple types of data stores can be supported, all transparent to the user.

The cons of this pattern are:

- **Adds an extra layer of objects.** An extra layer of command beans must be written to separate the persistence logic from the other layers.

- **Doesn't support advanced JDBC features.** Features such as batch updating are not explicitly supported by the data access command bean (as illustrated here).

The Data Access Command Bean pattern provides a simple extensible way to decouple persistence logic from enterprise beans, making it an attractive mechanism for handling persistence behind the session façade and BMP entity beans. DACBs should be used in parallel with the JDBC for Reading pattern. The interface of the command beans can also be slightly modified to support returning RowSets directly, for the Data Transfer RowSet pattern.

Related Patterns

Data Access Command Bean (Matena and Stearns, 2001)
Data Access Object (J2EE Blueprints; Alur, et al., 2001)

Dual Persistent Entity Bean

An EJB developer needs to write entity bean components that support both CMP and BMP.

How can an entity bean be designed to support either CMP or BMP at deployment time?

* * *

The environment in which an entity bean component will be deployed can vary widely from project to project. In the best case, a team will have access to an application server with a good CMP implementation, which they can use to gain significant performance enhancements that are not possible when using BMP. Often a team will be using an application server with poor CMP support or lack of support for their database. In this case, BMP is a requirement. This puts an entity bean component developer in a tough situation. How can they provide a component that can fit both situations?

One way to achieve this is to ship two separate versions of the same entity bean component. One packaged for CMP, the other for BMP. Unfortunately, this approach would require that the component developer maintain two separate code bases/components, making testing, debugging, and maintenance more difficult.

A truly portable EJB component should be deployable in any J2EE-compliant server, in a wide variety of environments and configurations. By portable, this means that the component should be customizable without any reprogramming or compiling. The only source of modification should be the deployment descriptors.

Therefore:

> **To build more portable components, write entity beans that support both CMP and BMP, by separating business logic into a CMP-compliant superclass and BMP persistence logic into a subclass. Deployment descriptor settings can be used to select between the two at deployment time.**

Entity beans can be made to support both CMP and BMP by splitting entity bean logic into two classes: a CMP-compliant superclass, and a subclass that extends the superclass implementations of *ejbStore*, *ejbLoad*, and other methods. This new component can be used to choose its persistence mode at deployment time, by making minor changes to the standard *ejb-jar.xml* file.

For example, consider an Account entity bean. The Account entity bean contains two attributes: an *account id* and a *balance*. It also has three business methods: *deposit*, *withdraw*, and *balance*, and one special finder method: *findByBalance(int)*. As a dual persistent entity bean, the Account entity bean would look like Figure 3.5. A full source code example is available in the appendix.

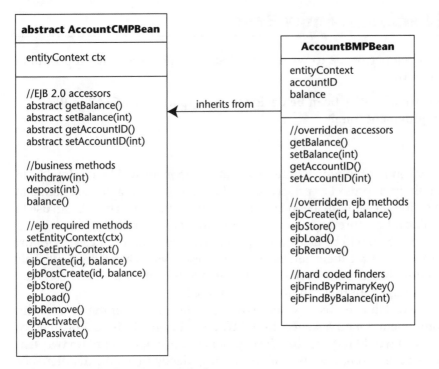

Figure 3.5   A dual persistent entity bean.

The CMP superclass contains the business methods and abstract *get/set* methods (abstract attribute accessors are required by EJB 2.X CMP), and simple implementations of required EJB methods such as *set/unSetEntityContext* and *ejbCreate()*. Note that the implementations of *ejbLoad*, *ejbStore*, and *ejbRemove* are empty implementations. Finder methods do not need to be implemented in the CMP class, since these are declared separately in the deployment descriptor.

The BMP subclass provides concrete implementations of the accountID and balance attributes, and their *get/set* accessors. Other than that the only extra logic this class requires is real implementations of persistence-related methods: *ejbCreate*, *ejbLoad*, *ejbStore*, and *ejbRemove*. Finder methods also need to be implemented, whereas the CMP superclass relied on *query* definitions in the *ejb-jar.xml* file. Note that the BMP does not need to reimplement the business logic methods, *set/unSetEntityContext*, or *ejbActivate/Passivate*, since these are inherited from the superclass.

At deployment time, the CMP or BMP classes can be chosen simply by changing the *ejb-jar.xml* file. Specifically, the *<ejb-class>* tag will need to refer to either the CMP superclass or the BMP subclass. Obviously, the *<persistence-type>* tag will need to select "container" or "bean managed" as well. If you choose CMP, the *ejb-jar.xml* will need to be configured with CMP specific tags to add a schema, attributes, finders, and so on. The schema will also need to be mapped to an underlying data store using the proprietary mechanism provided by the application server it is being deployed on. On the other hand, if you deploy with BMP, the *ejb-jar.xml* will likely need to add a SQL *DataSource* via the *<resource-ref>* tags, and that's it.

Besides creating more portable entity beans, another use of this pattern is migrating BMP entity beans to CMP. Many pre-EJB 2.0 applications were written in BMP. The CMP support provided by the EJB 1.X specifications were often insufficient for the needs of nontrivial applications, furthermore, many CMP implementations available on the market at the time suffered from poor performance. All of these *legacy* EJB applications could benefit by moving from EJB 1.X BMP to newer and more sophisticated CMP. Unfortunately, the migration process from BMP to CMP can be very tricky. One solution would be to completely rewrite the component using CMP. This option would require a lot more up-front work, and would essentially require cutting and pasting business logic from one entity bean to the other. This is hardly an efficient way to convert BMP beans to CMP. Using the Dual Persistent Entity Bean pattern, an existing BMP entity bean can be *refactored* into CMP by creating a superclass and moving code to it, leaving only the attributes, attribute accessors, and persistence-related methods in the subclass. The new superclass can be tested and deployed, and the subclass can be removed later if necessary.

CHAPTER 4

Client-Side EJB Interaction Patterns

Determining the best way to use EJBs is perhaps more complicated than writing them. The two patterns in this chapter outline how to improve the maintainability of your client-side EJB applications, as well as improve performance:

EJBHomeFactory. Provides a best practice for interacting with the EJB layer: caching the home objects in a singleton factory, which also encapsulates all the complexity involved with looking up EJBHomes and handling errors.

Business Delegate. Used to decouple the client layer from the session or message façade layers, abstracting away all the complexities of dealing with the EJB layer, enabling better separation of client and server development team concerns.

EJBHomeFactory

An EJB client needs to look up an EJBHome object, but multiple lookups of the same home are redundant.

> **How can a client look up an EJBHome only once in the lifetime of its application, and abstract the details of that lookup?**

* * *

The JNDI lookup of an enterprise bean's home method is the first step to getting access to the remote interface of an EJB. In order to get access to this interface, the client must go through the code-intensive and expensive process of getting access to the *InitialContext*, followed by performing the actual lookup of the EJBHome, casting it, and handling exceptions, as depicted in the following code:

```
try //to get the initial context

{
    Properties properties = new Properties();

    // Get location of name service
    properties.put(Javax.naming.Context.PROVIDER_URl,
            "some providers url");

    // Get name of initial context factory
    properties.put(Javax.naming.Context.INITIAL_CONTEXT_FACTORY,
      "some name service");

    initContext = new InitialContext(properties);
}
catch (Exception e) { // Error getting the initial context ... }

try //to look up the home interface using the JNDI name
{
     Object homeObject = initContext.lookup("aHomeName");
      myHome = (MyHome) Javax.rmi.PortableRemoteObject.narrow(
            homeObject, MyHome.class);
}
catch (Exception e) { // Error getting the home interface ... }

//get EJBObject stub
MyEJB anEJB = myHome.create();
```

The code example illustrates how complex and repetitive EJBHome lookups can be. The problem is that a typical application makes use of many EJBHome references—one for each EJB a client needs to access. Thus, writing lookup code for each EJBHome essentially duplicates code.

Furthermore, this code is complex and requires tedious error handling (ClassCastExceptions, NamingExceptions, and so on). Duplicating this code all over the clients is simply a messy affair.

Even worse, once the home is retrieved, it is only used once (to get the EJBObject stub). Performing a JNDI lookup every time an EJBHome is needed can be expensive for the following reasons:

- **Requires a network call if the JNDI server is on a different machine.** If the client is not collocated on the same machine as the JNDI server, then the call to JDNI will require a network call. This may occur, for example, in a clustered scenario, where the Web server/servlet engine is on a different box than the EJB server, where the JNDI server is usually part of the EJB server.

- **May require interprocess communication (IPC) if the JNDI server is on the same box.** If the client is running on the same box as the EJB server but is not running within the same virtual machine (VM), then there is IPC overhead in looking up an EJBHome.

Even if the client (such as a servlet client) is running within the same VM as the JNDI server, looking up an EJBHome for every Web request can only hurt performance, since an EJBHome never goes stale and can be reused for the life-time of the client application. Imagine a highly trafficked Web site (such as TheServerSide.com), in which a particular page may be viewed about 500 times per minute. The performance overhead of looking up the same object 500 times for 500 different clients is significant, and completely unnecessary.

A better way is needed to look up an EJBHome, one that allows lookup code to be abstracted, and one that can reuse the same EJBHome instance through-out the lifetime of the client.

Therefore:

Abstract EJBHome lookup code into a reusable EJBHomeFactory, which can cache EJBHomes for the lifetime of a client application.

An EJBHomeFactory is a plain Java class implemented as a singleton, as in Figure 4.1. The factory encapsulates EJBHome lookup logic (making lookup logic reusable for any type of EJBHome) and caches homes internally, passing the cached home to clients upon subsequent requests. An EJBHome factory is generic, the same class is reusable across any application. This reusability is achieved because it does not contain any domain-specific lookup code, such as *getAccountHome*, or *getXXXHome*; rather, it defines a single *lookUpHome* method. The factory is intended to be used from EJB clients such as applets, servlets, and standalone applications, but can also be used by EJBs (EJBs usually simply cache the required homes in *setSession/Entity/MessageContext* method), as a method to encapsulate and optimize EJBHome lookups.

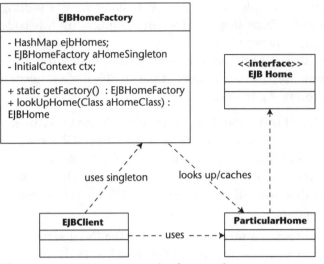

Figure 4.1 EJBHomeFactory implementation.

A simple implementation of the factory is included in the *EJB Home Factory* section of the appendix. Using an EJBHomeFactory is simple. A client is completely abstracted from the home lookup and creation logic, reducing client lookup code to just one line. For example, an Account bean client would call the following code (exception-handling code left out for clarity):

```
AccountHome accountHome = (AccountHome)EJBHomeFactory.getFactory()
                    .lookUpHome(AccountHome.class);
```

HOME CACHING AND STALENESS, CLUSTERING ISSUES

Questions have been raised as to whether this pattern invalidates clustering, or whether it is possible for cached EJBHomes to go stale in a clustered or nonclustered environment. The truth is that clustered servers almost always implement cluster-aware home stubs (Weblogic and Webshere, at least, take this approach), meaning that a home is not tied to a particular server in the cluster. Servers can fail and restart, and the cached home stubs will be able to communicate with the live or restarted servers in the cluster. As for single-server deployments, again, the home stubs of majority of servers can survive redeployment and even server restarts. However, you should verify the semantics of your particular application server and code the HomeFactory defensively if your server can allow stale homes.

The first time a client calls the EJBHomeFactory for a particular home object, the factory will look up the home through JNDI, and then cache the home object internally in a HashMap. On subsequent calls, the factory will pass out the cached copy of EJBHome, completely optimizing on home calls.

Note that the client passes in the *.class* qualification on the AccountHome interface, instead of a JNDI name. Using the EJBHomeFactory, the client is further abstracted from even the JNDI names of the EJBs. All a client needs to know is the interface of the home object in question (to pass in as a *.class* parameter, and then to cast the *EJBHome* returned). Since the client needs to use this EJB's home interface anyway, by passing in the class to lookupHome, the amount of information the client needs to know is minimized, thus keeping client code simple and lean. In order to allow the factory to find a home via JNDI using only a class as a parameter, one of three things must be true:

1. **JNDI name of deployed EJBs must be equal to the fully qualified names of the EJBs' home interfaces.** If you have control over the deployment properties of the EJBs in your application, then adopting a naming convention of using the fully qualified class name of an EJB's home interface (that is, com.xxx.xxx.xxxHome) as the EJBs JNDI name will allow you to use the xxxHome.class alone as a parameter to *lookUpHome*. On large projects, this may be too much to ask for.

2. **Use the EJB-REF tag to decouple the JNDI name.** By far the most elegant solution is to use an EJB-REF tag in your web.xml file to map com.xxx.xxxHome to the actual deployed JNDI name of the EJBs you need to use. Note that this implies that the EJBHomeFactory class must be deployed in the WEB-INF\lib directory of your application, in order for the singleton to make use of the web.xml's ejb-ref mappings. For EJBs making use of EJBHomeFactories, using EJB-REFs in the ejb-jar.xml can also be used for this purpose (and likewise, the factory class will need to be packaged with the ejb-jar in-order make use of the ejb-ref mappings defined in this layer).

3. **Read in .class to JNDI name bindings from a resource file.** If you are working with older application servers and don't have access to EJB-REFs, then you can code the EJBHomeFactory to read in .class to JNDI name bindings from a factory file.

By far the most elegant and portable solution is Option 2, using the EJB-REF tags to map the EJB's home class name to the actually JNDI name. This allows the home factory to be written with the assumption that the JNDI name of the EJB is the fully qualified name of its home interface, because the deployer can perform this mapping from home class name to JNDI name at deployment time. The EBJHomeFactory example in the appendix is written with this assumption. To illustrate how the ejb-ref mapping works, consider a bank account example. The following ejb-ref tag would be placed in the web.xml file, which would define `com.bankapp.AcccountHome` as the logical JNDI name for the Account:

```
<ejb-ref>
    <ejb-ref-name>
        com.bankapp.AcccountHome
    </ejb-ref-name>
    <ejb-ref-type>
        Session
    </ejb-ref-type>
    <home>
        com.bankapp.AcccountHome
    </home>
    <remote>
     com.bankapp.Acccount
    </remote>
</ejb-ref>
```

This declaration of `com.bankapp.AccountHome` as the logical JNDI name for the account is then mapped to the actual JNDI name at deployment time. In Weblogic, this is achieved by placing the following code in the weblogic.xml descriptor (which is used for WARS):

```
<reference-descriptor>
    <ejb-ref-name>
        com.bankapp.AcccountHome
</ejb-ref-name>
<jndi-name>
    AccountHomeActualJNDINAme
        </jndi-name>
</reference-descriptor>
```

Using this scheme allows EJBHomeFactory to simply lookup a home object by passing in the fully qualified class name of the home class passed in by the client in *lookUpHome*, while behind the scenes, the servlet or EJB container will map this string to the real JNDI name declared in the ejb-ref tag.

Note that the choice of using the home interface class as a mechanism for requesting a home is an implementation decision designed to simplify the client and factory, but it is not necessary. You could easily change the lookup method to take in a class and a JNDI name, as follows:

```
AccountHome accountHome = (AccountHome)EJBHomeFactory.getFactory()
                .lookUpHome("AccountHome", AccountHome.class);
```

The disadvantage of this approach is that the client is burdened with the hard-coded JNDI names of the homes that need to be looked up, which diminishes the maintenance benefits of the EJBHomeFactory pattern.

A SERVLET-CENTRIC ALTERNATIVE

A common practice among servlet developers is to place EJB home initialization logic in *Servlet.init()*, and cache EJB homes in the *ServletContext* object, since it is shared across the application. This approach shares the same benefits as EJB home factory (performance, simplicity), but complicates code a bit more. Common presentation layer constructs—such as Java bean helpers—do not have access to the ServletContext, and would have to be manually passed one in, in order to get access to an EJB home. Since the home factory is a singleton, it can exist anywhere in your Web application and can thus simplify your code.

The EJBHomeFactory pattern is a simple and efficient way to abstract EJB-Home lookup complexity from the client in a completely generic, reusable format. By caching EJBHomes, performance is increased significantly by eliminating costly redundant home lookups. The EJBHomeFactory provides a consistent interface to home object lookup, and is reusable in any environment (applet, servlet, standalone, even in between EJBs).

Related Patterns

Service Locator (Alur, et al., 2001)

Factory (Gamma, et al., 1995)

Business Delegate

When using session and/or message façade, the client is tightly coupled to the EJB layer, creating dependencies between client and server that affect development, run-time, and project management concerns.

How can an intermediary between a client and the session façade be created to facilitate decoupling the client from the EJB layer?

* * *

In a good EJB design, use cases should be divided up over a layer of session and/or message-driven beans, as described in the Session and Message Façade patterns, respectively. A common way to interact with this layer is via direct invocation from client code. That is, your presentation layer will directly interact with EJBHomes, and EJBObjects for session beans, and send JMS messages when talking to message-driven beans.

Ironically, programming directly to the EJB APIs is not always the best way to program EJB applications. Various issues can arise, all of which revolve around the problems created by tightly coupling the client layer to the EJB layer:

- **Reduces separation of roles between client programmers and server programmers.** On large projects, speed and efficient project completion depend upon the ability of the client tier (that is, servlet/JSP) developers and the server-side EJB developers to work independently. One common dependency that can arise between teams is the availability of the complete and compiled session bean layer. Client programmers depend on the implementation of the session façade in order to compile and test their code, creating a terrible bottleneck between the two teams.

- **Places optimistic concurrency recovery responsibility on clients.** Often a transaction will fail due to an optimistic concurrency conflict at the application server or database level, catchable by the client as TransactionRolledBackException or TransactionRolledBackLocalException. For certain types of use cases (such as idempotent operations), it may *not* be necessary to propagate this error down to the end application users and ask them to retry (usually by clicking submit again on a Web form). Instead, client code should automatically reexecute the transaction. When coding directly to the EJB APIs, client code needs to explicitly catch these exections and retry the transaction, which places a large responsibility on the client developer (who may not fully understand the nature of the use case implementation, since they didn't write the EJB layer), as well as cluttering up their code.

- **Complicates client logic with complex error handling.** Clients need to be burdened with the ability to catch and react to the myriad number of errors that can occur when looking up and using EJBs, including exceptions thrown when looking up components, RemoteExceptions, EJBException (when using local interfaces), and so on. Remote or EJBExceptions in particular can occur for a variety of different reasons (such as optimistic concurrency conflicts described above), placing the responsibility on the client to implement messy code required to parse an exception and determine how to react to it.

- **Couples the clients directly to EJB and JMS APIs.** Even when executing simple use cases, clients need to be loaded with EJB- or JMS-specific code required to discover, create, execute, and recover from business logic implemented in the session or message façade layers. This creates inconsistency in the client code (different types of business services are explicitly executed with very different APIs) and complicates even the simplest of use cases, resulting in lower maintainability as a whole.

Despite the performance and maintenance benefits of the Session/Message Façade patterns, using these layers explicitly from the clients creates a tight coupling that affects project development and overall maintainability of client code.

Therefore:

> **Create a layer of business delegates: plain Java classes that hide EJB API complexity by encapsulating code required to discover, delegate to and recover from invocations on the session and message façade EJB layers.**

A business delegate is a plain Java class that serves as an intermediary between client and server. Clients locally invoke methods on the business delegate, which then usually delegates directly to a method with the same signature on the session façade, or populates a JMS message and send it off to the message façade.

Business delegates map one-to-one to session beans on the session façades and can be written to wrap multiple message-driven beans. For example, consider a forum message board application. Here we could expose our use cases (postMessage, addReply, and so on) on a ForumServices session bean, or each use case could be asynchronously executed by using separate message-driven beans. Figure 4.2 illustrates how business delegates would map to both architectures.

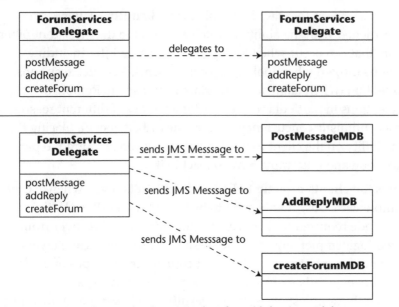

Figure 4.2 Fronting session/message façades with business delegates.

In either case, the client code interacts only with the business delegate, oblivious to the APIs and processes being executed by the delegate itself. When a method is executed on a business delegate, it can perform the following functions:

- **Delegate method calls to an EJB.** The delegate will take all the parameters passed in from the client and simply delegate this call to a method on the session façade, or pack the parameters into a JMS message and send them to a message-driven bean.

- **Hide EJB-specific system exceptions.** API-specific system exceptions such as RemoteException, EJBException, or JMS exceptions are caught in the business delegate and rethrown to the client as a non-ejb-specific exceptions, such as a BusinessDelegateException. Application-level exceptions are still passed to the client.

- **Cache data locally.** A business delegate can cache the return results from a session bean method call locally and pass that out to clients on subsequent requests.

- **Transparently retry failed transactions.** Business delegates can implement the complicated error-handling code required to determine the cause of a failed transaction (such as an optimistic concurrency conflict, described above), and retry the transaction by reexecuting the method on the session façade. Business delegates shield clients from this delicate, complicated process.

■ **Execute business logic locally or create dummy data for clients.** As mentioned in the first problem with coupling clients to EJB APIs, the client-side project team is dependent on the existence of the session façade in order to compile and test their code. Business delegates provide a way for client programmers to write, compile, and test working code without the existence of the session façade. Prototype business delegates can be written that simply return dummy data (very useful for unit testing), or even execute business logic locally (good for quickly creating a working prototype). As the server-side EJBs get built, the business delegate classes can be refactored to work with the EJB layer, all transparently to the client developers, who are no longer dependent on the EJB project team.

Implementing business delegates is simple. For every session bean in your application, simply create a local Java class with the same method signature. Internally, the business delegate can perform any of the tasks outlined above, within its business methods. The only other piece of code that needs to be written is a constructor and a reference to the session bean that this delegate is fronting. In the delegate's constructor, it should call an EJBHomeFactory (see the EJBHomeFactory pattern) to acquire a home for the session bean it represents and create an instance of the session bean, storing it locally as a member variable. On subsequent calls to business methods on the delegate, it should delegate these calls to the session bean reference stored internally, as in the following code:

```
public class ForumServicesDelegate
{
    ForumServices sb;

    public ForumServicesDelegate() throws DelegateException
    {
      try
      {
        ForumServicesHome home = (ForumServicesHome)
            EJBHomeFactory.getFactory().lookUpHome
                          (ForumServicesHome.class);

        this.sb = home.create();
      }catch(Exception e)
      {
          throw new DelegateException();
      }
}

public long addForum(long categoryPK, String forumTitle,
                  String summary)
throws NoSuchCategoryException,DelegateException
{
```

```
try
{
    return sb.addForum( categoryPK, forumTitle, summary);
}
catch(CreateException e)
{
    throw new DelegateException();
    //log errors, etc
} catch(RemoteException e)
{
    throw new DelegateException();
    //log errors, etc
}
}
... //more similarly implemented business methods

}//ForumServicesDelegate
```

For message-driven beans, the business delegates are created to group similar use cases (that map to different message-driven beans, as shown in Figure 4.2), together in one class. Implementation is similar to that in the session bean example, except that all methods return void.

The client view of a business delegate is simple. When a method needs to be executed, it simply creates a *new* delegate and calls a method on it. Behind the scenes, the business delegate initializes itself (using an EJBHomeFactory) in the constructor, and then delegates the method call. Since EJB homes are cached in the EJBHomeFactory, creating and using a business delegate is relatively lightweight.

The only time when the semantics of using a business delegate change is when using them to front stateful session beans. In this case, a client does not create new business delegates upon every request, rather, it needs to create it once and then cache it locally, reusing the same delegate (which internally maintains a reference to the same stateful session bean). In a servlet application, delegates are cached in the *ServletSession*. In order to support storing the stateful Business Delegate in the HTTPSession, some changes need to be made to the way the business delegates are written:

- **Business Delegate must be serializable.** Since the delegate is stored in the *ServletSession*, it should be declared as Serializable, in order to support servlet engines that passivate HTTPSessions, or support session replication in a cluster.

- **Must use an EJB handle to support serialization.** Since the delegate can be serialized, it cannot simply contain a reference to the EJBObject, as in the code sample shown earlier. EJBObjects are not guaranteed to be serializable, thus the delegate must be written to use a handle object so that the reference to the stateful session bean will remain intact, even through serialization.

A source code example of a business delegate for a stateful session bean that can be serialized is included in the section *Business Delegate* in the appendix. This example provides serializability in a completely transparent fashion—other than throwing it into an HTTPSession, the client of the business delegate doesn't need to handle it any differently than it would a delegate for a stateless session bean.

One important side effect of using a business delegate to front a stateful session bean is that the class and its methods can be *synchronized*, which protects a client from making concurrent calls to the same stateful session bean (which is disallowed by the EJB specification, since EJBObjects are not threadsafe). This problem can occur in Web sites that use frames (where each frame needs to make a request that ends up going through the same stateful session bean), but is corrected transparently to the developer by using a business delegate.

Another atypical use of the Business Delegate pattern is as a method for integration between non-Java applications and EJB. Since business delegates are just simple Java objects, they can easily be wrapped with non-Java code using JNI or some Java-com bridge. Because all the J2EE Javax interfaces are hidden from the client, you don't have to provide non-Java versions of them. This approach to integration removes the dependencies between non-Java applications and the application server vendor's ORB. Because of the age-old ORB interoperability problems, having non-Java applications communicate with EJB via business delegates guarantees that clustering and security will function correctly.

When should the Business Delegate pattern be used? For projects in which the same developers are writing both the client- and the server-side code, the benefits of decoupling the client code from the server APIs may not be large enough to warrant the extra legwork in writing and maintaining this layer. However, for large projects, where the Web team is separate from the EJB team, business delegate can result in better decoupling between client and server-side developers which can more than make up for the implementation work.

Related Patterns

Business Delegate (Alur, et al., 2001)

CHAPTER 5

Primary Key
Generation Strategies

Generating primary keys (PK) in a portable, scalable, and reliable fashion is a great challenge in EJB. Many application servers provide a proprietary way to create primary keys for entity beans. For example, Weblogic allows you to automatically generate a primary key by transparently using your database's built-in sequence/counter. While in many cases this is a simple and viable solution, the problem with this approach is that when migrating code from one application server to another, the PK generation mechanisms between the different CMP implementations may not be compatible. The only way to achieve true portability for entity bean primary key generation is to call some external, user-created structure.

This section will go over three different primary key generation best practices, used in creating primary keys for entity beans:

Sequence Blocks. Provides a pattern for creating incrementing, integer primary keys with very few database accesses. The pattern uses a stateless session bean and a CMP entity bean in its solution.

UUID for EJB. Provides an algorithm and implementation for a PK-generation service that creates string-based primary keys in memory, without the need for a database- or an application-wide singleton.

Stored Procedures for Autogenerated Keys. Describes when to use your database's built-in key generation service, and how it can be used in a portable fashion from a BMP entity bean.

Sequence Blocks

An entity bean developer needs a way to generate integer-based primary keys in an incrementing fashion and doesn't mind possible gaps between keys.

> **How can integer-based incrementing primary keys be generated in a portable, efficient manner?**

✳ ✳ ✳

Using a simple incrementing number as a primary key mechanism provides a very efficient and maintainable solution for primary keys. Integers are efficient from a database perspective because they are more easily and efficiently indexed than large string-based integers (such as those generated by the Universally Unique Identifier [UUID] for EJB pattern or the High/Low pattern). They are more maintainable from a developer's perspective because the primary keys start from 0 and increment upwards, resulting in short keys that can easily be manipulated by a database administrator (DBA) for quick and easy reporting purposes.

The Stored Procedures for Autogenerated keys pattern provides an easy solution for working with autoincrementing keys built into an RDBMS database, but this pattern only works for BMP entity beans and requires a database that supports autoincrementing keys, and requires the writing of an extra layer of stored procedures in between your entity beans and the database.

What is needed is some way to create sequences of integer primary keys, callable from CMP or BMP entity beans. One solution is to create an entity bean that represents a sequence. That is, an entity bean that simply stores an integer in the database and increments it every time a client requests a primary key. An example Sequence entity bean is shown in Figure 5.1. The entity bean's primary key would be a string that represented its name, allowing the existence of multiple sequences, each maintaining a different *currentKeyValue.*

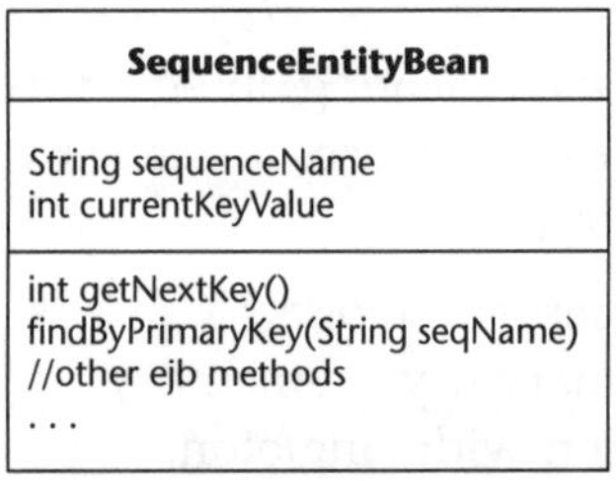

SequenceEntityBean
String sequenceName int currentKeyValue
int getNextKey() findByPrimaryKey(String seqName) //other ejb methods . . .

Figure 5.1   Simple incrementing Sequence entity bean.

Other entity beans would call the Sequence entity bean from their *ejbCreate* methods. For example, a Bank Account entity bean would execute code similar to the following pseudocode:

```
int ejbCreate(attrib1, attrib2, ...)
{
Sequence aSequence = SequenceHome.findByPrimaryKey("Account");
this.id = aSequence.getNextKey()

...
}
```

There are many problems with this approach:

- **Performance.** The Accounts *ejbCreate* will result in four database calls, breaking down as follows: one call each to *SequenceHome.findBy*, *Sequence.ejbLoad*, *Sequence.ejbStore*, and, finally, one to the Account entity bean's insert. To optimize the process, the reference to the "Account" sequence could have been cached in the Account entity bean, but that would still result in database three calls.

- **Scalability.** If the *getNextKey* method is running with an isolation level of serializable, this will result in an unacceptable loss of scalability, as there could potentially be hundreds of entity beans waiting in line to get their primary key.

- **Need to code optimistic concurrency logic into ejbCreate.** If the application server or underlying database uses an optimistic concurrency strategy, then the entity beans making use of the sequence entity bean will have to catch TransactionRolledBack exceptions and retry the call to *getNextKey()*, resulting in cluttered ejbCreate code and many retries, as many entity beans fight to make use of the same sequence.

A Sequence entity bean would provide a simple way to generate integer-based primary keys, but having clients directly interact with this entity bean to increment keys one by one results in poor performance and encapsulation of code. A better mechanism is needed, one that allows entity beans to make use of incrementing integers as primary keys but optimizes on the mechanism used to generate those numbers.

Therefore:

> **Front a Sequence entity bean with a session bean that grabs blocks of integers at a time and caches them locally. Clients interact with the session bean, which passes out cached keys and hides all the complexity from the other entity bean clients.**

The previous solution of using a sequence entity bean to increment a counter can be improved upon by modifying the Sequence entity bean to increment by blocks of integers (instead of one number at a time), and using a session bean to front the entity bean and cache blocks of keys locally, as shown in Figure 5.2. The Session bean becomes a primary key generation service, maintaining blocks of keys for any number of different sequences, and providing fast access to new keys in memory, without having to access the Sequence entity bean (and thus the database) every time some entity bean needs a primary key.

When an entity bean needs a primary key in *ejbCreate*, it will call the local interface of the Sequence session bean and ask it for the next available key. Using the Bank Account example, *ejbCreate* in the Account entity bean would contain the following code:

```
//home and sequence session lookup (this could be done just one
//once and cached in setEntityContext)
SequenceSessionLocalHome ahome = (SequenceSessionLocalHome)
        (new InitialContext()).lookup("SequenceSessionLocal");
SequenceSessionLocal aSequence = aHome.create();

//get next key
this.id = aSequence.getNextNumberInSequence("Account"));
```

A complete implementation is included in the *Sequence Block* section in the appendix, based on a submission from Jonathan Weedon at Borland.

A pseudocode description of *getNextNumberInSequence* is provided:

1. Check its local cache of blocks for a block corresponding to the Sequence "Account."

2. If none exists or if the cached block has run out of keys, then the Sequence Session will call the Sequence entity and get the next block of integers available for sequence "Account."

3. When grabbing the next block, catch any transaction rollbacks (explained below) and retry a specified number of times.

4. Pass a key from its local block of keys directly to the client entity bean. The session bean will pass out keys from its local block for all subsequent requests, until the block runs out, at which point repeat Step one.

The Sequence entity bean can be implemented as a simple CMP bean whose primary key is a string corresponding to the *name* of the sequence (see appendix). The only other value it needs to maintain is the current highest key. As in Figure 5.2, the Sequence entity exposes only one method—*getNextKeyAfterIncrementingBy- (block- size)*. This method simply takes in a block size, and increments itself by that size, returning the new highest key to the Sequence session bean that called it. The Sequence entity bean maps to a simple column in the database, whose rows correspond to the current value of different sequences, as shown in Figure 5.3.

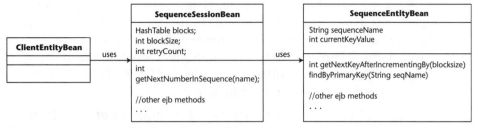

Figure 5.2　Sequence blocks architectural layout.

SEQUENCES TABLE

name	value
Account	80
Person	30
Country	100

Figure 5.3　Mapping of a Sequence entity bean to a database table.

Despite the ultimate simplicity of this CMP bean, special care must be taken to mark the *getNextKeyAfterIncrementingBy* method as TRANSACTION_ REQUIRES_NEW in the deployment descriptor. Without this special setting, the block increment would be part of the transaction initiated by the original client entity bean, which could be a long one depending on the use case. To limit locking and increase performance, the act of acquiring a new block should be an atomic operation, kept as short as possible.

The transaction and concurrency semantics of this pattern depend on the application server and database combination in use. In order to make the sequence session portable across different systems, it should be encoded to with a try/catch block that catches *TransactionRolledBackLocalExceptions*, in order to catch possible optimistic concurrency conflicts. An example of such a conflict is two Account entity beans in a cluster that both request a primary key at the same time, and in both servers, the Sequence session bean needs to grab the next *block* at the same time. If not properly configured, the two instances of Sequence session beans may end up getting the same block of keys. The configuration required to correct this depends on how your database or application server handles concurrency:

1. **Isolation of READ_COMITTED with application server CMP verified updates.** In this case, the application server will compare the contents of

the Sequence entity bean to that in the database *before* transaction commit time. If it is discovered that a previous transaction has already gotten the next block, an exception will be thrown. This is an optimistic concurrency check implemented at the application server level, allowing you to use a transaction isolation level of just READ_COMMITTED, since the application server guarantees consistency.

2. **Isolation of SERIALIZABLE with a DB that supports optimistic concurrency.** If optimistic concurrency is not implemented at the application server level, then a transaction isolation of SERIALIZABLE must be used to ensure consistency. If the database itself implements optimistic concurrency checks, then it will automatically roll back the transaction of the *second* sequence entity bean when it detects that *ejbStore* is trying to overwrite the data inserted by the first transaction.

3. **Isolation of SERIALIZABLE with a DB that uses pessimistic concurrency.** Again, SERIALIZABLE must be used since the application server won't enforce consistency. However, since the database is using a pessimistic concurrency strategy, it will lock the "Account" row in the sequences table, forcing the SequenceEntity.*ejbLoad()* of the second transaction to *wait* until the SequenceEntity.*ejbStore()* from the first transaction completes and commits.

4. **Isolation of SERIALIZABLE with a SELECT FOR UPDATE.** Some application servers allow the CMP engine to be configured to issue a *SELECT FOR UPDATE* during ejbLoad, by editing a deployment descriptor setting. The purpose of this is to force a database that uses optimistic concurrency to actually lock the underlying row, as in Option 3.

For Options 3 and 4, it is guaranteed that every SequenceSession will get a unique block of keys, since a second transaction will not be allowed to read the same row until the first transaction has completed its ejbLoad-inrementBlock-ejbStore cycle. However, for Options 1 and 2, a try/catch block is necessary in the sequence session, to retry the call. The takeaway point of this discussion is that if you keep the try/catch coded in the session bean, then the code itself will be portable across all possible configurations. Only the isolation levels and possible vendor-specific CMP options described previously need to be changed in a deployment descriptor.

The advantages to the Sequence Block pattern are:

- **Performance.** Despite the fact that this pattern requires a database, with a high setting for block size, this pattern approaches the performance of the UUID for EJB pattern, since most of the generated primary keys are occurring in memory.

- **Scalability.** Even with a transaction isolation of serializable (on the Sequence entity), this pattern scales well since calls to *getNextKeyAfter-IncrementingBy* don't occur often.

- **Easy reuse.** The Sequence Block pattern uses completely generic code. Once implemented, this pattern can be reused across projects with no problems.

- **Simplicity.** The amount of code required to implement this pattern is very low. Furthermore, CMP can be reliably used for the Sequence entity bean.

- **Generates simple keys.** The pattern generates simple integer-based keys, which allows databases to efficiently index primary key columns, and DBAs to easily work with the primary keys.

The trade-offs are:

- **Keys not guaranteed to be ordered.** The primary keys of four different entity beans that are created one after the other (but that went through two instances of Sequence session beans) can be 10, 20, 11, 12 respectively, using a block size of 10. This is because different Sequence session beans in the pool all have different blocks assigned to them.

- **Keys can be "lost" during pool resizing.** Using a stateless session bean to maintain a cache of keys, keys will be lost when the application server decides to remove session bean instances. Most application servers use pools of session beans that are demand based—new beans are created based on current traffic and removed when traffic subsides. This loss of keys is, practically speaking, not a point of concern (there are a lot of numbers in the world); it will not affect the uniqueness of keys passed out to entity bean clients.

Overall, the Sequence Block pattern provides a simple, cluster-safe mechanism for generating integer-based primary keys in a efficient, portable manner.

UUID for EJB

An entity bean developer needs a way to generate a string-based, universally unique primary keys in memory, without a database or a globally unique singleton.

How can universally unique primary keys be generated in memory without requiring a database or a singleton?

* * *

For many primary key generation schemes, the database is used to maintain the state of the primary key and is used to synchronize access to the key, such as in the EJB Sequence pattern. While these schemes work, the very fact that they require database infrastructure makes them difficult to implement, because they need to be coded to be portable across different databases, which becomes difficult due to the different ways in which databases handle issues such as row locking, and so on.

Many non-database primary key generation schemes require the use of a *Singleton*, that is, an object of which only one instance exists across an entire application. Instead of a database, a singleton could now manage primary keys and be the point of synchronization for any clients (such as entity beans) that require a primary key.

The problem with this approach is that it is difficult to create a true single instance of an object across a J2EE application. A traditional Java singleton (a class which contains a synchronized static instance of itself) only guarantees one instance per *classloader*, and a typical J2EE server will contain multiple running classloaders per VM. Another approach is to use a *networked RMI object singleton*, that is, an object that only lives on one server in your application, callable via RMI, thus achieving only one instance across your entire application. The problem now becomes scalability: every entity bean in your potential cluster of servers must synchronize access to this one RMI object, which can become a bottleneck, and also a single point of failure.

Another solution is to use the java.rmi.server.UID class, which is provided with the JDK. The problem with IDs generated via this class is that they are not unique across boxes, they need to be appended to an InetAddress to achieve such uniqueness. More importantly, the implementation of the UID class makes use of *Thread.sleep()*, which is not allowed in an EJB environment.

A better approach would be a primary key generation mechanism that does not require synchronization around a database or a global singleton. Such a mechanism would need to be decentralized (since there is no point of synchronization), allowing multiple instances of it to concurrently generate primary keys that are still unique.

Therefore:

Create primary keys in memory by creating a universally unique identifier (UUID) that combines enough system information to make it unique across space and time.

A UUID is a primary key encoded as a string that contains an amalgamation of system information that makes the generated UUID completely unique over space and time, irrespective of when and where it was generated. As a completely decentralized algorithm, there can be multiple instances of UUIDs across a cluster and even in the same server, allowing for fast and efficient primary key generation.

The original UUID specification is available in a Network Working Group Internet Draft by Paul Leach and Rich Salz[1], however the algorithms defined in that original work will not work in an EJB context. The various implementations described there require proper singletons, access to a synchronized shared resource (database), and often to the IEEE 802 address hard-coded into your servers network card. None of these features are possible in an EJB context, but it is still possible to create an equivalent GUID in EJB, which is the focus of this pattern.

A UUID is a string-based primary key consisting of 32-digits (spaces inserted only for clarity), encoded in hexadecimal, as in Figure 5.4. The string is composed as follows:

1. **Unique down to the millisecond.** Digits 1–8 are the hex-encoded lower 32 bits of the *System.currentTimeMillis()* call.

2. **Unique across a cluster.** Digits 9–16 are the hex-encoded representation of the 32-bit integer of the underlying IP Address (an IP address is divided into four separate bytes, appended together they form 32 bits).

3. **Unique down to the objects within a JVM.** Digits 17–24 are the hex representation of the call to System.identityHashCode(this), which is guaranteed to return distinct integers for distinct objects within a JVM. Even with multiple VMs on the same machine, it is highly unlikely that two UUID generators will return duplicate UUIDs (explained later).

4. **Unique within an object within a millisecond.** Finally, digits 25–32 represent a random 32 bit integer generated on every method call using the cryptographically strong java.security.SecureRandom class. Thus, multiple calls to the same method within the same millisecond are guaranteed to be unique.

Altogether, a UUID created using this algorithm is guaranteed to be unique across all machines in a cluster, across all instances of UUID generators within a JVM on a machine, down to the millisecond and even down to the individual method call within each millisecond.

[1] "UUIDs and GUID," http://casl.csa.iisc.ernet.in/Standards/internet-drafts/draft-leach-uuids-guids-01.txt.

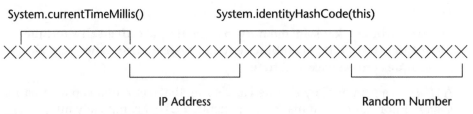

Figure 5.4 Layout of GUID in EJB.

There are two ways to implement the UUID pattern in an EJB context: as a plain Java singleton class or as a stateless session bean. The choice between implementations is really up to the developers, according to their tastes. The UUID algorithm is safe no matter how many instances of it are running within a VM. Implemented as a stateless session bean, the EJB server would pool instances of the UUID generator and have to intercept requests and perform the usual server overhead such as security checks, session bean creation, and so on. As a plain Java singleton there is none of this overhead, entity beans simply call the singleton instance that lives in their class loader (see the EJB Strategy *Using Java Singletons Is OK if They're Used Correctly* in Chapter 9).

A sample implementation of the UUID as a stateless session bean is provided below (utility and EJB methods left out for clarity), based on an implementation by Steve Woodcock (www.activescript.co.uk):

```
public class UUIDBean implements javax.ejb.SessionBean {

    // secure random to provide nonrepeating seed
    private SecureRandom seeder;

    // cached value for mid part of string
    private String midValue;

    public void ejbCreate() throws CreateException {
        try {
            // get the internet address
            InetAddress inet = InetAddress.getLocalHost();
            byte [] bytes = inet.getAddress();
            String hexInetAddress  = hexFormat(getInt(bytes),8);

            // get the hashcode for this object
            String thisHashCode =
            hexFormat(System.identityHashCode(this),8);

            // set up mid value string
            this.midValue = hexInetAddress + thisHashCode;

            // load up the randomizer first
```

```
            seeder = new SecureRandom();
            int node = seeder.nextInt();

    } catch (Exception e) {
        throw new CreateException ("failure to create bean " + e);
    }
}


public String getUUID() throws RemoteException
{

    long timeNow = System.currentTimeMillis();

    // get int value as unsigned
    int timeLow = (int) timeNow & 0xFFFFFFFF;

    // get next random value
    int node = seeder.nextInt();

  return (hexFormat(timeLow, 8) + mid + hexFormat(node, 8));

}
}
```

When the session bean is first created, the hex format of the system's IP address and hashCode, as well as the SecureRandom seeder are created and cached for performance. On subsequent calls to getUUID() only the current time in milliseconds and the current random number need to be hex-formatted and added with the cached IP and hashcode, to efficiently create a primary key in memory.

Theoretically, the one problem that could break this pattern is a clock setback. If somehow the clock on the server got setback *and* the UUID generators within the server JVM happen to have the SAME hash codes as any generators that existed at the new setback time, *and* the generators create *the same random numbers* within *the same milliseconds* as their counterparts in the past, then there is a remote possibility of generating a duplicate key.

The other theoretical problem this pattern may have occurs when a cluster of application servers are on the same machine (multiple VMs per machine). On single machines that run multi-JVMs under Sun's JDK 1.3.x and 1.4, the object identifier used as the middle eight characters of the UUID string (gathered from System.identityHashCode(this)) will be the same for two objects *if* application server(s) create the two objects in exactly the same order in the two JVMs. However, to clash UUIDs, the two objects would need to be called in the same millisecond *and* generate the same secure random number, which makes an UUID clash an extremely remote possibility.

The advantages of the UUID for EJB pattern are:

- **Performance.** Primary keys are generated in memory, without requiring any synchronization around global singletons or databases.

- **Simplicity.** The UUID pattern does not require complicated databases access and synchronization code, and can be deployed as a plain old Java singleton class.

The trade-offs are:

- **Reliance on IP addresses.** UUIDs generated on your local LAN will be encoded with local 192.168... addresses. However even on the local LAN, all IP addresses are guaranteed to be unique.

- **Use of 36-digit strings for primary keys.** The large strings generated by the UUID pattern may result in slower indexing capabilities on some databases. The long strings also make it difficult for DBAs to manipulate primary keys (that is, performing regular maintenance tasks, reporting, and so on).

Stored Procedures for Autogenerated Keys

A BMP entity bean developer using a JDBC 2.X or 1.X driver needs a way to create a simple integer-based primary key, unique to each entity bean. Most relational databases offer a proprietary, built-in autogenerated key feature.

How can an entity bean make use of a relational database's built-in autogenerated keys in a portable, efficient fashion?

* * *

Most databases offer a primary generation service that automatically generates a primary key for a newly inserted row. The most common such facility is an autoincrementing counter (often called a sequence or an identity column), which allows you to create primary keys by simply incrementing a number, starting from zero. Autoincrementing counters can be queried for the next available number, which can then be used to populate the primary key column in a database table. Often, the autoincrementing counter can be directly attached to the primary key column in a table, and will automatically populate the primary key field of an inserted row, with the next number in the sequence. For BMP programmers, autogenerated keys provide a simple, powerful, built-in mechanism for creating primary keys.

The EJB specification requires that the primary key of a newly created entity bean be passed to the container as a return value on the *ejbCreate* method. This presents a problem for BMP developers wanting to use autogenerated keys. When performing a JDBC insert, the returned result set contains a count of the number of rows inserted, not the primary keys of the inserted rows. The act of inserting does not give the developer the primary key that was generated. Given this restriction, how can a developer programmatically retrieve the value of the row that was just inserted?

In JDBC 3.0 (part of JDK 1.4) this problem has been solved. JDBC 3.0 extends the statement interface by adding the capability to return the primary key of any inserted rows using standard API methods, as in the code example below:

```
PrepartedStatement pstmt = conn.prepareStatement();

stmt.executeUpdate("insert Into sometable(field1 ,field2)" +
    "values ('value1', 'value2')", Statement.RETURN_GENERATED_KEYS);

ResultSet rs = pstmt.getGeneratedKeys();

if ( rs.next() ) {
    int myPrimaryKey = rs.getInt(1);
}
```

Unfortunately, developers who do not have access to JDBC 3.X drivers for their database cannot make use of this standardized method for using an auto-generated key.

One solution is to code *ejbCreate* to perform a SQL select immediately after the insert, to get the primary key of the row that was just inserted. The problem with this approach is that there is that there may be no way to uniquely select the row that was just inserted. Remember that only the primary key is guaranteed to be unique in a row. If the other inserted fields are not guaranteed to be unique, it may be impossible to populate the *where* clause of the SQL select with parameters unique enough to select the row that was just inserted. Even if every inserted field is then used in the where clause (which will result in a long and poor performing query), it is possible that there may be more than one such row in the table with the same fields. Another problem is that this approach would require two database calls (which are network calls when the database is on a separate machine from the application server): one to perform the insert and one to retrieve the key of the last inserted row.

Many databases that support sequences (autoincrementing counters) allow the creation of a sequence that is not tied to a particular table. Using this approach, a developer can ask for the next available number in one database call [usually by selecting on a DB provided procedure such as *nextval("sequence-name")*], which will both increment the counter and return the next number at once, and then use this generated number to insert the primary key along with other contents of the entity bean in the insert call. The primary key can then be returned from *ejbCreate*. Along with the fact that this approach requires two database calls, the main problem with this approach is that it is not portable across databases. Some databases that provide incrementing counter facilities (most notably SQLServer) do not allow you to create sequence counters that are not tied to a particular table. Thus it is impossible to get the next free primary key *before* performing an insert.

Autogenerated keys provide a powerful built-in mechanism for creating primary keys, but hard-coding your entity beans to access a generated key through some DB-specific mechanism limits their portability and often requires the use of multiple database calls in *ejbCreate*. An entity bean's persistence code should ideally be portable across application servers *and* databases.

Therefore:

> **Use stored procedures to insert data into the database and return the generated primary key in the same call. Entity beans can be written to use the standard and portable JDBC CallableStatement interface, to call a stored procedure.**

Stored procedures are a feature that all SQL-compliant databases have. They allow the encoding of complex data access logic directly into the database, where they are compiled for optimum performance. In JDBC, stored procedures can be accessed in a completely database-independent format, using the

CallableStatement interface. Stored procedures can thus be used to provide a database-independent method of inserting a row into a database and retrieving the autogenerated primary key within one database call. By writing your entity beans to use the standard CallableStatement API, portability across databases can be achieved, since the database vendor specific coding is stored in the database, not the EJB layer. Thus, any relational database that supports autogenerated keys can be used in a standard way, without requiring repro-gramming of your *ejbCreate* method if your database needs to be changed.

Using a stored procedure, the code in *ejbCreate* would execute a JDBC CallableStatement by passing in all of the entity bean's attributes that need to be inserted as parameters. On the database side, the stored procedure would use vendor-specific mechanisms to perform the insert and get the generated key, all within one stored procedure.

Using the Bank Account example, the *ejbCreate* for an Account entity bean would look like this:

```
public AccountPK ejbCreate(String ownerName, int balance) throws
CreateException
{
      PreparedStatement pstmt = null;
      Connection conn = null;
      try
      (
            this.ownerName = ownerName;
            this.balance = balance;

            conn = getConnection();

            CallableStatement call = conn.prepareCall(
                  "{call insertAccount(?, ?, ?)}");

            call.setString(1, this.ownerName);
            call.setInt(2, this.balance);
            call.registerOutParameter(3, java.sql.Types.INTEGER);

            call.execute();
            this.accountID = call.getInt(3);

            return new AccountPK(accountID);
      }
      catch (Exception e)
 . . .
```

In the above code example, a CallableStatement is created that calls an *insert-Account* stored procedure. All the entity bean attributes passed in through *ejbCreate* are then passed into the *insertAccount* procedure for insertion. On the database side, the *insertAccount* procedure will insert the passed-in data into the appropriate table, while at the same time determining the autogenerated key using vendor-specific hooks. The stored procedure will then return the generated key to the client by placing it in the OUT parameter (in this case the last question mark in the procedure call), allowing Java code in ejbCreate to access it after the call has been executed (see appendix).

The advantages of this approach are:

■ **Simplicity.** If you are using BMP entity beans and an RDBMS with an autogeneration facility there is little reason to implement more complicated primary key generation tactics such as those described in the UUID for EJB and Sequence Blocks patterns.

■ **Portability.** The CallableStatement interface is a standard JDBC API that is portable across any database.

The trade-offs are:

■ **Increased database infrastructure maintenance.** A new *insertXXX* stored procedure must be created for every entity bean in the application, in order to do the inserts on behalf of *ejbCreate*. Whenever a column is added to the underlying table or an attribute added to an entity bean, the associated insert stored procedure will also have to be updated. This may not be such a major issue though, since stored procedure creation code is usually stored in the same scripts as the table creation code, which will need to be updated anyway.

■ **Not all databases support autogenerated keys.** All enterprise-class databases support some form of primary key autogeneration facility. For the ones that don't, a simple incrementing counter can be manually manipulated behind a stored procedure if necessary. For example, a table that maintains the current highest primary key in use by all other tables in the database can be maintained, and the *insertXXX* procedures can manually increment those rows to maintain a primary key.

When writing BMP entity beans, the Stored Procedures for Autogenerated Keys pattern provides a fast and portable way to make use of your RDBMS's built-in key generation facility. Two other alternatives that are useable in both BMP and CMP beans are explored in this chapter: the Sequence Blocks and UUID for EJB patterns.

PART

Two

Best Practices for EJB
Design and Implementation

CHAPTER 6

From Requirements to Pattern-Driven Design

So you have this great idea for an application, and you have already gone through the process of outlining all the use cases that your application must support. How do you actually map this conceptual understanding of the business problem to a J2EE application design? How do the patterns presented in this book fit in?

Different processes and best practices have been established for going from a business problem to a concrete design. This chapter will not illustrate any one process and will not recommend any methodology. Rather, we will take a set of real-world requirements and show how they can be realized as pattern-driven architectures.

I recommend that you browse the patterns in Part One before reading this chapter. You may also need to periodically refer back to the patterns while reading this. This chapter is also a walk-through of all the patterns presented in this book. Thus, after having read this chapter, you should have a very good idea of how all the patterns of this book can be applied to your own real-world projects.

The application we will design together is the forums subsystem of TheServerSide.com J2EE Community, the industry's source of J2EE news, discussions, patterns, application server reviews, and articles. Note that this book does not have a long-running example—TheServerSide will only be used in this chapter to illustrate how pattern-driven designs can be achieved using a real-world application.

Launched in May 2000, TheServerSide.com was among the first deployed J2EE-based Web sites that included an EJB based back end. Funded and created by The Middleware Company, an enterprise Java training and consulting company with Ed Roman (author of *Mastering EJB* (2002)) as its CEO, the purpose of TheServerSide was to create a community Web site for J2EE developers. On the back end, this community was basically just a message-board-style application based on EJB. In fact, the very first version of TheServerSide only had one session bean fronting a simple domain model of four entity beans. Since then, this portion of the site has been localized into a *forums* component, and other pieces of functionality (such as surveys, polls, e-mail, and more), were added to the system as separate components, with session beans as the interface into these components.

TheServerSide's Forum Messaging System Use Cases

In our experience, a use-case-driven approach is the most effective approach to take when designing any software application. In order to build a successful application, we need to understand the wants and needs of the users of the application (Carey, et al., 2000). For TheServerSide, this mantra was taken to the extreme, because it helped us focus on getting a lean and useful Web site up and running quickly, rather than spend too much time focusing on cool features and back-end infrastructures that would have delayed the launch of the portal (back in a time when several similar J2EE community portals were in the works).

For TheServerSide, we needed to build a forum/message board system that would allow developers to post messages to each other in a way that could be organized by topic (forum). Furthermore, replies to messages had to be organized together along with the original message in order to create a thread of discussion within a topic. TheServerSide also had to support administration functions to allow managing of the topics of discussion (forums), managing of messages posted, and so on.

Using this requirements-first approach, we came up with a set of use cases that the system needed to support in order to fulfill its purpose. A subset of these use cases is presented in Figure 6.1. *Pay special attention to these use cases, because we will frequently refer to them when making design decisions in the rest of this chapter.*

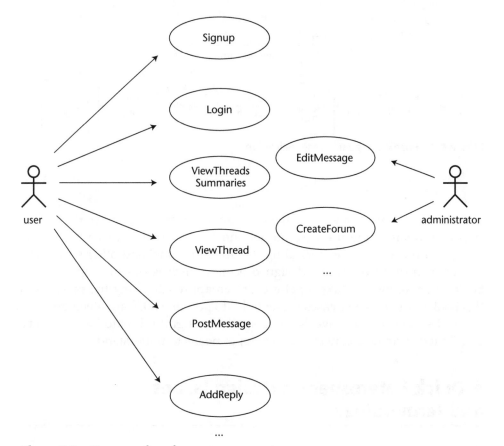

Figure 6.1   Use cases for a forum message system.

The rest of this chapter will show you how to take these requirements and map them to designs. Each use case should have its semantics and user interactions specified in detail at this point, to make sure that all the architects and other project members (and particularly the clients) understand and agree upon what each use case means. One such tool that was used when specifying TheServerSide was a home-brew use case diagram, such as the one illustrated in Figure 6.2.

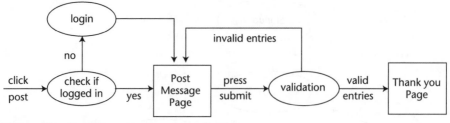

Figure 6.2   Post Message use case realization.

With a solid understanding of the use cases a system must support, the next step is to analyze the use case model and begin coming up with concrete designs of the application, including the domain model and other structures. Rather than go through this design process (which is out of scope for this book), we will instead take a pattern-driven approach, using the patterns in this book to map the use cases presented into possible J2EE architectures.

But first, we need to cover some essential background material that every distributed systems architect and developer needs to understand.

A Quick Referesher on Design Issues and Terminology

When we discuss architecture and design, it is necessary that we agree on some basic terminology, in order to be able to treat this subject with the detail it needs. If you haven't been involved in the design and architecture of large object-oriented systems before, we strongly suggest reading this section before continuing, because the rest of the chapter (and Chapter 7) makes heavy use of the concepts covered in this section. If you have designed many systems in the past, we recommend you still read this section as a refresher.

What Is a Domain Model?

A domain model represents all the *nouns* in a business problem: the people, places, things, and ideas. Domain objects in the model are most often derived by inference from the use cases in an application, or by consultation with the *domain experts*, people who understand the business problem really well (for example: the customer who is sponsoring your project).

Using TheServerSide's use case model as a starting point, we can derive all of the domain objects in the application. For example, taking the PostMessage use case, we can infer the existence of and the need to model a *Message*. Also, Messages need to be posted into some sort of topical category, which we can call a *Forum*. Taking the AddReply message, we know that we need a way to string together a message and its hierarchy of replies. A *Thread* is the mechanism by which we can do this, hence the ViewThread use case. Finally, Messages need to be associated with the identity of the person who posted them (there is no anonymous posting on TheServerSide), thus we need to model the main actor in this drama: the *User*.

The end result is the realization of our domain model, which usually maps directly to a similarly structured model of entity beans (or other persistent object technology). Figure 6.3 illustrates the domain model that would be derived after analyzing the use cases in Figure 6.1.

Understanding the Layers in a J2EE System

A J2EE-based application (or any distributed system for that matter) can in general be classified into a set of layers corresponding to Figure 6.4. These layers will be referred to frequently in the rest of this chapter and Chapter 7.

Domain Model

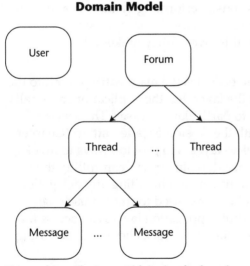

Figure 6.3 TheServerSide's simple domain model.

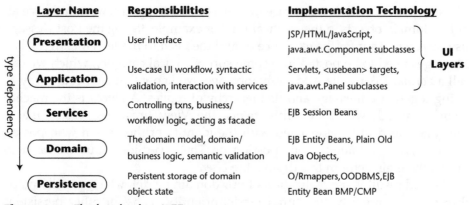

Figure 6.4 The layering in a J2EE system.

The layers break down as follows:

Presentation. All the actual UI parts of an application, such as HTML, JSP, Flash, Swing, or AWT classes. JSP Tag Libraries (when used only for formatting purposes) can also be considered to be part of this layer.

Application. The application layer binds an application together by providing the *glue* and workflow between components on the presentation layer and the services layer. In general, this layer is responsible for managing client-side state (HTTPSessions), performing syntactic validation on client input, and delegating to the services layer for business logic. Taglibs can be considered part of this layer if they make calls to the EJB layer.

Services. The services layer (session beans) is the main entry point into the EJB side of things, and serves as the layer that the application layer calls to invoke business logic specific to particular use cases. The services layer is usually implemented with the Session Façade pattern (Chapter 1). The main function of the services layer is to provide ways to invoke the business logic of a use case (on a domain object), controlling the transactions that the use cases run under, and handling any delegation and workflow between domain objects required to fulfill a use case. A key distinction here is that multiple application layers can access the same services layer, such as a Web site and a thick client both accessing the same session bean layer.

Domain. The domain layer (for example, entity beans) is where all the objects that came out of an object-oriented analysis of the business problem (the domain model) reside. The services layer *delegates* many of the requests it receives to the domain layer (Fowler and Mee, 2001). Thus, the domain layer is definitely where the *meat* of the business problem resides, and is often application-independent (reusable across applications/projects).

Persistence. The persistence layer contains all of the plumbing logic required to make your domain model persist in a data store. For CMP entity beans, JDO, and O/R, the developer does not need to do any coding for this layer, rather, external tools are used to map domain objects to a data store. For BMP entity beans, and session beans, this layer can be implemented with the Data Access Command Bean pattern in Chapter 3.

BUSINESS LOGIC VERSUS DOMAIN LOGIC

There is a great deal of confusion about the meaning of business logic and domain logic, and where each type of logic resides in the five-layer system described earlier.

Domain logic is logic that acts upon the domain objects in a system. Most of the logic in an application is logic that acts upon the domain objects (the business *things* in an application), and thus belongs on the domain objects themselves (if you care about good OO principles such as encapsulation, that is). However, since this logic solves a business problem, it is also considered by many to fit the description of business logic. For example, the *PostMessage* use case would be implemented by a PostMessage method on a forum object, since only a forum should know how to post messages to itself. Thus the logic that posts a message in a forum is domain logic and belongs in the domain layer.

But if business logic and domain logic are the same thing, then what goes on the session bean methods in the services layer? Oddly enough this logic is also a form of business logic, but is can be differentiated from business logic in the domain layer if you think of *workflow.* That is, business logic in the services layer is logic that acts across multiple (possibly unrelated) domain objects, or external systems (systems exposed via JMS or Java Connector Architecture) in order to fulfill a use case. For example, before calling Forum.postMessage-(aMessage), the session bean must first create the Message in question and then pass it to the Forum (a trivial example of workflow). Other examples of business/workflow logic is sending JMS messages to message-driven beans, e-mails, transaction logging, interactions with legacy systems via Java Connector Architecture, and so forth. Business/workflow logic on the services layer is basically any sort of logic that is needed to fulfill a use case, that simply doesn't match the concepts embodied by a domain object (and thus shouldn't be encapsulated behind a domain object).

The answer to the original quandary is that there are two kinds of business logic, one that basically *is* domain logic, and one that involves workflow that doesn't belong in the domain model (and thus lives in the services layer).

Pattern-Driven EJB Architectures

Now that we have the use cases and necessary architectural background in hand, we are ready to apply the design patterns in this book to a real application design. The approach we will take is to design TheServerSide layer by layer, applying the most essential patterns in this book and looking at all the alternate architectures that these patterns will allow.

Since all the other layers in our system depend on the domain and persistence layers, this is the best place to start.

Domain and Persistence Layer Patterns

When we design the back end of our system, the architecture and patterns that we use will vary depending on whether our application has a domain layer (such as entity beans) or no domain layer at all (such as session beans using JDBC, or stored procedures. Let's explore both approaches: first we'll design a system without a domain layer, and then again with a domain layer

---

WHY GO STRAIGHT TO THE DATABASE?

Some nonreligious reasons why one might opt for direct database calls are:

Enables quick building of prototypes. Direct database access can help when throwing together quick prototype applications that are not intended to have a long life span or be changed much over time.

Provides trivial domain models. If an application is very simple, then it can be very quick to hack together an application by not putting in the up-front time to build a nice domain model. For example, the forums subsystem of TheServerSide is extremely simple—there are only four domain objects. Thus, the initial launch of TheServerSide (which only had a forums subsystem at the time), could have arrived a lot quicker if time wasn't spent writing a nice BMP-entity-bean-based domain model. Luckily, this course of action was not taken. TheServerSide ended up growing and changing with the times, and the OO domain model back end helped ease the maintenance burden along the way.

Able to circumvent the domain model for performance reasons. Developers may want to at least *circumvent* a domain model and write persistence logic themselves when implementing a use case that is read-only in nature, such as ViewThreadSumaries or ViewThread. For the reasons expressed in the JDBC for Reading pattern (Chapter 3), it can be a lot faster to circumvent the domain model and go straight to the database for these types of operations.

Persistence Layer Patterns without a Domain Layer

When designing a system without a domain layer, then the Data Access Command Bean pattern (Chapter 3) provides a best practice for architecting a persistence layer. Using this pattern, the persistence layer implementation of the PostMessage and ViewThreadSummaries use cases would be implemented using data access command beans, as shown in Figure 6.5.

In a similar fashion, all of the use cases in our system would eventually map down to a DACB that handles its persistence. Data access command beans provide a standard and efficient way to completely encapsulate persistence logic behind a set of command beans. In effect, they become the persistence layer and the domain layer in an application.

Persistence Layer Patterns with a Domain Model

If you have made the good decision to model your business problem with an object-oriented domain model, then the question of what patterns apply in the persistence layer depends on what technology you are using to implement your domain model. The domain model implementation technology choices can be divided into two types: those that generate the persistence code for you and those that do not, as explained below:

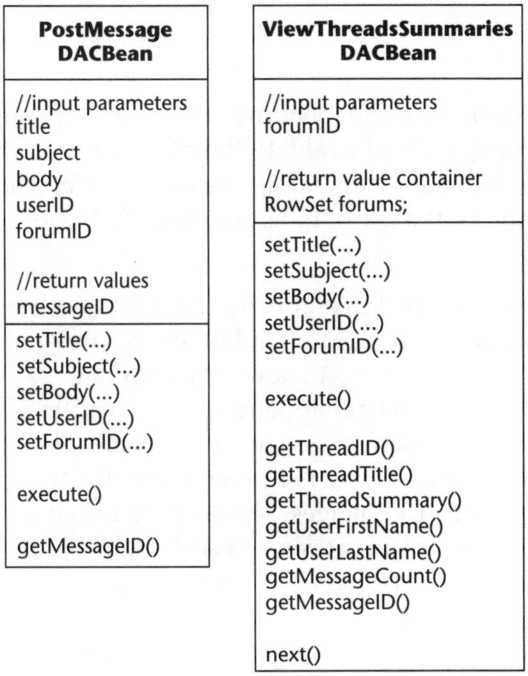

PostMessage DACBean	ViewThreadsSummaries DACBean

//input parameters
title
subject
body
userID
forumID
 	
//return values
messageID
	//input parameters
	forumID
	
	//return value container
	RowSet forums;

setTitle(...) setSubject(...) setBody(...) setUserID(...) setForumID(...) execute() getMessageID()	setTitle(...) setSubject(...) setBody(...) setUserID(...) setForumID(...) execute() getThreadID() getThreadTitle() getThreadSummary() getUserFirstName() getUserLastName() getMessageCount() getMessageID() next()

Figure 6.5   Persistence layer with data access command beans.

Use generated Persistence Logic. CMP entity beans, JDO, and the use of object/relational mapping tools provide you with a technology for implementing your domain model without having to write any persistence logic. They allow you to write your domain objects and have a tool automatically persist your domain objects to a data store. Since the persistence layer is generated, there is no place for developers to apply any patterns.

Do it yourself. Bean-managed persistent entity beans are an example of a domain model technology that requires the developer to write all the persistence logic. Despite the fact that BMP beans allow (and encourage) you to write your persistence code directly into the domain object itself (in the ejbLoad/Store/Create/Find/Delete), developers should still consider creating a separate persistence layer, and here there are design patterns to help you out.

A persistence layer can be created beneath a BMP entity bean domain layer using the Data Access Command Bean pattern (Chapter 3), much in the same way that it was applied in Figure 6.5. This will allow you to keep your BMP entity beans free of any persistence logic, localizing the logic to its own well-encapsulated layer of classes. Another useful pattern for this is the Data Access Object pattern (Alur, et al., 2001).

Patterns for the Domain Layer

At the domain layer, numerous patterns apply, depending on the context and problem being solved. In this section, we will evaluate the requirements of TheServerSide and choose implementations depending on factors affecting concurrency, portability, maintainability, the use of tools, and the need to generate primary keys.

Concurrency. Among the use cases outlined in Figure 6.1, the EditMessage use case opens the potential for corruption of the underlying database unless special precautions are taken. Figure 6.1 shows that only site administrators can edit a message. But what happens when two different administrators attempt to edit the same message? As explained in the Version Number pattern (Chapter 3), there is a potential for the two administrators to overwrite each other's changes. The solution is to use the Version Number pattern, which would cause us to add optimistic concurrency checks to the domain objects that have use cases that could potentially result in database corruption.

Tools. Most modern EJB development tools automate many of the tedious development tasks required to use EJB—including maintaining consistent business method signatures between the remote/local interface and the bean class. If, however, you find yourself in need of writing your EJBs with a text editor (VI is my favorite), then the Business Interface pattern (Chapter 1) can help you catch errors that occur between inconsistent method signatures on the remote/local and bean classes. This pattern applies to all EJBs, not just entity beans.

Portability. If you are in a situation in which you are designing an entity bean domain model that could potentially be used in diverse and unpredictable application server environments, then it is likely that the different application servers will have different levels of support for CMP and BMP. The Dual Persistent Entity Bean pattern (Chapter 3) presents a solution this problem. Since The Middleware Company (who built TheServerSide.com) is in the training business and not the component resale business, there is no use case on TheServerSide that requires portability across CMP and BMP, thus this pattern won't affect the designs in this chapter.

Maintainability. If you are programming in an EJB 1.X environment (without remote interfaces) and want to make use of the Data Transfer Object pattern, or if you are working in an application with very large entity beans (with many attributes), then the Generic Attribute Access pattern shows how to give your entity beans a generic, HashMap-based interface, thus reducing simplifying the implementation and interfaces of your entity beans.

Primary Key Generation. Domain objects in a distributed system require the use of primary keys in order to be able to distinguish one instance of an object from another. In particular, entity beans require that a primary key be returned to the container when ejbCreating an entity bean. But how does a developer generate primary keys for their entity beans? Chapter 5 offers three design patterns, none of which change the architecture of the entity beans themselves, but some of which provide some pretty creative utility EJB to generate primary keys.

Services Layer Patterns

When deciding how to design the architecture of the services layer of our use cases, a simple first question to ask is whether the use case is synchronous or asynchronous in nature.

Asynchronous Use Cases

Asynchronous use cases are those that a client can initiate but doesn't need to wait for a response for. That is, once the client initiates the use case, he or she can continue using the application, while the use case executes in parallel. Developers can identify asynchronous use cases as those that don't require returning any sort of immediate return value or confirmation to the user. For example, most online bookstores implement the equivalent of the *purchase-Books* use case asynchronously. Once users have entered in all the information and clicked the final submit button, they don't sit and wait while their credit card gets billed or the book is located in inventory and wrapped for shipping. Instead, the use case is triggered in the back end, and then the users are free to browse the rest of the site.

On TheServerSide, the PostMessage and AddReply use cases could be executed asynchronously, because once a message is typed in and submitted to the server, the client doesn't necessarily need to wait for it to be added to the forum. For these use cases, the Message Façade pattern (Chapter 1) provides an architecture for implementing the business logic for these use cases asynchronously. The Message Façade pattern advocates using a message-driven bean to encapsulate the business logic for a use case. Thus, the PostMessage and AddReply use cases could have their services layers implemented as in Figure 6.6.

Synchronous Use Cases

Synchronous use cases require the client to block and wait while a use case executes. All use cases that read in data from the server are synchronous, as are other use cases such as CreateForum or EditMessage, which require that the administrator know if the use case executed successfully.

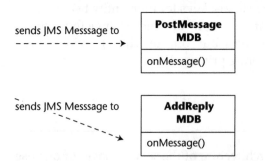

Figure 6.6   Services Layer with Message Façade pattern.

Accounting for the vast majority of use cases, synchronous use cases can have their services layer implemented with one of two patterns, the Session Façade pattern, and the EJB Command pattern (Chapter 1).

Session Façade

The Session Façade pattern is the most commonly used EJB design pattern, and is a building block for other patterns in this book. In fact, the Session Façade pattern *is* the services layer. It advocates hiding the domain layer in an EJB application behind a layer of session beans that encapsulate all the business logic in a J2EE system from the application layer.

For example, if we needed to change the specification of the PostMessage and AddReply use cases to allow the user to browse the message that he just submitted, then the user would have to block and wait while the back end actually added the message to the forum (and thus these use cases would now become synchronous in nature).

In the services layer, these use cases would be implemented as two methods on a stateless session bean: *postMessage* and *addReply*. For example, the business logic of the postMessage use case would be encapsulated on a session bean method, and consist of creating a Message and passing it to the postMessage method on a Forum. Thus, domain logic is maintained on the domain model, but the workflow required to fulfill the use case (creating the Message and then passing it to the Forum), is on the session bean, as in Figure 6.7.

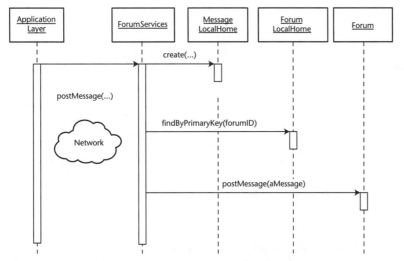

Figure 6.7 Post Message use case on a session façade.

When we use the Session Façade pattern to design the architecture of a services layer, use cases and processes of a similar nature should be grouped together as methods of the same session bean (see the Session Façade pattern for more info). Thus, services layer of our application could potentially be split into two session beans, one that contains all the use cases that are forum-message board related, and one that is related to users and use cases surrounding users, as shown in Figure 6.8.

The only other way to implement the architecture of the services layer is by using the EJB Command Pattern, which replaces the session façade.

EJB Command Pattern

The EJB Command pattern (Chapter 1) is an alternate way to implement a use case's services layer business logic. The easiest way to think of the Command pattern is as a lighter-weight session façade, that also has the benefit of decoupling the client from the details of EJB (similar to the Business Delegate pattern, covered later in this chapter).

Using the Command pattern, the business logic from each use case is encapsulated into small, lightweight command beans, resulting in a services layer consisting of many fine-grained commands (one per use case) that looks like Figure 6.9.

ForumServices
postMessage
addReply
updateMessage
createForum
...

UserServices
createUser
editUser
editUserPreferences
getUserProfile
...

Figure 6.8   Session Façade Services Layer for TheServerSide.

Figure 6.9   Services Layer with Command pattern.

Other Services Layer Patterns

The Session Façade, Message Façade and Command patterns illustrated how our use case's business logic could be constructed on the services layer. However, certain use cases require that the business logic within the façade and command patterns be designed differently, to address performance and maintainability concerns:

Performance. As mentioned in the persistence layer pattern, for use cases that are read-only in nature, the JDBC for Reading pattern (Chapter 3) can help improve performance by circumventing the entity bean domain layer in favor of direct database access. Using this pattern, the ViewThread and ViewThreadSummaries use cases would have their services layer business logic skip the Forum and Thread domain objects, in favor of interacting directly with the persistence layer (using the Data Access Command Bean pattern).

Maintainability. The Data Transfer Object pattern suggests particular best practices for how the services layer should construct data transfer objects and return them to the client. The implementation of this pattern lives in the services layer, but we will cover it in the next section, after introducing the Data Transfer Object pattern in relation to our sample case.

Inter-Tier Data Transfer Patterns

Each use case in our application involves communication between the application layer and the services layer, and needs a mechanism to transfer data from one layer to the other.

The Data Transfer Object pattern in combination with the Session Façade pattern is the most commonly used architecture among EJB developers. The DTO pattern advocates creating a plain, serializable Java class that acts as an envelope, carrying large amounts of data (in one network call) from server to client and from client to server. As an alternative, HashMaps can also be used in place of DTOs (explained below).

RowSets also provide an excellent alternative to DTOs, when transferring read-only data intended for tabular display (explained below).

Data Transfer Objects

Applied to TheServerSide, a DTO would need to be created for almost every use case, since all of them (except for the login use case) require some transfer of data between application and services layer. Using the DTO pattern, a layer of DTOs would be created, as shown in Figure 6.10. Note the method names on the ForumServices class.

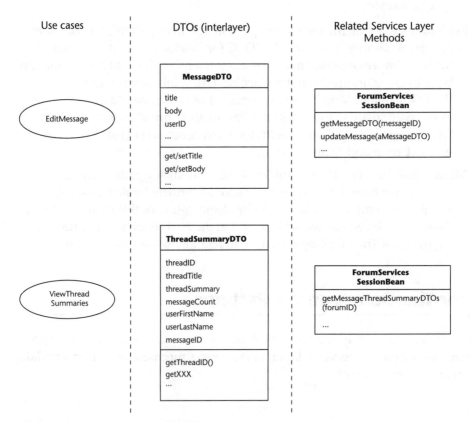

Figure 6.10 Message Domain DTO.

Here we show the two types of data transfer objects: domain and custom. Message DTO is a domain DTO, because it maps directly to a Message domain object. It is used both for retrieving a Message's data on the client and for sending an updated version back to the server. ThreadSummary DTO on the other hand, is a custom DTO that contains attributes from three different domain objects: Thread, User, and Message. The ThreadSummary DTO is completely UI-specific and is used to show a summary of threads, such as on TheServerSide.com's home page.

Data Transfer Object Factory

The Data Transfer Object pattern advocates encapsulating DTO creation and consumption logic into a DTOFactory, which keeps entity beans clean of DTO creation and consumption logic. Applied to our example, a DTOFactory would extract DTO-related method from the ForumServices session bean, either by implementing DTOFactory as another session bean, or as a plain Java class that ForumServices delegates to, as shown in Figure 6.11.

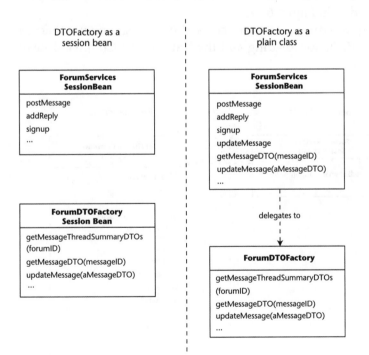

Figure 6.11 DTOFactory Implementation options.

Note that the main takeaway point of the Data Transfer Object pattern is that DTOs should not be used between the services layer and the domain objects, as was common in EJB 1.X, rather, domain objects should be kept clean of DTO knowledge.

Data Transfer HashMaps: A DTO Alternative

The examples shown above only show a limited number of DTOs to keep the chapter more manageable, but often developers need to deal with an explosion of DTOs. The Data Transfer HashMap pattern (Chapter 2) discusses how a generic HashMap can be used to replace the entire DTO layer.

Data Transfer RowSets

As a Web-based site, almost every UI on TheServerSide is tabular in nature, since HTML tables are the main way of organizing data on a Web page. Furthermore, as a forum-messaging system, users of the site only have read-only access. Thus, all use cases involving browsing the site (such as ViewThread, ViewThreadSummaries) are read-only in nature and will be represented in tabular form on TheServerSide. Thus, the ViewThreadSummaries use case could be implemented as in Figure 6.12.

Using RowSets requires direct database access, thus, you should use them in conjunction with the JDBC for Reading and the Data Access Command Bean patterns.

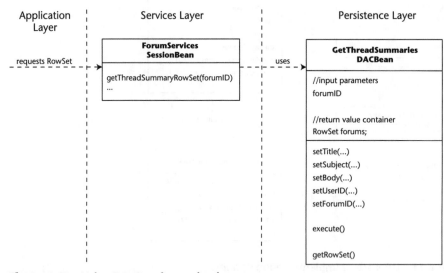

Figure 6.12   Using RowSets for read-only use cases.

Application Layer Patterns

Because this book is about EJB design patterns, it does not contain any patterns that would change the actual architecture of the application layer (see Core J2EE patterns [Alur, et al., 2001] for an excellent set of presentation and application layer patterns), however, the book contains two important patterns that provide best practices for how the application layer should interact with the services layer:

EJBHomeFactory pattern. This pattern provides a clean, encapsulated and high-performance mechanism for application layer clients to find EJB-Homes. For example, rather than look up the home for ForumServices, our use cases can simply call `EJBHomeFactory.getFactory().` `lookUpHome(ForumServicesHome.class).` This also further simplifies application layer logic by removing the burden of remembering JNDI names (these are extracted into ejb-ref tags in web.xml).

Business Delegate. The Business Delegate pattern advocates creating a thin plain Java class that hides the details and complexities of EJB from the application logic. Using this pattern, application logic would interface only with the business delegate, as shown in Figure 6.13. Note that business delegates can be optimized by using the EJBHomeFactory.

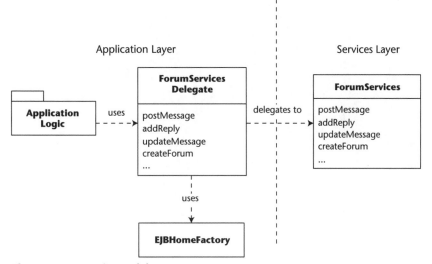

Figure 6.13   Business delegate.

The business delegate is most useful in large projects where there is a separation between presentation/application layer programmers and EJB developers working on the service/domain layers, as a mechanism to shield the details of EJB from the presentation/application layer programmers.

Summary

Up to this point, we took the use cases for TheServerSide.com's forum-messaging component and observed how the patterns in this book affect the implementation of the use cases at each layer in the system. You may feel a bit unsure about which patterns to choose, because many patterns are mutually exclusive. I would recommend paying close attention to the context and problem each pattern solves, as well as the pros and cons. There is a best-fit pattern for your needs; you must simply evaluate it along with the alternatives, to discover which one best applies to your particular use case.

Luckily, patterns tend to have an affinity for one another, which results in our seeing particular combinations of patterns being used again and again across projects. I like to think of those types of patterns combinations as *reference architectures*. That is, certain combinations of patterns give rise to certain *architectures* that are consistent across projects.

Probably the most common reference architecture used to build J2EE systems is the Data Transfer Object + Session Façade pattern combination, which enforces a strictly distinct and clean services layer. On TheServerSide, the reference architecture we use is the EJBHomeFactory + DTO + Session Façade + DTOFactory + Sequence Blocks pattern combination (with a domain model of course).

EJB Development Process: Building with Ant and Unit Testing with Junit

Suppose that you have a conceptual design in mind for your system. You know the use cases it must support, and you know the mapping from the use cases to the methods of the session beans that are on your services layer. You know the domain model the system will manipulate, at least from the conceptual perspective (Fowler, et al., 1997). You also know the approach your system will use for persistent storage.

Now the question arises of how best to develop the system you've designed. Which code should you write first? How will you deploy the system into the containers of your J2EE environment? What about unit testing? In general, what kind of tools and procedures will you need to support the processes of development, environment administration, testing, and the like?

This chapter provides pragmatic, best practice answers to these questions, guiding you from a conceptual application design to a running, working, J2EE system. We will consider real-world topics such as the order of code development, what it means to administer a J2EE application environment, unit-testing best practices, and tools and procedures supporting J2EE development.

We assume that a number of potentially conflicting forces are at work around you. You have selected the J2EE platform for the implementation of your system, and have designed it consistent with industry best practice patterns such as the ones outlined in this book. However, you have likely committed to some sort of schedule, so it is important that your development process be efficient. But at the same time, you care about your craft (Hunt, et al., 1999) and are therefore motivated to maintain a professional level of quality in your work.

The solution presented in this chapter attempts to strike a balance among these conflicting forces. Lest anyone form the impression that our advice is overly prescriptive, let us assure you that our intent is exactly the opposite. We want developers to be free to do what they do best, which is creatively solving business problems. We don't want development teams to become inefficient as a result of inconsistent environments, breakage of previously working functionality, and general lack of repeatability. On the contrary, we sincerely believe that adopting certain habits, as presented in this chapter, frees us to be as productive as we can be.

Order of Development

Which code should you write first? Whether you are the solo developer of an entire project, or a member of a team that has adopted some strategy for organizing itself and dividing labor, this question must be confronted. Fortunately, the forces at work around you combine to suggest a natural solution, which works for teams of various sizes and organization strategies.

Before proceeding, we assume that you have designed your system with an architecture that should be conceptually separable into at least five layers, as illustrated in Figure 7.1 (see the section entitled *Understanding the Layers in a J2EE System* in Chapter 6 for a quick refresher).

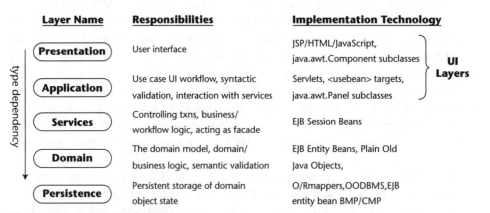

Layer Name	Responsibilities	Implementation Technology	
Presentation	User interface	JSP/HTML/JavaScript, java.awt.Component subclasses	UI Layers
Application	Use case UI workflow, syntactic validation, interaction with services	Servlets, <usebean> targets, java.awt.Panel subclasses	
Services	Controlling txns, business/ workflow logic, acting as facade	EJB Session Beans	
Domain	The domain model, domain/ business logic, semantic validation	EJB Entity Beans, Plain Old Java Objects,	
Persistence	Persistent storage of domain object state	O/Rmappers,OODBMS,EJB entity bean BMP/CMP	

type dependency

Figure 7.1   Layered architecture.

One consequence of this layering is that the Java types (classes and interfaces) that you will write to implement the layers will exhibit "downward" type dependencies. That is, at both compilation time and run time, types in "higher" layers will depend on types in "lower" layers. But per industry best practices, the converse is not true—objects and layers should not encode knowledge, via "upward" type dependencies, of the client objects or layers that use them.

Furthermore, Java compilers are driven by type dependencies. When compiling a given source file, a Java compiler will first search the classpath for compiled classes corresponding to types referenced within that source file, compiling the referenced types if necessary and possible. This depth-first traversal of the typegraph means that persistence classes must be compiled before domain classes, and domain classes before services classes, and so on.

These phenomena suggest writing your code in order from "lowest" layer to "highest" layer. And that, tempered with a few pragmatic alterations, is exactly what you should do. The first pragmatic alteration is that you may have some types (notably, exceptions and "utilities") that transcend layers— they are used from within various layers. Therefore, they could be coded first. Second, in order to facilitate user interface development in parallel with persistence layer development, it is helpful to get to a working services layer as quickly as possible. One way to accomplish this is to initially stub out the persistence layer, returning example data for "read" requests, and implementing "create," "update," and "delete" requests with "no-op" implementations. Then the "real" persistence layer implementation can be programmed while the user interface is developed against the service layer API.

Third, and finally, we assume that you are working in the context of an iterative, incremental process—so you don't need to develop the entire breadth of a given layer, but only as much breadth as is necessary to support the use cases you're working on for the current iteration. The resulting solution—which might be termed "domain-out development"—is detailed in the following subsections.

Layer-Independent Code

As mentioned, you may come up with some Java types that do not properly belong to any "layer"—they are used from within multiple layers. Two primary examples of these types are "utilities" and exceptions. It is difficult to predict in advance what "utilities" you may need; they tend to emerge as coding proceeds. A common example is a class implementing static Foreign Methods (Fowler, 1999) for string manipulation. But you at least need to have an idea in mind for where to collect such methods, and in which package to put classes collecting such methods (see the sidebar that follows on choosing a Java package structure). One approach is to create a class named Strings (note the pluralization) for collecting static Foreign Methods that manipulate strings, and put the Strings class in some likely package (that is, util).

Exceptions are another matter. You would be wise to give some forethought to the types of exceptions you will use in your codebase, and which packages will contain your exception types. Since you won't be able to compile any class whose methods reference your exception types until you code your exception types, this is an unfortunate but necessary starting point. There is a great deal of discussion on the topic of exception handling in Java on Ward Cunningham's Portland Pattern Repository (Exception Patterns, 2001), and a large number of valuable documented patterns as well. We recommend that you pay particular attention to the patterns named Don't Throw Generic Exceptions, Let Exceptions Propagate, Homogenize Exceptions, and Convert Exceptions.

Domain First

Once you have settled on a package structure and approach to exception handling, you are ready to begin coding your domain layer (see the *What Is a Domain Model* discussion in Chapter 1). The first choice that will need to be made is whether to implement the domain model as entity beans or plain Java objects (see Chapter 8 "Alternatives to Entity Beans"), because each choice has obvious implications for how you will implement your persistence layer.

Regardless, the domain layer is the proper place to begin, because you will not be able to compile the session beans in your services layer until you've compiled the domain layer (because your session bean business methods need to use the classes in the domain layer). Furthermore, domain objects are fairly straightforward to implement, in either choice of implementation technology.

At this stage, your main objective should be to implement the domain object classes needed for the current iteration of your project, and get them to compile. Don't worry too much at this early stage about the persistence of your domain objects; you can just leave the *ejbLoad/Store/remove/find* methods empty for now.

Persistence Second

Once you have a compiling domain layer, your next step is to begin implementing the persistence layer. Experience has shown that implementing persistence layers can be very time-consuming, especially when relational databases are used for persisting domain object state. Effort is required to develop the database schema corresponding to the domain model, and to develop the mapping from the domain model to the database schema (Brown and Whitenack, 1995; Stafford, 2001). While all of this development is going on, your user interface developers are not as productive as they otherwise might be. Even if they can implement and compile the classes for the UI, they cannot truly test the UI until some form of persistence is working.

CHOOSING A JAVA PACKAGE STRUCTURE

Another decision you'll face in your EJB application development process is how to separate your classes into Java packages. What set of packages will you use? How will the package structure be organized?

Ideally, you want to group "logically related" classes together into packages in such a way that the dependencies between classes in different packages are minimized.

One obvious solution is suggested by the layering of your architecture: create a package per layer, plus a couple of additional packages for layer-independent code. This results in a set of packages such as the following:

```
com.mycompany.mysystem.domain
com.mycompany.mysystem.exceptions
com.mycompany.mysystem.persistence
com.mycompany.mysystem.services
com.mycompany.mysystem.util
com.mycompany.mysystem.web (assuming a web-based application layer)
```

Another worthwhile approach is to insert an additional level of packaging according to the container (or tier) in which the packages will be deployed at run time. In this approach, one must allow for code that will be deployed in more than one container or tier, hence a "common" package. The resulting structure is as follows:

```
com.mycompany.mysystem.common.exceptions
com.mycompany.mysystem.common.util
com.mycompany.mysystem.common.datatransferobjects
com.mycompany.mysystem.ejbcontainer.domain
com.mycompany.mysystem.ejbcontainer.persistence
com.mycompany.mysystem.ejbcontainer.services
com.mycompany.mysystem.webcontainer.web
```

Within the per layer packages, you may choose to create additional subpackages as needed—if you have a bunch of conceptually related groups of classes within a layer, that are distinct from each other, then it makes sense to add an additional level of packaging within that layer. This often occurs as a result of "vertical subsystems" within the overall system, that tend to slice through the layers and derive their names from major "subjects" in the domain model that they deal with.

Services Third

It can be surprising that all of the foregoing work is required in preparation for implementing the session-bean-based services layer of your system, but that is just a fact of J2EE development. Nevertheless, the services layer is perhaps the most important layer in the system, and its implementation definitely represents a culmination, a milestone, in the EJB development process. In addition to the fact that it defines the API used by clients of the system (including user interfaces), and sees into the domain and persistence layers, one of the primary reasons for its importance is that it forms a very high-leverage test point for your unit test suites—a point we will revisit later in this chapter.

So, given a compiling domain layer, and a working persistence layer, service layer implementation can be completed. Because service layer "business methods" are generally drawn from use case names in the system's requirements model (or system responses in the use case scenarios), it is very common to have service layer "business methods" that reflect Create, Read, Update, Delete (CRUD) operations on domain objects. Even though it may seem mundane, creating and updating and deleting business objects in a system are common user goals, which translate into use cases (Cockburn, 2000). Typically the implementations of these business methods will merely delegate to the CRUD API in the domain and/or persistence layer.

Clients Last

Finally, with a unit-tested services layer supported by a real persistence layer, you are ready to complete the development and integration of client layers—including user interfaces, external system interfaces, and so on. There are definite advantages, in terms of consistent validation, transaction control, and response coordination, to integrating all such clients against your services layer. After all, the services layer defines the behavioral boundary of your application.

Be all that as it may, the most significant client of your services layer is usually your user interface. In fact, the user interface's needs often inform the set of business methods required at the services layer, just as much as the system's use cases do. The services layer exists to serve clients of the system, and if the primary client is a user interface, then the services layer API is tailored to the user interface's needs. So while the compilation dependency factor has a major influence on the order of development, the needs of the user interface must be taken into consideration throughout the process of designing the service layer API.

And just as the service layer API forms a high-leverage test point, so does the application layer API. Suppose that the user interface is Web-based, implemented with JSPs and servlets. Chances are the JSP/Servlets use JavaBeans for access to the data they display (if not, they should—the division of overall system responsibility into the five previously mentioned layers of architecture is a very well-established pattern within the industry). In fact, the data needs of the JSP pages form the basis for the contract between the JSP pages and the JavaBeans they use—and the method signatures making up this contract should return simple data types only, and not domain objects. Furthermore, chances are that the servlets in the architecture will delegate to "controller" (Brown, 2001) classes within the application layer. These JavaBeans, servlets, and controller classes will have their own APIs, which can be subjected to unit test suites in an effort to automate regression testing as close to the "glass" as is possible with Java-based unit test tools.

We will return to the unit-testing discussion later in the chapter, after delving into deployment of your application into the J2EE containers in your environment, and how to automate that.

Automating Environment Administration with Ant

As soon as you begin writing the code for your system, you will need a way to compile it, package it for deployment, and deploy it into the containers in your J2EE environment. How best to do this? Our preferred way to do these things is with Ant (http://jakarta.apache.org/ant). Ant is a cross-platform, XML-driven build automation tool from the Apache Jakarta project (http://jakarta.apache.org), which is very useful for administering the environments of J2EE applications. After explaining what we mean by these terms, we'll show how Ant is used to do these things, and provide template Ant build file targets for administering J2EE application environments.

What Is a J2EE Application Environment?

A typical J2EE project utilizes multiple application environments in the life cycle of the product it produces. Each environment serves a different purpose—it facilitates a different activity in the software development life cycle. Code and data are promoted from one environment to the next, in an orderly progression. A typical, minimal set of environments for a J2EE project consists of:

- Development environments (typically one or more per developer)
- QA environment
- Production environment

The definition of *environment* is important because it sets the stage for the definition of what is involved in administering an environment.

As used herein, an environment refers to the hardware/OS platform(s), and the collection of processes, files, and environment variables that make up a running installation of an application. For applications with two or more tiers of architecture, it is possible, if not likely, that these processes, files, and environment variables are divided amongst multiple (heterogeneous) hosts in a network.

J2EE-based applications generally reflect an architecture defined by the J2EE platform. This application architecture largely determines the coarse-grained components (for example, containers, servers, systems, and so on) found in any environment of such an application. Figure 7.2 illustrates the J2EE platform that forms the basis of J2EE application architecture by JavaSoft's Blueprints team (Kassem, 2000).

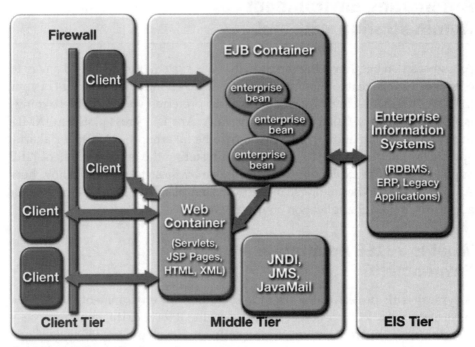

Figure 7.2 J2EE application environment.

What Does It Mean to Administer a J2EE Application Environment?

There is a frequent need during the development of a J2EE application to administer environments of various types: development environments, QA environments, production environments, and the like.

The administration of a J2EE application environment consists of a number of steps. In general the assumed starting points are a new (virgin) machine, and a corporate source code control system (we assume that you're using a source code control system; if you're not, then get one, immediately). The goal is to get a running configuration of the application onto the machine. The steps are as follows:

1. **Install Environment Components.** This step involves installing third-party products on which the application and its development environment depend. In the process it may involve creating directory structures, environment variables, and so on.

2. **Check out the application's codebase.** This involves doing transactions with the corporate source code control system. The transactions need to be parameterized to allow specification of which projects/modules to get, and which versions.

3. **Compile the checked-out codebase.**

4. **Package the application and code upon which it depends for deployment into the containers in which it runs.** For example this probably involves the creation of at least one jar file.

5. **Deploy the application into its containers.** This may involve configuring the containers for the application.

6. **Initialize or update databases.** This step involves initializing or updating any persistent stores or other resources the application may depend on. For example this may involve running DDL scripts, and loading any data the application might require to operate.

7. **Start the application running.**

8. **Test the installation, perhaps, using a unit test suite or perhaps even a load test harness.**

The administration of environments needs to be as reliable, repeatable, and efficient as possible. Few things are more frustrating than spending hours chasing down an apparent bug in some environment, only to discover the root cause is some configuration difference or deficiency. Automation via scripting is the best approach for achieving these goals, and all but the first step are scriptable. But to realize the benefits, environment administrators, including developers, have to consistently use and maintain the scripts—and different environments use slightly different configurations (partly because developers have a tendency to like to do things their own way).

Therefore, in order to accommodate different configurations (and developer preferences) while still delivering the benefits of automation by holding certain things constant, automation scripts need to offer a fair degree of flexibility—especially in the areas of being property-driven and location-independent (with respect to the locations of installed third-party products and directories checked out from the corporate source code control system). The design of the environment administration scripts for a J2EE application needs to account for these conflicting goals.

Using Ant

Ant build files can offer this degree of flexibility and account for these conflicting goals. The trick is to set things up so that your Ant build file can hold certain things constant—such as the steps necessary to administer an environment, the directory structures that are used in the process, the set of third-party products (and versions) that are depended upon, and the classpaths required to compile and run your application—while at the same time accommodating configuration differences and location independence by exploiting properties files and environment variables during environment administration. Basically the goal is to encode as much knowledge as possible into the Ant build file about what is involved in environment administration, while simultaneously minimizing the dependencies and expectations of the Ant build file on the environment.

To use Ant most effectively for J2EE application environment administration, you have to take care in the initial setup of your source code control system and application environments, and you have to organize and implement your Ant build file with consistency and flexibility in mind. The following subsections expand on these themes.

Initial Setup

Your Ant build file will need to make a certain minimal set of assumptions about the organization of directory structures and files within your source code control system and on the filesystems of the hosts in the environments you're administering. Likewise, it will need to make a certain minimal set of assumptions about the existence of installed third-party products in the environment. Therefore, the first step in using Ant effectively for J2EE application environment administration is to set up your source code control system with certain directory structures, and your application environments with certain installed products and environment variables.

Source Code Control System Setup

Source code control systems typically operate on a client/server paradigm. On the server, there is a repository containing all the versions of all the files in your codebase. These files are checked out onto a client's filesystem. The files in the server's repository are organized into some directory structure of your invention, which is preserved when you check out the codebase to a client. The client typically hosts an application environment (or portion thereof) and, during the process of administering that environment, the Ant build file may need to create additional directories (to hold compiled class files, packaged jar files, third-party library files, and so on). So, one of the questions that comes up is how to organize the required directory structures, both in the server repository and on the client filesystem.

Our answer, which we believe to be representative of industry best practice, is tabulated in Table 7.1. We assume that there is a top-level project directory, referred to as <project_dir>, in the server repository, which is checked out into some parent directory on the client filesystem. It is the structure under this top-level project directory that is of interest.

We also assume the existence of a "third-party" directory structure in the server repository. The purpose of this directory structure is to organize, and store in the source code control system, certain third-party files upon which your application depends (jar files and product license files being primary examples). Storing these in source code control and checking them out into the client environment is a best-practice approach, because it relieves your build file from having to expect that they exist in the environment, and it allows your build file to encode which files and which versions are depended upon by the version of the application you're administering into the environment. Another best-practice approach is to organize this third-party directory structure using a three-level scheme to reflect the vendor, product, and version represented by third-party file. Doing so relieves you of later having to reverse-engineer, based on file size and modification date, the API version corresponding to some jar file (for example, jaxp.jar) laying around in some environment.

Table 7.1 Project Directory Structure

DIRECTORY	LOCATION	CONTENT/USAGE
<project_dir>	Server and Client	The top-level directory under which the entire application codebase is organized. The Ant build file lives at this level.
Bin	Server and Client	Any shell scripts or executables upon which your application depends.
Build	Client Only	A directory created during environment administration, to hold compiled class files and Java archive files generated for deployment.
Archives		The location of generated jar files.
Classes		The compilation destination directory.
Conf	Server and Client	Any configuration files used by your application or third-party products upon which it depends.
Data	Server and Client	Any data files that may be required by your application, for example, reference data files that are used during database initialization.
Doc	Server and Client	Documentation files associated with your project, for example, package-level Javadoc files.
Lib	Client Only	A directory to hold third-party library files depended upon by your application. Your Ant build file creates this directory and populates it with the correct third-party files and versions stored in the source code control system. Used in classpaths for compiling and running the application.
Src	Server and Client	The top-level directory under which the (non-test-related) source code of your application is organized.
Java		The root directory of your Java source code tree.
Sql		Contains any DDL scripts used to initialize your application's database.
Web		Contains all of your application's Web content, including JSPs, static HTML, graphics, JavaScript files, and so on.

DIRECTORY	LOCATION	CONTENT/USAGE
Test	Server and Client	Contains all code implementing test harnesses for your application.
Java		Contains your JUnit test suite.
Third-party	Server Only	Top-level directory structure for third-party product files upon which your application depends.
<vendor>		Names the vendor of the third-party product.
<product>		Names the third-party product.
<version>		Contains files associated with the indicated version of the product.

Standard Environment Setup

While some third-party products upon which your application depends (such as "minor" APIs and products distributed as jar files) can be stored in your source code control system, other third-party products, such as database management systems, application servers, and Web servers simply must be installed in the environment you're administering.

In order to deploy your application into these products, and invoke executables distributed with these products, your Ant build file needs to know the filesystem location of the installations of these products. While there are platform-specific conventions that should be followed for product installation locations (for example, /usr/local on Unix, and \Program Files on Windows), the Ant build file would be inflexible if it hard-coded expected locations. The preferred method for passing these installation locations to the Ant build file is via environment variables. An Ant build file can get access to the environment variables defined in the shell in which it is run. Therefore, you should define an environment variable for each installed third-party product whose location needs to be known by your Ant build file (JAVA_HOME is one example). This set of environment variables forms almost the entire contract needed between an Ant build file and the environment in which it is used.

The only other bit of information needed by the Ant build file is the location on the client filesystem where the project directory was checked out from the source code control system. All path computations made by the Ant build file can be made relative to this location. This bit of information is available to the Ant build file via the basedir attribute of its <project> tag, which defaults to the directory containing the build file itself.[1] Since the Ant build file is kept at the root level of the project directory structure, the checked-out location is therefore available trivially.

Build File Organization and Implementation

An initial setup such as that described above allows the implementation of the Ant build file to make a great number of simplifying assumptions, which enables reliable, repeatable, efficient administration of J2EE application environments. Consistency is also facilitated by a strong organizing principle within the Ant build file.

Ant build files are composed of "targets" (conceptually similar to makefile targets, but specified in XML), which are categorized as "main" targets and "subtargets." So, what set of targets is necessary in an Ant build file to accomplish J2EE application environment administration? The answer, and organizing principle, is one main target (perhaps with supporting subtargets) for each step involved in the administration process enumerated earlier. Experience across multiple projects has shown this set of steps to be relevant and appropriate, regardless of which products have been selected for source code control, application serving, and database management. While the implementation details of certain steps may differ from product to product, the need for those steps does not. Therefore, let us examine in turn each step and its automation via Ant.

The Checkout Targets

The first scriptable step of the environment administration process is checking out the application's codebase into the environment. Of course this can be done manually, outside of Ant. But one of the reasons for automating it with Ant is to also automate checking out the correct versions of required third-party files into the client's "lib" directory, which makes your administration process more self-sufficient than it would be if every such file was expected to preexist in every environment. The following code shows sample checkout target implementations, assuming CVS as the source code control system, and an application dependency on JAXP. Note that the checkout target invokes the checkout.lib target:

```
<!-- Checks out the application codebase from the CVS repository.
     If property tag is not defined, will check out head revisions
     of the main branch.
```

---

[1] See the Ant User Manual at http://jakarta.apache.org/ant/manual/index.html.

```
-->
<target name="checkout" description="Checks out the application
 codebase">
    <property name="tag" value=""/>
    <cvs package="<project_dir>" tag="${tag}" dest="${basedir}/.."/>
    <antcall target="checkout.lib"/>
</target>


<!-- Checks out third-party jar files on which the application
     depends into a local "lib" directory which is then included in
     classpaths, deployable archive files, etc.
-->
<target name="checkout.lib" description="Checks out third-party jar
 files">
    <delete dir="${basedir}/lib"/>
    <mkdir dir="${basedir}/lib"/>
    <!--- insert here: cvs export tasks for required jar files -->
</target>
```

Of course, using a build file target to check out the codebase creates a bit of a bootstrapping problem, since the build file itself is kept in the source code control system. However this can be easily solved with command macros on windows or command aliases on Unix: simply set up a command macro or alias that checks out only the build file to some local directory, then changes to that directory—at which point you're ready to issue `ant checkout`.

The Compile Targets

Ant's javac task makes compiling your codebase pretty easy. It works by recursively descending whatever directory tree you give it, looking for Java source files with stale or nonexistent class files, and compiling those source files to the supplied destination directory. Thus, by default, it only compiles source files that have been modified since their last compilation: to force recompilation of the entire codebase, one must clean the destination directory of class files. Since both of these compilation scopes are desirable, we use two targets (*compile* and *recompile*) in our Ant build file, as shown in the following Ant script. To make it easy to clean away class files (and for other reasons), we keep our class files in a separate directory tree from our source files.

```
<path id="classpath.compilation">
    <pathelement location="${basedir}/build/classes"/>
    <pathelement location="${basedir}/lib/jaxp.jar"/>
    <pathelement location="${env.WL_HOME}/lib/weblogic.jar"/>
</path>


<target name="compile" description="Compiles only modified source
 files">
```

```
    <mkdir dir="${basedir}/build/classes"/>
    <javac classpathref="classpath.compilation"
       srcdir="${basedir}/src/java"
       destdir="${basedir}/build/classes"/>
    <antcall target="compile.resources"/>
</target>

<!-- Forces recompilation of the entire codebase by deleting the
     classes directory before invoking compile.
-->
<target name="recompile" description="Recompiles the entire
 codebase">
   <delete dir="${basedir}/build/classes"/>
   <antcall target="compile"/>
</target>

<!-- "Compiles" (in the collection sense) any additional resources
     (besides java class files, i.e., product license files, application
     properties files, etc.) upon which the application depends, that
     need to be collocated with class files due to being accessed through
     class loaders.
-->
<target name="compile.resources">
   <copy todir="${basedir}/build/classes"
includes="${basedir}/src/java/**/META-INF/**"/>
</target>
```

Note that the compile target references a <path> element as its classpath. This is one of the benefits of using Ant—classpaths defined in the build file serve as precise specifications of the dependencies of your codebase. Note also the invocation of the compile.resources target, which is intended to copy any classpath-relative resources, loaded at run time, to the root of the classes directory.

The Package Targets

There are many different ways to package a J2EE application for deployment into containers. At one end of the spectrum, you could use a single Enterprise ARchive (ear) file, containing a single Web ARchive (war) file, a single EJB jar file with all your EJBs, and supporting code. At the other end of the spectrum, you could deploy everything "exploded," in which case your "packaging" step is trivial. Perhaps you'll use different approaches for different environments. Depending on which EJB container you use, you may or may not have to include generated EJB stubs and skeletons in your archive files. These sources of variability make it difficult to provide a universal template Ant build file target for packaging, but the following Ant script shows an example of packaging for deployment of a war file into Tomcat and an ear file (containing multiple EJB jar files and supporting code) into WebLogic:

```
<target name="package" description="Packages the application for
 deployment">
    <delete dir="${basedir}/build/archives"/>
    <antcall target="package.ejb.jars"/>
    <antcall target="package.ejb.ear"/>
    <antcall target="package.web.war"/>
</target>

<target name="package.ejb.jars">
    <antcall target="packageExampleEJB"/>
    <!-- insert calls for other EJBs here -->
    <antcall target="generate.ejb.ear.DD"/>
</target>

<target name="packageExampleEJB">
    <antcall target="package.ejb">
        <param name="package.ejb.ejbname" value="Example"/>
        <param name="package.ejb.directory"
          value="com/mycompany/mysystem/services/example/"/>
        <param name="package.ejb.implclass"
value="com/mycompany/mysystem/services/example/ExampleBean.class"/>
        <param name="package.ejb.remoteIFclass"
value="com/mycompany/mysystem/services/example/Example.class"/>
        <param name="package.ejb.homeIFclass"
value="com/mycompany/mysystem/services/example/ExampleHome.class"/>
    </antcall>
</target>

<target name="package.ejb">
    <mkdir dir="${basedir}/build/archives/temp"/>
    <jar
        jarfile="${basedir}/build/archives/temp/temp.jar"
        basedir="${basedir}/build/classes"
        includes="${package.ejb.implclass},
                  ${package.ejb.remoteIFclass},
                  ${package.ejb.homeIFclass},
                  ${package.ejb.directory}/META-INF/**"
    />
    <java classpathref="classpath.compilation"
          classname="weblogic.ejbc" fork="yes">
        <arg line="${basedir}/build/archives/temp/temp.jar
            ${basedir}/build/archives/${package.ejb.ejbname}.jar"/>
    </java>
    <delete dir="${basedir}/build/archives/temp"/>
</target>

<target name="generate.ejb.ear.DD">
    <java classpath="${basedir}/lib/weblogic.jar"
     classname="weblogic.ant.taskdefs.ear.DDInit" fork="yes">
        <arg line="${basedir}/build/archives"/>
    </java>
```

```
    </target>

    <target name="package.ejb.ear" if="isNonDevelopmentEnvironment">
        <jar
            jarfile="${basedir}/build/archives/myapp.ear"
            basedir="${basedir}/build/archives"
            includes="**"
            excludes="myapp.ear, myapp.war"
        />
    </target>

    <target name="package.web.war" if="isNonDevelopmentEnvironment">
        <mkdir dir="${basedir}/build/archives/temp/WEB-INF/classes"/>
        <mkdir dir="${basedir}/build/archives/temp/WEB-INF/lib"/>
        <copy todir="${basedir}/build/archives/temp/WEB-INF">
            <fileset dir="${basedir}/src/web" excludes="**/CVS/**"/>
        </copy>
        <copy todir="${basedir}/build/archives/temp/WEB-INF/classes">
            <fileset dir="${basedir}/build/classes"/>
        </copy>
        <copy todir="${basedir}/build/archives/temp/WEB-INF/lib">
            <fileset dir="${basedir}/build/archives" includes="*.jar"
              excludes="*.ear"/>
        </copy>
        <java classpath="${env.WL_HOME}/lib/weblogic.jar"
              classname="weblogic.ant.taskdefs.war.DDInit" fork="yes">
            <arg line="${basedir}/build/archives/temp"/>
        </java>
        <jar
            jarfile="${basedir}/build/archives/myapp.war"
            basedir="${basedir}/build/archives/temp"
        />
        <delete dir="${basedir}/build/archives/temp"/>
    </target>
```

The Deploy Target

The meaning of "deployment" differs from container to container. With some EJB containers, deployment consists of copying files into directories known to the container; with others, it consists of using a vendor-provided deployment utility or interface. Furthermore, your approach to deployment may differ depending on the type of environment you're administering.

For a development environment, you'll probably want to "deploy" your application in exploded form, and avoid copying files to the container's directory structure from your local project directory structure. You'll inform the container of the location of your application via configuration files and virtual machine classpaths. The reason for this approach to deployment in a development environment is efficiency: when you're in the "development loop," repeatedly editing and testing code, you'll frequently need to redeploy your edited code to the container for testing. And each time you do, you may have to stop and restart (bounce) the container to make it load your edited code. The most efficient way to do this loop, it seems, is to deploy your code as described above, edit the source files in your project directory structure, compile them if necessary, and bounce the container.

For a nondevelopment environment, however, efficiency is not the emphasis. Instead, it is more important to know the exact configuration of code deployed into the environment, and secure that configuration from modification. These concerns suggest that you should deploy archive files into nondevelopment environments, by copying them from the location where they are prepared.

Ideally your Ant build file's deploy target will be sensitive to the type of environment being administered, and do the right thing for the current environment type. Once again it is difficult to provide a universal template deploy target because of differences between containers; but the following ant script shows a deploy target that assumes Tomcat as the Web container and WebLogic 6.1 as the EJB container:

```
<target name="deploy" description="Deploys the application to this
 host's servers">
    <antcall target="deploy.ejbcontainer"/>
    <antcall target="deploy.webcontainer"/>
    <antcall target="deploy.webserver"/>
</target>


<target name="deploy.ejbcontainer">
    <antcall target="create.weblogic.domain"/>
    <antcall target="deploy.ejbcontainer.earfile"/>
    <antcall target="touchRedeployFile"/>
</target>


<target name="create.weblogic.domain">
    <mkdir dir=
     "${env.WL_HOME}/config/${weblogic.admin.domain}/applications"/>
    <copy overwrite="yes" filtering="yes"
        file="${basedir}/conf/WebLogic/config.xml"
        todir="${env.WL_HOME}/config/${weblogic.admin.domain}"
    />
    <copy overwrite="yes"
        file="${basedir}/conf/WebLogic/fileRealm.properties"
        todir="${env.WL_HOME}/config/${weblogic.admin.domain}"
    />
    <copy overwrite="yes"
        file="${basedir}/conf/WebLogic/SerializedSystemIni.dat" \
        todir="${env.WL_HOME}/config/${weblogic.admin.domain}"/>
</target>


<target name="deploy.ejbcontainer.earfile"
```

```
                if="isNonDevelopmentEnvironment">
        <copy todir=
          "${env.WL_HOME}/config/${weblogic.admin.domain}/applications">
            <fileset dir="${basedir}/build/archives"
                      includes="myapp.ear"/>
        </copy>
    </target>

    <target name="deploy.webcontainer">
        <copy filtering="yes"
              file="${basedir}/conf/Tomcat/tomcat.conf"
              todir="${env.TOMCAT_HOME}/conf"
        />
        <copy filtering="yes"
              file="${basedir}/conf/Tomcat/server.xml"
              todir="${env.TOMCAT_HOME}/conf"
        />
        <copy
              file="${basedir}/conf/Tomcat/web.xml"
              todir="${env.TOMCAT_HOME}/conf"
        />
        <antcall target="deploy.webcontainer.war"/>
    </target>

    <target name="deploy.webcontainer.war"
              if="isNonDevelopmentEnvironment">
        <copy todir="${env.TOMCAT_HOME}/webapps">
            <fileset dir="${basedir}/build/archives"
                      includes="myapp.war"
            />
        </copy>
    </target>
```

The Start/Stop Targets

Using Ant build file targets to start and stop the servers in your environments provides another example of how Ant centralizes and encodes the knowledge of what is necessary to administer an environment of your application. Container vendors typically encourage us to hack the start scripts they supply, to add our own classpaths and so forth. A more manageable approach is to include start and stop targets in our Ant build files, and to regard the vendor-supplied startup/shutdown classes and executables as examples of the usage of vendor-supplied classes and executables. In this approach the implementation of the targets can be sensitive to context, such as the type of host or environment, and can leverage everything known within the build file in passing parameters to vendor-supplied classes and executables. Classpaths, in particular, which are specifications of the dependencies of your application, can leverage the environment-variable-based location independence and the "lib" subdirectory of the project directory. The following and script shows the implementation of start/stop targets for Apache, Tomcat, and WebLogic across the Windows and Unix platforms:

```
<target name="start.apache" description="Starts the Apache Server in
 this environment">
    <antcall target="start.apache.unix"/>
    <antcall target="start.apache.windows"/>
</target>

<target name="start.apache.unix" if="isUnix">
    <exec executable="${env.APACHE_HOME}/bin/httpd"
          dir="${env.APACHE_HOME}/.."/>
</target>

<target name="start.apache.windows" if="isWindows">
    <exec executable="${env.APACHE_HOME}/apache.exe"/>
</target>

<target name="stop.all" description="Stops all servers in this
 environment">
    <antcall target="stop.apache"/>
    <antcall target="stop.tomcat"/>
    <antcall target="stop.weblogic"/>
</target>

<target name="stop.apache" description="Stops the Apache Server in
 this environment">
    <antcall target="stop.apache.unix"/>
    <antcall target="stop.apache.windows"/>
</target>

<target name="stop.apache.unix" if="isUnix">
    <echo file="tempKill" message="kill "/>
    <exec vmlauncher="false" executable="cat tempKill
        ${env.APACHE_HOME}/logs/httpd.pid" output="tempKillApache"/>
    <chmod file="tempKillApache" perm="+x"/>
    <exec vmlauncher="false" executable="tempKillApache"/>
    <delete file="tempKillApache"/>
    <delete file="tempKill"/>
</target>

<target name="stop.apache.windows" if="isWindows">
    <exec executable="${env.APACHE_HOME}/apache.exe">
        <arg line="-k shutdown"/>
    </exec>
</target>

<target name="start.tomcat" description="Starts Tomcat in this
```

```
                   environment">
                 <java classname="org.apache.tomcat.startup.Tomcat" fork="yes"
                       dir="${env.TOMCAT_HOME}">
                     <classpath>
                         <pathelement location="${basedir}/build"/>
                         <pathelement
                           location="${basedir}/build/applications/myEJB.jar"/>
                         <pathelement
                           location="${env.TOMCAT_HOME}/lib/webserver.jar"/>
                         <pathelement
                           location="${env.TOMCAT_HOME}/lib/jasper.jar"/>
                         <pathelement location="${env.TOMCAT_HOME}/lib/xml.jar"/>
                         <pathelement
                           location="${env.TOMCAT_HOME}/lib/servlet.jar"/>
                         <pathelement location="${env.TOMCAT_HOME}/classes"/>
                         <pathelement location="${env.JAVA_HOME}/lib/tools.jar"/>
                         <pathelement
                           location="${env.WL_HOME}/lib/weblogic.jar"/>
                     </classpath>
                     <sysproperty key="tomcat.home" value="${env.TOMCAT_HOME}"/>
                 </java>
             </target>

             <target name="stop.tomcat" description="Stops Tomcat in this
              environment">
                 <java classname="org.apache.tomcat.startup.Tomcat" fork="yes"
                       dir="${env.TOMCAT_HOME}">
                     <classpath>
                         <pathelement
                           location="${env.TOMCAT_HOME}/lib/webserver.jar"/>
                         <pathelement
                           location="${env.TOMCAT_HOME}/lib/jasper.jar"/>
                         <pathelement location="${env.TOMCAT_HOME}/lib/xml.jar"/>
                         <pathelement
                           location="${env.TOMCAT_HOME}/lib/servlet.jar"/>
                         <pathelement location="${env.TOMCAT_HOME}/classes"/>
                         <pathelement location="${env.JAVA_HOME}/lib/tools.jar"/>
                     </classpath>
                     <sysproperty key="tomcat.home" value="${env.TOMCAT_HOME}"/>
                     <arg line="-stop"/>
                 </java>
             </target>

             <target name="start.weblogic" description="Starts the WebLogic
              Server in this environment">
                 <java classname="weblogic.Server" fork="yes"
                       dir="${env.WL_HOME}">
                     <classpath>
                         <pathelement location="${basedir}/build/classes"/>
                         <pathelement location="${basedir}/lib/toplinkall.jar"/>
```

```
            <pathelement
                location="${env.WL_HOME}/lib/weblogic.jar"/>
        </classpath>
        <sysproperty key="bea.home" value="${env.WL_HOME}/.."/>
        <sysproperty key="weblogic.Domain"
                     value="${weblogic.admin.domain}"/>
        <sysproperty key="weblogic.Name"
                     value="${weblogic.admin.server.name}"/>
        <sysproperty key="weblogic.management.password"
                     value="${weblogic.admin.password}"/>
    </java>
</target>

<target name="stop.weblogic" description="Stops the WebLogic Server
 in this environment">
    <java classpath="${env.WL_HOME}/lib/weblogic.jar"
        classname="weblogic.Admin">
        <arg line="-url localhost:${weblogic.admin.server.port}
            SHUTDOWN -username ${weblogic.admin.username} -password
            ${weblogic.admin.password}"
        />
    </java>
</target>
```

The Initialize Database Target

When you readminister a J2EE application environment, you'll typically need to reinitialize, or perhaps update, the database in that environment. Perhaps your application requires certain "reference" data to function correctly. Perhaps your development process benefits from certain example data always being available for testing and debugging and new development purposes. Perhaps you develop and test new functionality against an imported copy of a production database, and apply migration scripts to implement schema and data migration. All of these scenarios require the database in an environment to be properly initialized before the application can be run.

Assuming an RDBMS, database initialization conceptually consists of two steps. For the migration scenario, the steps are importing the database of record, and running the migration scripts. For the nonmigration scenario, the steps are loading the schema, and loading the reference/example data. The steps for both scenarios can be implemented by Ant build file targets. The following Ant script shows the implementation assuming Oracle as the RDBMS in use:

```
<target name="load.database" description="Loads schema and generated
  data into DB">
    <antcall target="load.schema"/>
```

```xml
        <antcall target="load.data"/>
</target>

<target name="load.schema">
    <exec dir="${basedir}/src/sql"
          executable="${env.ORA81_HOME}/bin/sqlplus">
        <arg line="-s
         ${database.username}/${database.password}@${database.name}
         @createtables.sql"/>
    </exec>
</target>

<target name="load.data">
    <java
       classname="com.mycompany.mysystem.persistence.DataGenerator"
       fork="yes">
        <classpath>
            <pathelement location="${basedir}/build"/>
            <pathelement location="${basedir}/lib/toplinkall.jar"/>
            <pathelement location="${basedir}/lib/weblogic.jar"/>
        </classpath>
        <arg line="jdbc:weblogic:oracle:${database.name}
                   ${database.username} ${database.password}
                   weblogic.jdbc.oci.Driver"/>
    </java>
</target>

<target name="export.database" description="Exports the database to
 a dump file">
    <exec dir="." executable="${env.ORA81_HOME}/bin/exp">
        <arg
line="${database.username}/${database.password}@${database.name}
file=exp.${database.username}.${app.version}.${date}.dmp
owner=${database.username} consistent=y buffer=102400 compress=n"/>
    </exec>
</target>

<target name="import.database" if="import.file" description="Import
 DB dump (set import.file, import.fromuser)">
    <property name="import.fromuser" value="${database.username}"/>
    <exec failonerror="true" dir="${basedir}/src/sql"
          executable="${env.ORA81_HOME}/bin/sqlplus">
        <arg line="-s
         ${database.username}/${database.password}@${database.name}
         @droptables.sql"/>
    </exec>
    <exec executable="${env.ORA81_HOME}/bin/imp">
        <arg line="${database.username}/
                   ${database.password}@${database.name}
               file=${import.file} fromuser=${import.fromuser}
               touser=${database.username} analyze=no"/>
```

```
        </exec>
    </target>


<target name="update.database" description="Updates DB using
 appropriate update scripts">
    <exec dir="${basedir}/src/sql"
          executable="${env.ORA81_HOME}/bin/sqlplus">
        <arg line="-s
          ${database.username}/${database.password}@${database.name}
          @migrate.sql"/>
    </exec>
</target>
```

The Test Targets

Last but not least, it is convenient to implement a target in your Ant build file to run your unit test suite. This gives you the opportunity to ensure that any necessary preconditions for running your test suite (for example, started servers) have been met. Your target will also, once again, encode a required classpath—in this case, the classpath required to run your top-level test suite. We will have much more to say about unit testing in the following section; meanwhile, the following example shows a template Ant build file target for running your unit test suite, assuming JUnit as the unit test framework:

```
<path id="classpath.compilation.test">
    <pathelement location="${basedir}/build/classes"/>
    <pathelement location="${basedir}/lib/junit.jar"/>
    <pathelement location="${basedir}/lib/toplinkall.jar"/>
    <pathelement location="${env.WL_HOME}/lib/weblogic.jar"/>
</path>


<path id="classpath.runtime.test">
    <pathelement location="${basedir}/build/classes"/>
    <pathelement location="${basedir}/lib/junit.jar"/>
    <pathelement location="${basedir}/lib/toplinkall.jar"/>
    <pathelement location="${env.WL_HOME}/lib/weblogic.jar"/>
</path>


<target name="compile.test">
    <javac
        srcdir="test/java"
        destdir="build/classes"
        classpathref="classpath.compilation.test"
    />
</target>


<target name="test" depends="compile.test" description="Runs the
 project's test suite">
```

```
<java classname="junit.textui.TestRunner"
      classpathref="classpath.runtime.test">
    <arg value="com.mycompany.mysystem.MySystemTestSuite"/>
</java>
</target>
```

As can see, the test target depends on compilation of the test suite, and we've introduced classpaths to use for compiling and running the test suite. The observant reader may also notice that we compile the test suite classes into the same directory as the code they're testing. This begs the question of where to locate your test suite within your project directory and within your set of Java packages, which are two of the many points on using JUnit that we'll address in the next section.

Unit Testing with JUnit

Unit testing—it's one of those things (like JavaDoc'ing) that we all know we should do, but that tend to get left behind in the race to revenue. Unfortunately this haste leaves us exposed; the lack of a unit test suite is one example of "technical debt" (Brown, 2000) that projects and organizations get into.

Let's face it: developing and maintaining and repeatedly running a worthwhile unit test suite costs a nontrivial amount of time and money. But the appropriate way to view this cost is as an investment—in the effectiveness of your development organization, both now and in the future. As it is made, this investment pays recurring dividends by reaffirming the confidence of developers, managers, and customers in the correctness of your application's codebase.

It is a significant milestone on a new project to be able to show successful execution of a service layer test suite, since this also validates the domain and persistence layers. Going forward, every time you merge new functionality into your codebase your unit test suite will tell you whether you have broken previously working functionality. Later, any time you have to merge code lines that may have been forked off to support parallel development (of production bug fixes versus new features, or next-release functionality versus future-release functionality), your unit test suite will tell you whether you have merged correctly. The confidence you'll gain from seeing successful runs of your unit test suite in these circumstances is the return on your investment in unit testing.

The risk associated with your investment is that you will pay more than necessary to realize the return; you'll spend too much time and money developing and maintaining and running your unit test suite. To minimize this risk, you'll need to decide how much test code is enough and who should write it. You'll need strategies for organizing your test suite so that it will be easy to understand and maintain, and quick to run at a selected level of granularity.

For that latter reason you'll also need approaches for efficiently setting up initial conditions before testing, and cleaning up afterward, especially where persistent storage is concerned. You'll need to know when to run your tests, and at what granularity. And you'll need to know what to do when tests fail and when bugs are found, so that your test suite (and codebase) remain in a state of good maintenance.

We will address all these issues below. Before you proceed, we assume that you have selected JUnit (www.junit.org) as your unit-testing framework, for which we are eternally grateful to Kent Beck (JUnit is a 1998 Java port, by Kent Beck and Erich Gamma, of Kent's original Smalltalk unit test framework, which debuted in 1995). We further assume that you are developing a J2EE system with a layered architecture as described earlier in this chapter. The following sections address each issue in turn.

How Much to Test?

The first question you will probably consider, as you contemplate unit testing, is how much unit test code you should write. How much is enough? How do we even define "enough"? The party line is to test "anything that could break" (Jeffries, et al., 2000). But following that to the letter could result in a prohibitively large unit test suite. Assuming that we trust only the simplest getter and setter methods not to break, we'd have to write at least one unit test for every other method in the codebase—and probably more than one unit test per method, in order to vary the inputs to cover all conditional paths and boundary conditions. The result would be a unit test suite method count that was a multiple of the codebase method count. Where is the point of diminishing return?

In our experience, the highest-value tests are those that test interfaces at significant layer boundaries. The services layer, for example, which forms the behavioral boundary of your application, is one of the highest-value test points in your architecture. This is true for several reasons:

The service layer interface is relied upon by numerous clients of your system. User interfaces, database loaders, and external system interfaces among them. Therefore it is critically important that every exposed service layer method function perfectly across the entire range of inputs, conditional paths, and normal and exceptional circumstances.

The service layer uses the domain and persistence layers. Since the services layer fulfills its responsibilities by delegating to the domain and persistence layers, tests of the services layer will indirectly test the lower layers upon which it depends. This central role, and leverage is what makes the services layer a high-value test point.

Beyond the services layer boundary, your next most significant layer boundary is probably your application layer, which controls your users' interaction with your system. The application layer consists of servlets and the controller classes they use, as well as the JavaBeans used by JSPs via <usebean> tags. Tests at this layer also wield a high degree of leverage, because this layer requires even more support underneath it than does the services layer. Furthermore, maintaining a unit test suite at this layer gets you very close to being able to regression test your user interface from within JUnit instead of a UI test tool. While tests at this layer are more focused and less general than tests at the services layer, they are still among the most valuable.

The persistence layer boundary, while crucial in terms of required correctness, offers less leverage than higher-layer boundaries. Given that there are some 104 scenarios that a persistence layer must support correctly, when one multiplies the various CRUD operations by interobject relationship types (association versus aggregation) by existence scenarios (all objects preexisting, no objects preexisting, some objects preexisting but not others) by other relevant factors, it would be very valuable to have a test suite to demonstrate correct behavior of the persistence layer in every scenario. On the other hand, the development of such a test suite would represent a significant investment and, in the end, the scenarios that you need to function correctly are the scenarios that are actually exercised by your service layer API (and tested by its test suite). The best approach to unit testing the persistence layer probably involves a compromise between extremes, which grows, over time, toward full coverage of all scenarios.

The domain layer doesn't have an obvious boundary against which a test suite can be written. Instead it consists of a large number of small objects, which may not have very many complex methods. Therefore developing an exhaustive test suite within this layer is not as urgent, in a relative sense, as developing test suites for the other layers. But ideally, you would want complete coverage, so implement it at your earliest opportunity.

What about framework code? What if your application depends on framework code of your own invention? In some cases, such as configuration frameworks, logging frameworks, and other such utilities, it is very clear how to test framework code—and very appropriate to do so. But in other cases, it may be difficult to test framework code except by subclassing it with application code, and testing the application code. And that's OK, in our experience. If the application uses the framework consistently with the framework's intentions, and the application passes its unit tests, then it seems reasonable to conclude that the framework correctly supports the application. Test as much as you can within the limits of pragmatism.

Thus, in general, we recommend concentrating your unit testing effort at layer boundaries, emphasizing the services and application layers to get the highest value and leverage, but not neglecting any layer (or layer-independent code or framework) if you can help it.

Test Suite Organization

The layering of the architecture, and the dependencies between layers, also forms the basis for the organization of your unit test suite. Furthermore, you will want to be able to run unit tests at different levels of granularity: perhaps for just an individual method or an individual class, or maybe an entire layer, and finally, for your entire application. JUnit facilitates this aggregation of granularity via the composite pattern (Gamma, Helm, Johnson, and Vlissides, 1995): the TestSuite class may contain TestCases, or other TestSuites, recursively, until a leaf level of all TestCases is reached.

So the organizing principles for your unit test suite are organization by layer of architecture, and then by classes within a given layer. The structure for applying the principles is a composition of TestSuites. Along the way, you'll need to decide which Java packages to put your TestSuites and TestCases in and also where in your project directory structure (in your source code control system) to put them. Each of these points is elaborated below.

Composition of Test Suites

Naturally, the granularity of your top-level test suite should be your entire application. It should be composed of layer-specific test suites, one for each layer except presentation. You may also wish to include test suites for layer-independent code. Within a given layer's test suite, you'll probably reference test suites on a class-by-class basis.

When it comes to ordering TestSuites within a containing TestSuite, keep two things in mind. First, one of the philosophical principles of JUnit is that every test should be independent from every other test. Therefore you shouldn't attempt to construct an ordering in which one test depends for its initial state on results left by a preceding test. Second, at the top level of granularity, you may wish to order your TestSuites from lowest layer of architecture to highest layer, on the assumption that failures in lower layers will probably cause failures in higher layers—so when you read the output of running the top-level TestSuite, you'll probably see root cause failures first among multiple failures (assuming you read from top to bottom). The template TestSuite classes shown in the following code block reflect this approach to test suite composition.

```
package com.mycompany.mysystem;

import com.mycompany.mysystem.domain.DomainLayerTestSuite;
import com.mycompany.mysystem.persistence.PersistenceLayerTestSuite;
import com.mycompany.mysystem.services.ServiceLayerTestSuite;
import com.mycompany.mysystem.web.ApplicationLayerTestSuite;
import junit.framework.Test;
```

```
import junit.framework.TestSuite;

/**
 * The MySystemTestSuite is a TestSuite that is specialized for
 * testing the behavior of My System.
 */
public class MySystemTestSuite
extends TestSuite {


    //PROTOCOL: SUITE

    /**
     * Returns a suite of tests for My System.
     *
     * @return a suite of tests for My System
     */
    public static Test suite()
    {
        MySystemTestSuite suite = new MySystemTestSuite();
        suite.addTest(PersistenceLayerTestSuite.suite());
        suite.addTest(DomainLayerTestSuite.suite());
        suite.addTest(ServiceLayerTestSuite.suite());
        suite.addTest(ApplicationLayerTestSuite.suite());
        return suite;
    }

}


package com.mycompany.mysystem.services;

import junit.framework.Test;
import junit.framework.TestSuite;

/** The ServiceLayerTestSuite is a TestSuite that is specialized for
 * testing the behavior of the services layer of My System.
 */
public class ServiceLayerTestSuite
extends TestSuite
{


    //PROTOCOL: SUITE

    /**
     * Returns a suite of tests for the Back Office System's
     * services layer.
     *
     * @return a suite of tests for the Back Office System's
     * services layer
```

```
    */
    public static Test suite()
    {
        ServiceLayerTestSuite suite = new ServiceLayerTestSuite();
        suite.addTest(MyEJBTestCase.suite());
        return suite;
    }


}
```

Packaging and Location Considerations

The observant reader will notice that the TestSuite classes in the code block above also reflect our preferences regarding the Java packages in which test code is placed. However it is not obvious from the listing where we put the test classes in our project directory structure. Both of these issues are the subject of mild debate in public Java-related forums.

It seems logical to put test classes in Java packages that are somehow related to the packages containing the code being tested. One school of thought would have you create "test" subpackages of the target packages, and place your test classes in those "test" subpackages. However, this only causes you to have to add numerous additional import statements to your test classes' source files; therefore we don't like it (we're lazy). We prefer to put our test classes directly into the packages containing the target classes, which eliminates the need for those extra import statements.

But wait, you say. Now, how do you separate your test code from your target code, especially for deployment or distribution purposes? Easy. We simply put all test code into a completely separate directory structure under the top-level project directory in the source code control system (refer to Table 7.1). Then our Ant build files can control which directory structures are copied from place to place, put in archive files, and so on. This approach gives us the best of both worlds.

It has never been necessary in our experience to "deploy" our unit test suites into any container or server; rather, the test code always acts as client code to the actual application code that gets deployed. Therefore the test code doesn't need to be packaged into archive files for deployment along with the application code. When it comes to distribution, if you need to distribute your test code to your consumers, you are certainly free to do so however you wish.

Naming TestCase Subclasses and Test Methods

As a final detail around test suite organization, we encourage you to think carefully about how you name your TestCase subclasses and the test methods they contain. Your primary heuristic should be to clearly communicate your intentions to whoever comes along later to read your code. The convention among JUnit users, which we follow, is to create one TestCase subclass per target class you are testing—and name the TestCase subclass by appending "Test" or "TestCase" to the target class's name. Of the two, we prefer "TestCase," since that is the superclass's name.

When it comes to naming test methods, the JUnit framework requires test method names to begin with the prefix "test." You are then free to append whatever you want to form the test method's name; the convention is to append the name of the target method tested by the test method. But you'll frequently need multiple test methods per target method, to cover the range of possible inputs, conditional paths, normal and exceptional circumstances, and so on. We suggest an intention-revealing suffix. For example, if you're testing a method named "createCustomers," you might have test methods named "testCreateCustomersWithEmptyCollection," and so on. Whatever you do, don't simply append a number to the end of your test method name—that doesn't do a very good job of communicating your intentions.

Test Case Setup and Tear Down

One of the challenges in using JUnit to test enterprise applications is in setting up the initial conditions required to test certain functionality. It is frequently the case that enterprise applications implement complex business logic manipulating complex domain models. The business logic likely implements responsibilities inherent in the workflows, or overall business processes, supported by the application. As a result, certain portions of business logic may not even be relevant unless certain workflows have advanced to certain stages, certain aggregation hierarchies of business objects exist in persistent storage, certain business objects have entered certain states, and so on. To test these portions of business logic, you must ensure that persistent storage is set up with the appropriate initial conditions.

How much should your test cases assume about persistent storage? One of the philosophical principles underlying JUnit is that tests are independent from one another—one test case should not rely on results left by some other test case that is assumed to have ran earlier in some sequence. But on the other hand, it would be prohibitive, in terms of time consumption at run time, for every TestCase to set up complex database states from scratch in its setUp() or test methods. When in the testing sequence, then, are tables created and data representing initial conditions loaded?

Our experience suggests that a reasonable compromise is to write test cases to assume that a standard test data set has been loaded (and perhaps also a standard reference data set). The test data set needs to be designed carefully enough to contain objects in all the right states, and all of the necessary aggregation hierarchies, associations, and so on, to support all of the functionality of the application (and therefore its testing). Of course the test data set, and the schema it populates, will evolve over time on your project—so they need to be maintained and enhanced as your application grows and changes.

There are two general approaches to creating and maintaining a test data set: you can write a program to generate it, or you can enter the data through your application's user interface into a database that you would maintain and migrate just as you would any other database (for example, a production, training, or demo database). Both approaches have advantages and disadvantages; but with the latter approach you may have the opportunity to get some repetitions in database migration before assuming the (serious) responsibility of maintaining and migrating a production database.

As test methods execute, they will likely cause transactional changes to the database containing the test data set. In keeping with JUnit's philosophy, your test methods should clean up after themselves and leave the test data set in the same state in which they found it. Given the approach of creating a TestCase class per target class being tested, this often means the cleanup logic has to be invoked from the test method itself—a TestCase class's tearDown() method won't necessarily know which test method was run and thus which of the target class's methods was tested and, therefore, what needs to be cleaned up.

Who Should Write the Tests?

The developer who wrote the code being tested is the person who should write the tests for that code. No one else has a better idea of what that developer's intentions were as the code was being written, and therefore what tests are indicated. No one else has a better understanding of the internal workings of that code, and therefore its input ranges, conditional paths, and normal and exceptional circumstances.

Some organizations suggest that junior programmers with time on their hands be assigned to write unit tests for other people's code. We feel this is an anti-pattern. It is likely that the resulting unit tests will not be complete or even correct; therefore, it is likely that the target code will not be adequately tested. Finally it is likely that productivity will decrease as a result of the unit test developer having to ask the target code developer about the latter's intentions.

Developers should be responsible for writing their own unit tests—period. It is just a regular part of being a professional software developer.

When to Run Tests?

Perhaps a better question to ask would be how often should we run tests of a particular granularity? We've seen that a J2EE application's unit test suite can test at different levels of granularity—from the entire application, to a certain layer of architecture, to a certain class within a layer, to even a certain method within that class.

Depending on how your team has chosen to organize and partition work, chances are that you are responsible for a given layer of architecture, or a given vertical subsystem that slices through all layers. As development proceeds, you'll likely run unit tests at the method or class level of granularity with very high frequency—because you'll be adding methods or classes to your layer, or functionality to your subsystem, and you'll want to test it as soon as you've coded and compiled it. Every time you complete the implementation of a method, or class, or development task, you will have also completed and run the concomitant additions to your unit test suite that test the code you completed. Occasionally you'll want to run an entire layer's test suite, or perhaps selected TestCase subclasses from the application layer or service layer test suites that exercise a specific subsystem.

When you're ready to check your code in to the source code control system, you should run the entire application's test suite. If you can't check in because your project directory isn't up to date with the repository, you should run the entire application's test suite after updating your project directory (and deconflicting any merges that occurred in the process).

Finally, after successfully checking in, you may want to take the opportunity to completely readminister your development environment, starting by deleting your local project directory and getting a "fresh checkout" from the source code control system. And, of course, the final step in readministering your environment is to run the entire application's unit test suite.

This goes for nondevelopment environments, as well. Any time any environment is readministered, the entire application's test suite should be run in that environment. Thus, when code is promoted from development to the QA, demo, or production environment, the unit test suite is run in that environment.

Basically the idea is to run tests, at the appropriate level of granularity, frequently enough to ensure that the codebase deployed in the environment (and certainly at the heads of the source code control system branches) is always in a state where it passes the entire unit test suite.

What to Do When Tests Fail

Fix something! There are only two possible reasons why a test might fail: either something is wrong with the test itself, or something is wrong with the code being tested. Both situations warrant your attention. If something is wrong with the code being tested, then your unit test suite has just done part of its job and given you partial return on investment (the other part is when it tells you everything is OK).

If something is wrong with the test itself, fix the test! It is very easy for test cases to fall out of maintenance as your application evolves. Don't just blow it off—keeping the test cases up to date is part of every development task. As soon as you establish the precedent for ignoring broken tests, the value of your test suite begins to diminish.

What to Do When Bugs Are Found

Inevitably, bugs will be found in your application that were not previously detected by anything that anyone did (including running a unit test suite). Maybe the bug is not in your application, but in a third-party product that you're using from some vendor.

In either case, the very first thing you should do is create a unit test that demonstrates the bug. Else how will you be able to state conclusively that you've fixed it? You've only fixed it when the unit tests that you just created now succeed, whereas they failed before. If the bug you found was in a third-party product, send the vendor your unit tests that demonstrate the bug. If they have some semblance of business sense and professionalism, they should be profoundly grateful to you for helping them QA their product.

Summary

We've covered a lot of ground. Hopefully by now you have a feel for what's involved in translating your conceptual design into a running, working J2EE application. You know the order in which to develop your code, you know how to administer an environment of your application using Ant, and you know how to unit test your codebase with JUnit. We'd like to close this chapter with an analogy for what happens in a software development process: that of nested loops in a program.

We see three levels of nesting. Within the innermost loop, every developer is repeatedly editing and testing code, perhaps doing domain-out development of new features, within some development environment—which may require repeated execution of some of the environment administration steps. Every so often, a developer will finish a task and pop out to the next level of nesting, in which she will do a transaction with the source code control system and then reenter the innermost loop. Around the transaction with the source code control system, the developer will (should) run unit test suites and readminister the development environment. Finally, at the outermost level, the project as a whole is repeatedly looping through a series of iterations. At the conclusion of each iteration, other (nondevelopment) environments will be administered, and test suites will be run.

CHAPTER 8

Alternatives to Entity Beans

Objects of love or hate, entity beans have been mired in controversy since their inception. Many claim that entity beans are simply a performance killer, not ready for prime time enterprise usage. Others claim that using entity beans is a good decision, when used in the correct circumstances. This chapter will discuss the pros and cons of entity beans and discuss common alternatives to entity beans that can be used behind a session façade just as well as entity beans can.

Entity Beans Features

Entity beans provide a standard way to create transparently persistent, container-managed, distributed, secure, transactional components. Note the choice of words:

A standard. Entity beans provide a standard way to create persistent domain objects. Before entity beans, people had to write their own persistence frameworks or rely on proprietary relational mappers.

Transparent Persistence. This means that business logic can be written that uses entity beans and business methods on entity beans without any knowledge of the underlying persistence mechanism (BMP or CMP;

RDBMS or OODBMS). This allows business logic to be business logic and not be mired with persistence code. Entity beans hide all the persistence logic from the entity bean client code.

Container Managed. When using Container-Managed Persistence (CMP) entity beans, it is a major plus that the container can handle all the persistence logic and O/R mapping, as well as data caching, on a developer's behalf. Persistence logic is notoriously long, tedious, and bug-ridden. Using CMP is a major plus for EJB developers.

Distributed. Entity beans are distributed objects, callable via RMI-IIOP from any Java or CORBA client on the network.

Secure. Like session beans, entity beans business methods can be configured with role-based security checks, configurable in the deployment descriptors.

Transactional. Entity beans provide developers with fine-grained transaction control. Deployment descriptors can be configured to assign different transaction semantics and isolation levels to different business methods on an entity bean, providing automatic, declarative transaction control.

Components. Entity beans are designed to be components. Deployment descriptors and all the declarative tagging that needs to occur to make an entity bean deployable is intended to make an entity bean into a self-contained component that is deployable in any J2EE application server without requiring any code changes.

These features represent a significant value add that was previously never available on this scale in other distributed frameworks. So with this rich feature set, why would people not want to use entity beans?

Entity Beans and Cognitive Dissonance

"Cognitive Dissonance is the inner conflict we experience when we do something that is counter to our prior values, beliefs, and feelings. To reduce our tension, we either change our beliefs or explain away our actions." The Complete Idiot's Guide to Psychology *(Johnston, 2000)*

Cognitive dissonance comes into play because entity beans are designed to be distributed components (with all the features outlined above), but developers really only want to use entity beans as lightweight domain objects. The limitations of early versions of the EJB specification, as well as the performance and development overhead required to support entity beans as components, are the main reason why opinions about entity beans have been so mixed.

So what are the features of entity beans that aren't practically used in most real-world projects?

1. **Distributed.** Communicating from a client directly with an entity bean is a performance and maintainability killer. See the Session Façade pattern (Chapter 1) for an in-depth explanation. Luckily, local interfaces alleviate the performance problems with entity beans, but in the pre-local-interface days, the fact that entity beans were remote was the de facto reason that many projects decided not to use them.

   Partially as a result of the remote nature of EJB 1.X entity beans, the Session Façade pattern became the de facto way to design EJB systems, both as a performance enhancer and also as way to design better systems. When using the Session Façade pattern, many of the other features provided by entity beans become redundant.

2. **Secure.** Since the session façade is the single point of access for the client tier, caller security checks are typically performed within the session bean method being called by the client. Thus container or programmatic security checks done when invoking entity beans, as well as any entity deployment descriptor tags used for security are not needed.

3. **Transactional.** Once again, behind a session façade, transactions are usually container managed, declared in the deployment descriptor of the session beans. Transactions begin when a client invokes a session bean method and ends when the method call has completed. Thus, since the session façade is where transactions are demarcated, there is no need for a developer to declare transactions for any business methods on an entity bean (in the deployment descriptor), there is also no need for the container to perform any transaction checks when an entity bean method is called.

4. **Components.** Much of the complexity and legwork required to write entity beans is plumbing infrastructure designed to make the entity beans' components, deployable independently in any application server. Much of the tags required in writing deployment descriptors are for this purpose. Cognitive dissonance comes into play here because developers are not using entity beans for components, they are using them as lightweight domain objects. The components are demarcated along session bean lines, and entity beans are simply the object model used by the session façade. Things such as entity bean relationships are more simply expressed in code, not in deployment descriptors.

Another major problem with entity beans is the *N+1 database calls problem* (see the JDBC for Reading pattern for an explanation). The N + 1 calls problem makes it very difficult to use entity beans in projects where the object model is complicated and where clients do not frequently read in the same data from the server (thus, caching of entity bean data would not really help). There are workarounds for this, which we will look at later in this chapter.

In Defense of Entity Beans

With the release of EJB 2.0, the following major problems with entity beans have been solved:

Remoteness. This has been solved with the introduction of local interfaces, allowing entity beans to be written in a fine-grained manner, callable only by the session façade.

Support for relationships and object modeling. Enhancements to CMP allow for a richer set of relationships between entity beans, making it possible to map a domain model directly to a hierarchy of entity beans. For example, entity beans can now be written with 1:N and N:M directionality, cascading deletes, and more features, which can be a great time saver.

The other two major problems with EJB are also being solved, as the EJB development platform matures:

N + 1 calls problem. The solution to this problem is to be able to load a set of entity beans in one bulk JDBC call, a feature that many modern application servers support for CMP. For BMP, Gene Chuang's Fatkey pattern (see TheServerSide.com patterns section) also solves the N + 1 calls problem.

Complex and slow development time. The complexity and development time overhead of programming with entity beans (explained in the previous section) has been alleviated by the maturity of EJB tools. New JSRs coming out of Sun will soon enable a tools market in which entity beans can be modeled, generated, and deployed into an application server without having to touch any XML or encode any of the home/component interfaces.

Despite the redundancy of many of the benefits of entity beans (when used behind the session façade) the practical benefits entity beans do provide (a standard, transparent persistence, container-managed persistence) are significant. Let's take a look at what these benefits will mean to your project:

Reduced ramp-up time. Because it's a well understood standard, people trained in EJB or people with an existing EJB skill sets are increasingly becoming more prevalent, reducing the amount of ramp-up time and the cost of new EJB projects.

Advanced O/R mapping out of the box. EJB CMP is essentially a standard persistence framework out of the box. Thus, when using CMP entity beans, there is no need to spend money and ramp-up time on buying a third-party O/R mapping product. *Reducing the number of moving parts in a software application can significantly ease the maintenance burden.*

Portability. Entity beans are guaranteed to be deployable in any J2EE-certified server, whereas plain ordinary Java objects (POJOs) developed with third-party persistence engines (such as O/R mappers/JDO engines) can only run in the application servers that your particular O/R mapper is certified on.

While EJB 2.0 has made entity beans a viable technology for building portable, scalable domain models to back a well-designed session façade, developing entity beans still remains fairly complicated compared to developing POJOs due to the fact that entity beans are components.

Despite the fact that this is a book on EJB design patterns, many of the patterns in this book that apply to entity beans also apply to any other domain model technology. Since many developers are still not using entity beans today, the rest of this chapter will discuss best practice alternatives to entity beans that support the use of POJOs for server-side domain models.

Alternatives to Entity Beans

Without entity beans, some other source of persistence is required to support any kind of business logic behind your Session Façade. The motivations for most of these options are the desire to achieve simplicity and performance by moving away from building your domain model with components (entity beans) and instead building them with plain ordinary Java objects (POJOs). POJOs are simply quicker, easier, and more object-oriented to implement than components. The options are outlined in the sections below.

Use Straight JDBC/Stored Procedures

This is a non-POJO approach, where session beans can be encoded to directly interact with the database to get things done. The Data Access Command Bean pattern (Chapter 3) provides a best practice for decoupling session bean business logic from persistence logic. However, even with the DACB pattern, splitting business logic across the session bean layer and a layer of stored procedures is simply bad separation of concerns and poor encapsulation. The argument against using straight JDBC/stored procedures boils down to a relational versus object-oriented design debate, which has been covered in depth in other publications.

Use a Third Party O/R Mapping Product

Using a third party O/R mapping tool that can plug into your J2EE application server, is the most common alternative to entity beans. These tools typically allow you to write your domain model as plain Java objects, using their tools to transparently persist the objects without any extra work on the part of the developer. O/R mapping tools are a very popular, widely used alternative to entity beans. The only drawbacks to this approach are the proprietary nature of the products and a potential lack of portability. That is, rather than use a well-understood standard such as entity beans; a proprietary product (which requires training) is used. Also, if you care about making your J2EE applications portable across application servers, then you will be limited to the specific application servers that your O/R tool supports.

Build a Custom Persistence Framework

Here the developer builds a custom persistence framework that can take POJOs and persist them behind the scenes. The benefits of this are that you can use POJOs without having to fork out money for an expensive third party O/R mapper. The disadvantage is that you need to implement the persistence layer yourself, which is a complicated and involved process.

Use Java Data Objects

Java Data Objects (JDO) is a new API from Sun whose purpose is to provide transparent persistence for POJO domain models. JDO provides all the practical benefits of entity beans (a standard, transparent persistence, container-managed) all packaged in a very lightweight framework that allows developers to quickly write complex domain models with simple POJOs.

Like entity beans, Java data objects are meant to represent persistent objects. Unlike entity beans, Java data objects can be developed as plain Java objects, completely independent of any container or API (JDOs don't even need to know about the JDO APIs). As a standard, JDO seems to be the most promising alternative to entity beans, so we will now spend the rest of the chapter reviewing it.

An EJB Developer's Introduction to Java Data Objects

JDO is a specification for the transparent object persistence. It allows you to create complex hierarchies of plain ordinary Java objects (POJOs) and have all of their persistence details handled with transparently. JDO defines a truly object-oriented persistence mechanism that can be used to persist JDOs to any type of data store (relational, object database, and so on).

With JDO, the developer doesn't need to write any persistence code, and business logic that uses Java data objects (and the data objects themselves) is completely hidden from the underlying persistence mechanism. Java data objects provide an attractive alternative to entity beans for making Java objects persistent behind a session façade, one that is lighter weight and leaves behind all the distributed component baggage typical of entity beans, while maintaining all the benefits of being a standard. At the time of this writing, it is being developed under the Java Community Process as JSR 12, and is in the 1.0 proposed final draft stage. Unfortunately, there are currently no plans to include JDO within the J2EE specification, likely due to the fact that JDO competes with entity beans. As a result, JDOs will not likely be part of the J2EE specification. The consequences of this is that J2EE application servers will not come with built-in JDO support, rather, third-party JDO engines will need to run alongside a J2EE server to enable JDO.

The remainder of this section will discuss JDO from the perspective of an EJB developer, showing how an EJB developer would use JDO and discussing issues that an EJB developer should be aware of. Detailed information about the various JDO APIs are beyond the scope for this section, instead we will focus on showing how JDO can be used in an EJB context to get the job done.

Class Requirements and Dependencies

Figure 8.1 illustrates a simple implementation of a bank account example, as a CMP entity bean and a JDO.

Account CMP Entity Bean   Account JDO

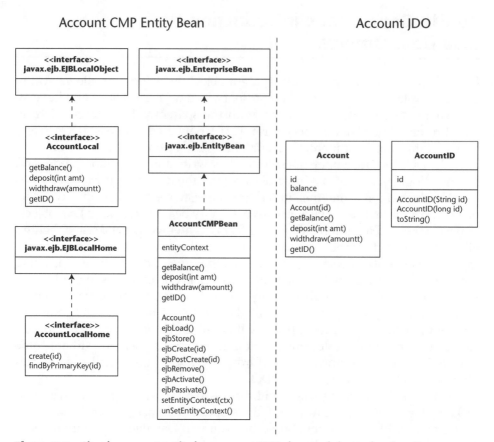

Figure 8.1 Simple account entity bean versus JDO class and dependencies diagram.

Figure 8.1 illustrates the classes that a developer would have to implement and the other dependencies (required implementation interfaces such as java.ejb.EntityBean) that need to be considered when developing a simple bank account. In the EJB case, three classes need to be written (home, local, and the bean class), all of which have dependencies on java.ejb interfaces and, in the case of the bean class, require the encoding of 10 EJB callback methods (ejbLoad, and so on). Compare this to the Java Data Object approach, which requires the simple coding of an Account java class, with no external dependencies on system APIs or callback methods. The only requirement for JDO is the writing of a primary key class (AccountID), which is required when attempting to *find* the JDO (explained later in this chapter).

Build and Deployment Processes

The build and deployment process for entity beans and JDO are loosely similar. The following section will compare and contrast the two approaches:

Write an XML descriptor for an object. This is done once, at the beginning of development for the object. The XML file is typically modified when major changes are made to the bean/object such as adding a new attribute. Entity beans require the writing of an ejb-jar.xml deployment descriptor (one per bean or set of beans). Ejb-jar.xml is where classes, transactions, security, jndi, persistent mappings, relationships and more are all localized via XML tags. Java Data Objects also require a <classname>.jdo or <packagename>.jdo XML file to be written (one per class or package of classes). The descriptor names which classes need to be made persistent as well as provides information about the class fields and any vendor extensions.

Compile the files with standard Java compiler. Entity Bean classes and JDO are now compiled using any standard compiler. With JDO, developers have the option to run a source code post-processor on their JDO java source files before compiling. The post processor modifies the source of the persistent objects names persistence-capable in the .jdo xml file, encoding them with the logic required to be persistent. If a developer does not want to run a source code post-processor, they can run a byte code enhancer, described below.

Once the JDOs have been compiled, it is possible to develop testing scripts which instantiate your JDOs and test all aspects of the code (without actually persisting any data). Entity beans cannot be tested in this manner because they depend on the EJB container.

Postcompile using vendor specific tool. At this step, a vendor-specific postcompilation tool is used to postcompile the entity bean or JDOs (unless the post-processor was already used) , using the XML descriptors for extra information. Note that the first time this is done, both entity beans and JDOs may need to be mapped to an underlying data store using a vendor specific tool (that is, mapping fields to columns in a RDBMS). Entity beans are compiled by an EJBC-like tool, which generates vendor-specific stubs, persistent subclasses of CMP entity. If the developer opted not to use the source code post-processor, then Java data objects need to be postcompiled by an *enhancer*, which modifies the byte code of the JDOs, making similar changes as the source post-processor. After postcompiling/post-processing, Java data objects can now be *fully tested* (persistence mappings, run-time behavior, and so on) within the environment of the JDO provider, without the use of an application server.

Package and deploy into the application server. Here we take our ready-to-run code and deploy it into the application server. Entity beans are usually packaged in the same ejb-jars as the session beans that call them through their local interfaces.

Java Data Objects can also be packaged in the ejb-jar of the session beans that make use of them, or they can be added to the J2EE ear as a library.

The build and deployment process for entity beans and JDO is pretty similar. The differences are in complexity of the deployment descriptors and also the fact that Java data objects can be tested earlier in the build cycle, since they don't rely on the existence of an application server.

Inheritance

Inheritance was never truly possible with entity beans, because entity beans were not meant to be domain objects, they were meant to be components. Basic code sharing can be accomplished via inheritance between entity bean classes or remote interfaces, but the overall components themselves cannot be inherited. That is, the run-time benefits of inheritance (that is, a client cannot down- or up-cast an entity beans EJBObject stub to a parent or subclass), are not achievable.

Java data objects, being just Java objects can easily make use of complex inheritance hierarchies. Classes can simply extend each other in the same way that normal Java objects can. At run time, clients can down- or up-cast JDOs without any problems. This makes JDO more suitable for building a proper domain model than entity beans with local interfaces.

Client APIs

The entry point into entity beans is the home interface, through which you can find, create, and delete, and modify (via home methods) entity beans. Home objects are as numerous as entity beans; that is, for every entity bean, there will be a different home object to access it, which needs to be looked up separately via JNDI.

Java Data Objects define a single entry point into all the JDOs in an application: the PersistenceManager (PM). The PM exposes interfaces to find JDOs, make JDOs persistent (create), delete JDOs, as well as performs cache management, life-cycle management, and transaction management functions. The PM has a significantly larger and more complex interface than an EJBHome. JDO developers may wish to wrap the PM with their own classes, hiding methods on it that are not commonly used.

Dynamic versus Static Discovery Mechanisms

When using EJB finders for CMP beans, the actual queries executed by the finders must be defined at development or deployment time in the deployment descriptors. This restricts CMP entity beans from making use of dynamic searches of entity beans at run time.

Java data objects express queries via loosely typed strings that can be constructed and executed dynamically, similar to strings used to execute JDBC queries. Thus, with JDO it is possible to create a dynamic query engine that can query the JDO engine for Java data objects based on different criteria dynamically at run time. This can open the door to solutions to difficult design problems not possible with the static "define at development time" finder mechanisms that entity beans use.

An EJB Developer's Guide to Using JDO

JDO and EJB are complementary technologies. Where JDO fits into the EJB picture is as a replacement for entity beans as the technology used to implement the domain model in your application.

JDO can also be used to provide persistence with BMP entity beans or transparently by your application server to make your CMP entity beans persistent, but these approaches entirely defeat the point. JDO is a lightweight mechanism for making plain ordinary Java objects (POJOs) persistent—to use them as an implementation detail of entity beans does not provide any real benefit from a design and development point of view.

The following sections discusses how to use JDO behind a session façade.

Preparing Your EJB Environment

The bootstrap interface to JDO is the PersistenceManagerFactory, which is required to get instances of PersistenceManagers—the main entry point into your JDO object model. EJBs making use of JDO need a way to get access to the factory in order to begin working with JDO.

The recommended approach for enabling JDO in your application server is by placing it in the JNDI tree, thus making it accessible from any session bean in your application. A named instance of a PersistenceManagerFactory can then be looked up via JNDI, similar to the lookup of a JDBC DataSource. PersistenceManagerFactory instances represent the data store and are configured by properties, such as data store name, user name, password, and options. PersistenceManagerFactory instances are typically instantiated one per data store in the VM.

Developers can add the PMF to the JNDI tree via startup classes, or via tool-specific mechanisms if available.

Configuring Session Beans

Session beans on the session façade (see the Session Façade pattern) need to access the PersistenceManagerFactory, as mentioned above. Session bean deployment descriptors need to be configured to use this resource, similar to how they would be configured to use a JDBC DataSource. It is recommended that the name space for JDO be java:comp/env/jdo. This is not a requirement, but a recommendation. For example, this may be in the session bean's deployment descriptor:

```
<resource-ref>
<description>The JDO PersistenceManagerFactory to access the Human
Resources database</description>
<res-ref-name>jdo/HumanResourcesPMF</res-ref-name>
<res-type>javax.jdo.PersistenceManagerFactory</res-type>
<res-auth>Container</res-auth>
<res-sharing-scope>Shareable</res-sharing-scope>
</resource-ref>
```

Within the session bean itself, one member variable needs to be used with JDO: a cached reference to the PersistenceManagerFactory. After the EJB container instantiates a session bean, it will call the *setSessionContext(...)* method. Here the session bean should look up and cache a reference to the Persistence-ManageFactory just once for the lifetime of the session bean, just as it would cache references to EJBHomes if you were using entity beans:

```
...
private PersistenceManagerFactory pmFactory = null;

public void setSessionContext (SessionContext ctx)
{
    this.ctx = ctx;
    InitialContext icx = new InitialContext();
    pmFactory = (PersistenceManagerFactory)icx.lookup("aPMFactory");
}
...
```

The session bean will acquire the reference to the PersistenceManager-Factory at session context time. The actual JNDI name of the Persistence-ManagerFactory can be mapped from "aPMFactory" to the correct JNDI name using the `<ejb-ref>` tags within the session bean's ejb-jar.xml.

Executing Use Cases and Transaction Management

The methods on the session façade usually map to individual use cases in your application design. Just as with entity beans, these use cases usually need to run within a transaction. When using JDO from a layer of session beans, developers must choose between container-managed transactions and bean-managed transactions just as they would for a session bean that queried the entity bean layer. With BMT, the bean developer chooses when to begin and end transactions, and may execute methods either inside or outside of transactions. With CMT, the container demarcates the transactions via transaction settings in the session bean deployment descriptor. The semantics and syntax of using JDO change depending on the choice.

Container-Managed Transactions

The preferred transaction model, using CMT, the container automatically begins a transaction, suspends an existing transaction, or uses an existing transaction prior to dispatch of the business method, and automatically commits, resumes, or rolls back the transaction at the end of the business method.

The impact on JDO is that when using CMT, each business method must acquire a PersistenceManager from the PersistenceManagerFactory at the start of the business method, and close it at the end of the business method. When the PersistenceManagerFactory is asked for a PersistenceManager, it automatically determines the transaction context of the calling thread, and attempts to find the PersistenceManager that is already bound to that transaction context. If there is none, the PersistenceManagerFactory will choose a PersistenceManager from the pool of available PersistenceManagers and bind it to the transaction context. Subsequent requests to the PersistenceManagerFactory for a PersistenceManager with the same transaction context will return the same PersistenceManager. At the transaction's completion (commit or rollback) the association between the PersistenceManager, and the transaction is broken, and the PersistenceManager is returned to the available pool.

This automatic behavior makes it easy to combine business methods from different beans into a single container-delimited transaction. Each business method that supports transactions will execute in the proper JDO transaction without any explicit logic written by the bean developer. For example, the *createAccount* and *deposit* methods (which live on a session bean) both use container-managed transactions:

```
void createAccount (acctId)
{
    PersistenceManager pm = pmFactory .getpersistenceManager();

    // get a new account id from somewhere
    Account acct = new Account (acctId);

    pm.makePersistent (acct);
    pm.close();

}

void deposit (long acctId, BigDecimal dep)
{
    PersistenceManager pm = pmFactory .getpersistenceManager();

    Account acct = pm.getObjectById ( new AccountId(acctId) );
    acct.deposit (dep);

    pm.close();
}
```

The bean developer can choose to be notified at completion of transactions when using CMT, by declaring that it implements SessionSynchronization interface. The method beforeCompletion will be called during the transaction completion phase. Similarly, all other components that registered for synchronization will be called, but there is no guarantee by the container as to the order of calling these methods. Therefore, no JDO accesses or entity bean accesses should be done during the beforeCompletion callback.

Bean-Managed Transactions

BMT gives greater flexibility to the bean developer, at the cost of more complexity and more decisions to take during development. The developer can use the container's UserTransaction instance to begin and complete transactions. This situation is similar to CMT in that the PersistenceManager needs to be acquired in the proper transaction context. Business methods acquire the PersistenceManager at the start of the method, and close the PersistenceManager at the end of the method. This is not strictly required, but is best practice, because then the methods can be freely mixed to construct larger-scale transactions.

For example, the following method combines the method calls defined in the CMT section into one transaction:

```
void openAccount (BigDecimal initialDeposit, int acctId)
{
    UserTransaction ut=icx.lookup("java:comp/UserTransaction");
    ut.begin();
    createAccount(acctId);
```

```
    deposit (acctId, initialDeposit);
    ut.commit();
}
```

Another technique is to use the PersistenceManager and the javax.jdo.Transaction instance directly. This allows the bean developer to acquire a single PersistenceManager and use it for several transactions without returning it to the PersistenceManagerFactory pool. In this case, the business methods do not acquire and close the PersistenceManager. The PersistenceManager is acquired by the transactional business method, as in the following example:

```
void openAccount (BigDecimal initialDeposit, int acctId)
{
    persistenceManager = pmFactory .getPersistenceManager();
    Transaction tx = persistenceManager.currentTransaction()
    tx.begin();
    createAccount(acctId);
    deposit (acctId, initialDeposit);
    tx.commit();

    // other transactions may be executed here with the same
    ...

}
```

Caching/Lazy Loading and Reference Navigation

With JDO, the PersistenceManager instance associated with a transaction manages a cache containing all of the persistent objects obtained during execution of the transaction. If persistent objects contain references to other persistent objects, then they can be navigated transparently. For example, if you have an instance of Account (with a reference to an Owner), you can navigate to the Owner instance simply by referring to the owner field in Account.

```
class Account
{
    long accountId;
    BigDecimal balance;
    Owner owner;

    Owner getOwner()
    {
        return Owner;
    }

}
```

```
class Owner {
    String name;
}
```

In the session bean, you can define a method that navigates to the Owner instance and executes a method on it.

```
String getOwner (long accountId)
{
    Account acct = persistenceManager.getObjectById (new
    AccountId(id));

    return acct.getOwner().getName();
}
```

Finding Java Data Objects

Finding JDOs can be done with one of two techniques: executing a query or looking up an instance by its JDO identity. As mentioned in the *Dynamic Discovery versus Static Discovery Mechanisms* section, JDO improves upon entity bean finders by allowing JDO find code to be constructed dynamically at run time.

Lookup by Identity

To look up an instance by identity, you must construct the equivalent of a primary key class (called identity class) corresponding to the Java data object you want to find. Although it is not a requirement, identity classes usually contain a constructor that takes a single string argument. Most identity classes will also contain convenience methods that take arguments corresponding to the key fields in the class. For example, the AccountId class might be defined as:

```
class AccountId
{
    public long id;

    public AccountId (String str)
    {
        id = Long.parseLong(str);
    }

    public AccountId (long id)
    {
        this.id = id;
    }

    public toString()
```

```
        {
            return Long.toString(id);
        }
    }
```

With this key class definition, getting an instance of Account is done by constructing an AccountId instance and asking the PersistenceManager to find the instance. Like JNDI, the return type of getObjectyById is Object, and it must be cast to the proper type.

```
AccountId acctId = new AccountId (id);
Account acct = (Account) persistenceManager.getObjectById(acctId);
```

Note that the toString method returns a String that can be used as the parameter to the constructor that takes a single String argument. This is a JDO recommendation for all key classes.

Lookup by Query

Another technique for finding instances to work with is by using the JDO query facility. The PersistenceManager is a query factory, which specifies the Extent in the data store and a filter to select the instance(s) of interest. A business method that finds all Accounts having a balance larger than some parameter and an owner name specified by another parameter would have a signature:

```
Collection getAccountByBalanceAndName (BigDecimal minBal,
                                       String name);
```

The Extent is an instance that represents all of the instances in the data store of the specified JDO class, possibly including subclasses. The Persistence-Manager is also the Extent factory, where the second parameter tells whether subclasses are to be included in the Extent:

```
Extent acctExtent = persistenceManager.getExtent
                                       (Account.class, true);
```

The Extent instance is a special instance that might not actually contain a collection of persistent instances. It might simply be used to hold the class name and subclasses flag. When the query is executed, the information in the Extent is used by the JDO implementation to pass the appropriate query to the database.

The Filter specifies a Java Boolean expression to be evaluated against all of the instances in the Extent. To find all Account instances that have a balance greater than some number and an owner whose name is specified, the following code would be executed:

```
String filter = "balance > balanceParameter & owner.name ==
                                      ownerParameter";
Query query = persistenceManager.newQuery (acctExtent, filter);
```

To declare the parameter types, we follow the Java syntax for declaring formal parameters to methods:

```
query.declareParameters ("BigDecimal balanceParameter, String
                    ownerParameter");
```

Finally, to actually find the accounts we are looking for, we execute the query to get a Collection of instances that satisfy the filter constraints:

```
Collection queryResult = query.execute (minBal, name);
```

The query result can be iterated; the iterator.next() values are persistent instances of type Account. Note that the queries filter and parameters are defined with strings. These strings can be dynamically created at run time, an improvement over the static entity bean finder mechanism.

Inter-Tier Data Transfer

The Data Transfer Object pattern applies equally well to a system that uses entity beans as well as Java data objects. With this pattern, DTOs are created to copy data from JDOs and send it to the client tier. On the client tier, updates can occur and DTOs can be sent back to the server, where the contents of the DTOs will be used to update JDOs.

JDO provides a unique value in that the JDO instances can themselves be used as DTOs, as long as they follow the rules for serializable objects. In fact, an object graph of JDO instances may be returned, allowing a complex collection of instances to be transferred to the client.

If you choose to use JDO persistent instances directly as value instances, then the process is slightly more complex, because persistent instances are bound to the PersistenceManager. In order to detach them from their PersistenceManager, the *makeTransient* method is used. The effect of this is method is to remove the persistent instance from the association with the PersistenceManager. Subsequent to the makeTransient call, the instance can no longer be used to refer to persistent data, so any association with persistent instances must be retrieved before the call.

For example, to return an Account directly to the user, with an associated Owner, define Account as a return value and make the Account and Owner classes available to the client of the application. The Owner will be serialized along with the Account when it is returned to the client.

```
Account getAccount (long id)
{
    Account acct = persistenceManager.getObjectById (new
                                      AccountId(id));
    Owner owner = acct.getOwner();
    Object [] objs = new Object[] {acct, owner};
    persistenceManager.retrieveAll(objs);
    persistenceManager.makeTransientAll (objs);

    return acct;

}
```

Summary

Entity beans have received a lot of mixed press since their inception, but with the maturity of the EJB tools market and the massive improvements brought on since EJB 2.0, entity beans have become a viable platform. Still, many prefer not to use entity beans, as they are still relatively heavyweight components, instead of lightweight domain objects. Instead, many have elected to make use of other technologies that allow you to create plain Java object models, including custom-built persistence frameworks, O/R mappers, and, most notably, Java Data Objects (JDO).

CHAPTER 9

EJB Design Strategies, Idioms, and Tips

This chapter contains a set of fine-grained strategies, idioms, and tips for effective EJB application design and implementation. While they may have been too simple or fine-grained to warrant being written as a full pattern, they are still important enough to include in the book.

Don't Use the Composite Entity Bean Pattern

The Composite Entity Bean pattern (also known as the Aggregate entity bean or Coarse-Grained entity bean pattern) was a common pattern for EJB applications built to the 1.x specification. The pattern arose in order to combat the performance problems associated with communicating with entity beans via the remote interface. To combat these problems, the pattern suggests creating a new entity type called a *dependent object*, a plain Java class whose life cycle is managed by the entity bean. The problem with dependent objects is that they are impossible to create using your application server's CMP engine, and are extremely difficult to implement using BMP. Managing the life cycle of a set of dependent objects in BMP is equivalent to writing your own persistence engine.

Entity beans were meant to model the "entities" or domain objects in an application. With the coming of EJB 2.0 CMP enhancements, including *local interfaces*, entity beans can now be used to model the domain objects in your designs as finely grained as you like. Thus, EJB 2.0 deprecates the notion of dependent objects, as well as the Composite Entity bean pattern. If you are concerned about the overhead of transaction and security checks that may take place when calling an entity bean—don't. Entity beans fronted with a session façade need only use tx_supports and do not need to use security at all, since security and transactions are declared and checked in the session façade. After speaking to numerous J2EE server vendors, it seems clear that it is common for an application server to not perform transaction and security checks if none were declared in the deployment descriptor.

Perhaps the only case in which the Composite Entity Bean Pattern should be used is for the 5 percent of the time when the data in the underlying database cannot map to a graph of entity beans. This can occur when building a new system on top of a legacy system that simply cannot be mapped to the new system's object model.

Use a Field-Naming Convention to Allow for Validation in EJB 2.0 CMP Entity Beans

As of EJB 2.0 CMP, entity beans must be written as abstract classes, since the CMP engine will implement all the persistence logic on behalf of the developer. One side effect this has had is that developers no longer have access to the implementation of *getXXX/setXXX* methods, since these must be declared abstract and implemented by the container. Since local interfaces make it acceptable to allow other EJBs to perform fine-grained *get/sets* on an entity bean, a developer will want to expose these *get/sets* on the local interface. The problem then becomes: how can a developer perform syntactic or business validation on data that is set, if they don't have access to the implementation of a set method?

The solution is to use a simple naming convention and delegation scheme for *set* methods. Instead of exposing a CMP-generated *setXXX* method (for an attribute called XXX) on the local interface, expose a method called *setXXXField* on the local interface. Inside the *setXXXField* method, a developer can implement proper validation checks and then delegate the call to the container-generated *setXXX* method.

Don't Get and Set Value/Data Transfer Objects on Entity Beans

Another deprecated pattern from the EJB 1.X days is the use of value objects (more properly known as data transfer objects) to get and set bulk sets of data from an entity bean. This pattern originally helped performance by limiting the number of *get/set* remote calls from clients to entity beans by instead getting and setting DTOs that contained bulk sets of entity bean attributes. This pattern resulted in some pretty serious maintenance problems for entity beans. For an in-depth discussion of the problems with using DTOs as an interface to entity beans, see the *Data Transfer Object Pattern* section (Chapter 2).

Luckily, local interfaces make it acceptable to perform fine-grained *get/set* calls on entity beans. Thus using DTOs to transfer data in and out of entity beans is a deprecated pattern. Developers should think of data transfer objects as envelopes of data, used to communicate between tiers (the client and the session façade).

Using Java Singletons Is OK If They're Used Correctly

There is a lot of fear, uncertainty, and doubt (FUD) about the role of singletons in EJB. The original Singleton pattern (Gamma, et al., 1995), suggests creating a Java class that contains a static instance of itself, so that only one instance of the class will run in an application. The EJB spec states that EJBs should not use static fields, nor should they use synchronization primitives (such as the `synchronized` keyword). Many developers have incorrectly assumed that this means that an EJB cannot call out to a singleton, since the singleton itself makes use of a static field and the `synchronized` keyword.

This assumption is false. There is nothing wrong with using a Singleton class, as long as developers DO NOT use it in read-write fashion, in which case EJB threads calling in may need to be blocked. It is this type of behavior that the spec is trying to protect against. Using a singleton for read-only behavior, or any type of service that can allow EJBs to access it independently of one another is fine.

One caveat with using Java singletons is that it is impossible to create a singleton in the classic sense—one instance of an object per application. At the very least, any singletons used will have one copy per server JVM, and usually will have one instance per class loader (each deployed ejb-jar will have its own separate class loader and its own Singleton if it uses one).

Use a Java Singleton class when you would like to create a nonblocking service in which you do not mind having a few copies of the singleton in-memory in the same VM, but do not want the pooling and memory overhead of implementing the service as a stateless session bean. For example, a primary key generator (such as the UUID for EJB or Sequence Block patterns) would provide a lighter-weight and more efficient implementation choice than a stateless session bean.

Prefer Scheduled Updates to Real-Time Computation

When building Web-based applications, it can often be extremely expensive to go through the EJB layer upon every single request to compute a value that needs to be displayed on the user interface (UI), if the computation is a time-consuming and resource-intensive process.

For example, on TheServerSide.com, the *membership count* number on the top right of the home page would require a delegation to the database to execute a `select count(*) from users` query, upon every single Web request. With over 140,000 users, and multiple page views per minute, executing this query in real time is significant performance bottleneck.

Instead, a sprinkling of realism can help. Instead of executing a computation in real time, use a scheduling tool such as Unix Cron or the J2EE Scheduler Flux to perform computations at regular intervals and cache output to disk. In the JSPs, simply do a jsp:include on this cached file, instead of delegating the query to the server. Significant performance boosts can be realized by taking this approach.

In general, ask yourself if the part of the UI being displayed really needs to be done in real time. For mostly read-only browsing types of UIs, it may not make sense to go through the EJB layer for every Web request. Therefore, you should prefer scheduled updates to real-time computation.

Use a Serialized Java Class to Add Compiler Type Checking to Message-Driven Bean Interactions

Message-driven beans consume JMS messages, all of which appear identical at compile time. This is in contrast to session/entity beans, which leverage Java's built-in strong typing of the methods and parameters of the remote and local interfaces to catch common errors at compile time.

One solution is to define JMS messages as serialized Java objects, mitigating this drawback. Establish the contract between the application layer and the business layer as a set of java objects simply containing the required member variables, getters and setters. Then use these objects in the JMS messages instead of free-form sets of fields. Doing so reenables compiler type checking. The overhead of serializing object does not impede performance, besides, it's all asynchronous anyway. A best practice when using this approach would be to give the classes *verbs* as names. For example, when creating a class to marshal data to a message-driven beans that *places an order*, the class would be called PlaceOrderAction, or something along those lines.

Always Call *setRollbackOnly* when Application Exceptions Occur

An important but unemphasized fact is that application exceptions (developer written exceptions) thrown from an EJB to the client don't trigger automatic rollbacks of the running transaction, in contrast to EJBExceptions, which automatically trigger the current transaction to roll back. Serious data consistency problems can arise if a use case fails without the transaction rolling back.

Therefore, always remember to first catch application exceptions and call `ctx.setRollbackOnly()` (where ctx is of type `javax.ejb.SessionContext` for session beans) before rethrowing or wrapping application exceptions to the client.

Limit Parameters to ejbCreate

When building entity beans, developers often incorrectly assume that they should add all the attributes of an entity bean to the *ejbCreate* method. While this method gets the job done, it often turns out that doing so makes it more difficult to make changes to an entity bean such as adding or removing an attribute. If an attribute is removed, then the entity beans ejbCreate, ejbPostCreate, and Home Interface need to be changed, and all the method signatures of those three definitions must be kept in synch. When adding an attribute, if all the other attributes are passed into ejbCreate, then out of consistency the new attribute should also be added, requiring changing all the other related method signatures as well.

One convention that can be adopted to reduce the amount of overhead required to change an entity bean's attributes is to limit the number of parameters for ejbCreate to just those that are mandatory or essential to its creation (with the assumption that mandatory attributes don't change that often). Thus, in the session bean that creates the entity bean, instead of passing in all the attributes to the *home.create* method, it would only pass in a subset, and then call *setters* on the entity bean to populate it with any other attributes that are required.

Don't Use Data Transfer Objects in ejbCreate

Another mistake that developers tend to make when programming an entity bean's *ejbCreate* method is passing in an entity bean's corresponding domain DTO as a constructor argument [Brown, 2000]. If you considered the five-layer J2EE architecture described in Chapter 6, data transfer objects live in between the application and services layers. Thus, passing in a DTO into an entity bean's ejbCreate method creates a dependency between the domain layer and the upper layers.

This can create a variety of problems. For example, often a domain DTO contains more attributes than are available to initially create an entity bean with, or even attributes that are not in the entity bean (such as computed values). Passing in a DTO that contains null values into an ejbCreate is using the wrong class for the wrong job.

Instead, only pass in primitives to an entity beans ejbCreate method, keeping in mind the *Limit Parameters to EJB Create* tip described above.

Don't Use XML to Communicate as a DTO Mechanism Unless You Really, Really Have To

XML is a very important technology for integration. The keyword here is integration, meaning integration between Java and non-Java systems. When communicating between two Java systems, XML doesn't really make sense; in fact it can result in unnecessary performance overhead and bloated code. In particular, using XML as a mechanism for transferring data between a client and server should only be done if you really, really have to. That is, unless you are actually persisting XML data in your database, generating XML in the EJB layer and passing it to the client layer is a poor substitute for simple and fast serialization of data transfer objects.

If your presentation layer uses XML to generate dynamic UIs, then consider transferring DTOs from the server to the client and performing your conversions to XML at this layer, where client-specific XML documents can be generated. Also, consider using the JAXB APIs, which can provide a standard way to achieve automatic DTO to XML conversions.

Pattern Code Listing

The purpose of the appendix is to provide complete sample code for patterns in the book that require the use of code for more explanation. Code is placed at the back of the book, in order to keep the pattern text itself clear and uncluttered.

Patterns that have sample code are included here. Refer to the table of contents for page numbers of all included code samples.

The book's Web site www.theserverside.com/patterns/ejbpatterns contains the running/compiling versions of all source code examples listed here, as well as a discussion forum for readers of the book.

EJB Command Pattern

Included here is a very simple implementation of the command pattern, including routing logic components (CommandExecutor and EJBCommand-Target) and a command server (CommandServerBean), including a bank account transfer command.

This source is a super simplified version inspired by IBM's Command framework, and is provided to illustrate the concepts of the command pattern only. Use it at your own risk.

Transfer Funds Command

```
package examples.command;

import examples.account.AccountHome;
import examples.account.Account;
import examples.account.ProcessingErrorException;

import javax.naming.InitialContext;
import javax.naming.NamingException;
import javax.rmi.PortableRemoteObject;
import javax.ejb.FinderException;
import java.rmi.RemoteException;

public class TransferFundsCommand extends Command implements
Serializable
{

    String withdrawAccountID;
    String depositAccountID;
    double transferAmount;

    double withdrawAccountBalance;
    double depositAccountBalance;

    public void execute() throws CommandException
    {
        //at this point we are inside the EJB Server
        try {

            InitialContext ctx = new InitialContext();
            AccountHome home = (AccountHome) PortableRemoteObject.narrow
                (ctx.lookup("Account"), AccountHome.class);

            //locate accounts and perform transfer
            Account account1 = home.findByPrimaryKey(withdrawAccountID);
            Account account2 = home.findByPrimaryKey(depositAccountID);

            account1.withdraw(this.transferAmount);
            account2.deposit(this.transferAmount);

            //populate command with final balances
            this.depositAccountBalance = account2.balance();
            this.withdrawAccountBalance = account1.balance();
        }
        catch (Exception e)
        {
            //wrap the exception as a command exception and throw
            //to client for interception
            throw new CommandException(e);
        }
```

```
        }

        public void setWithdrawAccountID(String withdrawAccountID) {
            this.withdrawAccountID = withdrawAccountID;
        }

        public void setDepositAccountID(String depositAccountID) {
            this.depositAccountID = depositAccountID;
        }

        public void setTransferAmount(double transferAmount) {
            this.transferAmount = transferAmount;
        }

        public double getDepositAccountBalance() {
            return depositAccountBalance;
        }

        public double getWithdrawAccountBalance() {
            return withdrawAccountBalance;
        }

        public TransferFundsCommand()
        {}
}
```

Command Superclass

```
package examples.command;

import java.io.Serializable;

public abstract class Command implements Serializable {

    public abstract void execute() throws CommandException;

}
```

CommandServer Session Bean

```
package examples.command;

import javax.ejb.*;
import java.rmi.RemoteException;
import javax.naming.*;


public class CommandServerBean implements SessionBean {

    SessionContext ctx;
```

```
    public void CommandServer() {}
                                       .
  public Command executeCommand(Command aCommand) throws
CommandException
    {
        try
        {
            aCommand.execute();
        }
        catch (CommandException e)
        {
            ctx.setRollbackOnly();
            throw e;
        }

        return aCommand;
    }

    public void ejbActivate() throws EJBException,
      java.rmi.RemoteException {}
    public void ejbCreate() throws CreateException {}
    public void ejbPassivate() throws EJBException,
      java.rmi.RemoteException {}
    public void ejbRemove() throws EJBException,
      java.rmi.RemoteException {}

    public void setSessionContext(final SessionContext p1)
      throws EJBException, java.rmi.RemoteException
    {
        this.ctx = p1;
    }

}
```

CommandException

```
package examples.command;

public class CommandException extends Exception  {

    Exception wrappedException;

    public CommandException(){}

    public CommandException(Exception e)
    {
        this.wrappedException = e;
    }
```

```
      Exception getWrappedException()
      {
          return wrappedException;
      }

      public CommandException(String s) {
          super(s);
      }
}
```

CommandTarget Interface

```
package examples.command;

interface CommandTarget {
        Command executeCommand(Command aCommand) throws
CommandException;
}
```

EJBCommandTarget

```
package examples.command;

import javax.rmi.PortableRemoteObject;
import javax.ejb.CreateException;
import javax.naming.Context;
import javax.naming.InitialContext;
import javax.naming.NamingException;
import java.rmi.RemoteException;

public class EJBCommandTarget implements CommandTarget {

    private CommandServerHome serverHome;

    public EJBCommandTarget()
    {
      try
      {
          Context ctx = new InitialContext(System.getProperties());
          Object obj = ctx.lookup("CommandServer");
          System.out.println(obj);
          this.serverHome = (CommandServerHome)
          PortableRemoteObject.narrow(obj, CommandServerHome.class );
      }
      catch (NamingException e)
      {
          e.printStackTrace();
      }
```

```
            catch (ClassCastException e)
            {
                e.printStackTrace();
            }
        }

    public Command executeCommand(Command aCommand)
    throws CommandException
    {

        try
        {
            CommandServer aCommandServer = serverHome.create();
            aCommand = aCommandServer.executeCommand(aCommand);
            return aCommand;

        }
        catch (Exception e)
        {
            throw new CommandException(e);
        }
    }
}
```

CommandExecutor

```
package examples.command;

public class CommandExecutor
{
    private static EJBCommandTarget ejbTarget = new EJBCommandTarget();

    //execute command, overwriting memory reference of the passed
    //in command to that of the new one
    public static Command execute(Command aCommand)
    throws CommandException
    {
        //at this point, a real implementation would use a properties
file
        //to determine which command target (EJB, Local, Corba, etc) to
        //use for this particular command, as well as which deployed
        //CommandServer to use (in order to run commands
        //under different transaction configurations)

        return ejbTarget.executeCommand(aCommand);

    }

}
```

Data Access Command Bean

The implementations of the abstract super classes BaseReadCommand and BaseUpdateCommand, as well as the InsertEmployeeCommand and QueryEmployeeByNameCommand classes are provided. Note that the BaseReadCommand uses a RowSet to simplify its implementation. RowSets are part of the JDBC 2.0 optional package, and joined core JDBC as of JDBC 3.0. The example here uses Sun's free CachedRowSet implementation of the RowSet interface.

BaseReadCommand.java

```java
package examples.datacommands;

import javax.sql.*;
import javax.naming.InitialContext;
import javax.naming.NamingException;
import java.sql.*;
import sun.jdbc.rowset.CachedRowSet;

/**
 * The Super class for any data command beans Read from the
 * database.
 */
abstract class BaseReadCommand {

    protected PreparedStatement pstmt;
    protected CachedRowSet rowSet = null;
    private Connection con;

    protected BaseReadCommand ( String jndiName, String statement )
    throws DataCommandException
    {
        InitialContext ctx = null;
        try
        {
            ctx = new InitialContext();
            DataSource ds = (javax.sql.DataSource) ctx.lookup(jndiName);
            con = ds.getConnection();
            pstmt = con.prepareStatement(statement);
        }
        catch (NamingException e)
        {
            throw new DataCommandException(e.getMessage());
        }
        catch (SQLException e)
        {
            throw new DataCommandException(e.getMessage());
```

```
            }
        }

    public void execute() throws DataCommandException
        {
            try
            {
                rowSet = new CachedRowSet();
                rowSet.populate(pstmt.executeQuery());
                rowSet.beforeFirst();
                this.release();
            } catch (SQLException e)
            {
                throw new DataCommandException(e.getMessage());
            }
        }
     public boolean next() throws DataCommandException
        {
            try
            {
                return rowSet.next();
            } catch (SQLException e)
            {
                throw new DataCommandException(e.getMessage());
            }
        }
        private void release() throws SQLException
        {
            if (pstmt != null) pstmt.close();
            if (con != null) con.close();
         }
}
```

BaseUpdateCommand.java

```
package examples.datacommands;

import javax.sql.*;
import javax.naming.InitialContext;
import javax.naming.NamingException;
import javax.ejb.EJBException;
import java.sql.*;

/**
 * The Super class for any data command beans that Create, Update or
 * Delete. This class is reusable across projects, all proj. specific
data
 * (Datasource JDNI and SQl String) are left to the subclasses
 */
abstract class BaseUpdateCommand {
```

```
    protected PreparedStatement pstmt;
    private Connection con;

    protected BaseUpdateCommand ( String jndiName, String statement )
throws DataCommandException
    {
        InitialContext ctx = null;
        try
        {
            ctx = new InitialContext();
            DataSource ds = (javax.sql.DataSource) ctx.lookup(jndiName);
            con = ds.getConnection();
            pstmt = con.prepareStatement(statement);
        }
        catch (NamingException e)
        {
            throw new DataCommandException(e.getMessage());
        }
        catch (SQLException e)
        {
            throw new DataCommandException(e.getMessage());
        }
    }
    public int execute() throws DataCommandException
    {
        try
        {
            //execute update, return the rowcount
            int updateCount = pstmt.executeUpdate();
            this.release();
            return updateCount;
        } catch (SQLException e)
        {
            throw new DataCommandException(e.getMessage());
        }
    }
    private void release() throws SQLException
    {
        if (pstmt != null) pstmt.close();
        if (con != null) con.close();
    }
}
```

InsertEmployeeCommand.java

```
package examples.datacommands;

import java.sql.*;
import javax.sql.*;

/**
 * InsertEmployeeCommand, this class
```

```java
 * is the usecase specific Command bean that
 * an application developer would write.
 */
public class InsertEmployeeCommand extends BaseUpdateCommand
{

    static String statement = "insert into Employees (EMPLOYEEID, NAME,
                                EMAIL) values (?,?,?)";
    static final String dataSourceJNDI = "bookPool";
    /**
     * Passes parent class the usecase specific sql statement to use
     */
    protected InsertEmployeeCommand() throws DataCommandException
    {

        super(dataSourceJNDI, statement);
    }

    public void setEmail(String anEmail) throws DataCommandException
    {
        try
        {
            pstmt.setString(3, anEmail);
        } catch (SQLException e)
        {
            throw new DataCommandException(e.getMessage());
        }
    }

    public void setId(int id) throws DataCommandException
    {
        try
        {
            pstmt.setInt(1, id);
        } catch (SQLException e)
        {
            throw new DataCommandException(e.getMessage());
        }
    }

    public void setName(String aName) throws DataCommandException
    {
        try
        {
            pstmt.setString(2, aName);
        } catch (SQLException e)
        {
            throw new DataCommandException(e.getMessage());
        }

    }
}
```

QueryEmployeeByName.java

```java
package examples.datacommands;

import java.sql.*;
import javax.sql.*;

/**
 * A usecase specific querying object
 **/
public class QueryEmployeeByNameCommand extends BaseReadCommand
{

    static final String statement =
    "select EMPLOYEEID, NAME, EMAIL from Employees where NAME = ?";
    static final String dataSourceJNDI = "bookPool";

    protected QueryEmployeeByNameCommand() throws DataCommandException
    {
        super(dataSourceJNDI, statement);
    }

    public String getEmail() throws DataCommandException
    {
        try
        {
            return rowSet.getString(3);
        } catch (SQLException e)
        {
            throw new DataCommandException(e.getMessage());
        }
    }

    public int getId() throws DataCommandException
    {
        try
        {
            return rowSet.getInt(1);
        } catch (SQLException e)
        {
            throw new DataCommandException(e.getMessage());
        }
    }

    public String getName() throws DataCommandException
    {
        try
        {
            return rowSet.getString(2);
        } catch (SQLException e)
        {
```

```
            throw new DataCommandException(e.getMessage());
        }
    }

    public void setName(String aName) throws DataCommandException
    {
        try
        {
            pstmt.setString(1, aName);
        } catch (SQLException e)
        {
            throw new DataCommandException(e.getMessage());
        }
    }
}
```

Dual Persistent Entity Bean

Included is the code example of the bank account entity bean inheritance relationship and deployment descriptors. These classes can be compiled and then deployed in CMP or BMP by swapping the provided deployment descriptors.

Account Deployment Descriptor for CMP

```
<ejb-jar>
    <enterprise-beans>
     <entity>
    <ejb-name>dualPersistent</ejb-name>
    <home>examples.dualpersistent.AccountHome</home>
    <remote>examples.dualpersistent.Account</remote>
    <ejb-class>examples.dualpersistent.AccountCMPBean</ejb-class>
    <persistence-type>Container</persistence-type>
    <prim-key-class>java.lang.String</prim-key-class>
    <reentrant>False</reentrant>


        <cmp-version>2.x</cmp-version>
    <abstract-schema-name>AccountBean</abstract-schema-name>
    <cmp-field>
        <field-name>accountId</field-name>
    </cmp-field>
    <cmp-field>
        <field-name>balance</field-name>
    </cmp-field>

       <primkey-field>accountId</primkey-field>
         <query>
```

```
                    <query-method>
                      <method-name>findBigAccounts</method-name>
                      <method-params>
                        <method-param>double</method-param>
                      </method-params>
                    </query-method>
                    <ejb-ql>
                      <![CDATA[FROM AccountBean AS a WHERE a.balance > ?1]]>
                    </ejb-ql>
                  </query>

            </entity>
        </enterprise-beans>

      <assembly-descriptor>
        <container-transaction>
        <method>
          <ejb-name>dualPersistent</ejb-name>
          <method-intf>Remote</method-intf>
          <method-name>*</method-name>
        </method>
        <trans-attribute>Required</trans-attribute>
        </container-transaction>
      </assembly-descriptor>
    </ejb-jar>
```

Account Deployment Descriptor for BMP

```
<ejb-jar>
    <enterprise-beans>
      <entity>
      <ejb-name>dualPersistent</ejb-name>
      <home>examples.dualpersistent.AccountHome</home>
      <remote>examples.dualpersistent.Account</remote>
      <ejb-class>examples.dualpersistent.AccountBMPBean</ejb-class>
      <persistence-type>Bean</persistence-type>
      <prim-key-class>java.lang.String</prim-key-class>
      <reentrant>False</reentrant>

        <resource-ref>
         <res-ref-name>jdbc/ejbPool</res-ref-name>
         <res-type>javax.sql.DataSource</res-type>
         <res-auth>Container</res-auth>
        </resource-ref>

      </entity>
    </enterprise-beans>
    <assembly-descriptor>
      <container-transaction>
```

```
      <method>
        <ejb-name>dualPersistent</ejb-name>
        <method-intf>Remote</method-intf>
        <method-name>*</method-name>
      </method>
      <trans-attribute>Required</trans-attribute>
       </container-transaction>
     </assembly-descriptor>
   </ejb-jar>
```

Account Remote Interface

```
package examples.dualpersistent;

import java.rmi.RemoteException;
import javax.ejb.EJBObject;

public interface Account extends EJBObject {

    public double balance() throws RemoteException;
    public double deposit(double amount) throws RemoteException;
    public double withdraw(double amount) throws
ProcessingErrorException, RemoteException;

}
```

Account Home Interface

```
package examples.dualpersistent;

import javax.ejb.*;
import java.rmi.RemoteException;
import java.util.Collection;


public interface AccountHome extends EJBHome {

  public Account create(String accountId, double initialBalance)
    throws CreateException, RemoteException;

    public Account findByPrimaryKey(String primaryKey)
          throws FinderException, RemoteException;

    public Collection findBigAccounts(double balanceGreaterThan)
          throws FinderException, RemoteException;

}
```

Account CMP Bean Superclass

```
package examples.dualpersistent;

import java.io.Serializable;
import java.util.Enumeration;
import java.util.Vector;
import javax.ejb.*;
import javax.naming.*;
import javax.sql.DataSource;

abstract public class AccountCMPBean implements EntityBean {

  protected EntityContext ctx;

    /**
     * container managed fields
     */
    abstract public String getAccountId();
    abstract public double getBalance();
    abstract public void setAccountId(String val);
    abstract public void setBalance(double val);

    /**
     * Developer implemented Business Methods
     */
    public double balance()
    {
        return getBalance();
    }

    public double deposit(double amount)
    {
        setBalance(getBalance() + amount);
        return getBalance();
    }

    public double withdraw(double amount)
    throws ProcessingErrorException
    {

        if (amount > getBalance())
        {
            throw new ProcessingErrorException("Attempt to withdraw too
                                               much");
        }

        setBalance(getBalance() - amount);
        return getBalance();

    }
```

```java
    public String ejbCreate(String accountId, double initialBalance)
     throws CreateException
    {
        setAccountId(accountId);
        setBalance(initialBalance);

        return null;
    }


    /**
     * Container required methods - implemented by the CMP engine
     */
    public AccountCMPBean() {}
    public void ejbActivate() {}
    public void ejbLoad() {}
    public void ejbPassivate() {}
    public void ejbPostCreate(String accountId,double initialBalance){}
    public void ejbRemove() throws RemoveException {}
    public void ejbStore() {}


    /**
     * The usual Plumbing
     */
    public void setEntityContext(EntityContext ctx)
    {
        this.ctx = ctx;
    }

  public void unsetEntityContext()
  {
        this.ctx = null;
  }


}
```

Account BMP Bean Subclass

```java
package examples.dualpersistent;

import java.io.Serializable;
import java.util.*;
import javax.ejb.*;
import javax.naming.*;
import java.sql.*;
import javax.sql.*;

public class AccountBMPBean extends AccountCMPBean implements EntityBean
{
```

```java
    private String accountId;
    private double balance;

    public String getAccountId()
    {
        return accountId;
    }

    public double getBalance()
    {
        return balance;
    }

    public void setAccountId(String val)
    {
        this.accountId = val;
    }

    public void setBalance(double val)
    {
        this.balance = val;
    }

    public String ejbCreate(String accountId, double initialBalance)
    throws CreateException
    {
        //delegate to super class for validation checks, etc.
        super.ejbCreate(accountId, initialBalance);

        Connection con = null;
        PreparedStatement ps = null;

        try
        {
            con = getConnection();
            ps = con.prepareStatement("insert into Accounts (id,
balance)
                values (?, ?)");
            ps.setString(1, accountId);
            ps.setDouble(2, balance);
            if (ps.executeUpdate() != 1)
            {
                throw new CreateException();
            }

            return accountId;
        } catch (SQLException sqe)
        {
            throw new CreateException();
        } finally
        {
```

```
                    try
                    {
                        if (ps != null) ps.close();
                        if (con != null) con.close();
                    } catch (Exception e)
                    {
                        throw new EJBException(e);
                    }
                }
            }


public Collection ejbFindBigAccounts(double balanceGreaterThan)
{
    Connection con = null;
    PreparedStatement ps = null;

    try
    {
        con = getConnection();
        ps = con.prepareStatement("select id from Accounts where
                                    balance > ?");
        ps.setDouble(1, balanceGreaterThan);
        ps.executeQuery();
        ResultSet rs = ps.getResultSet();
        Vector v = new Vector();
        String pk;
        while (rs.next())
        {
            pk = rs.getString(1);
            v.addElement(pk);
        }
        return v;
    } catch (SQLException e)
    {
        throw new EJBException(e);
    } finally
    {
        try
        {
            if (ps != null) ps.close();
            if (con != null) con.close();
        } catch (Exception e)
        {
            throw new EJBException(e);
        }
    }
}


public String ejbFindByPrimaryKey(String pk)
```

```
        throws ObjectNotFoundException
        {
            Connection con = null;
            PreparedStatement ps = null;

            try
            {
                con = getConnection();
                ps = con.prepareStatement("select balance from Accounts
where
                                                id = ?");
                ps.setString(1, pk);
                ps.executeQuery();
                ResultSet rs = ps.getResultSet();
                if (rs.next())
                    balance = rs.getDouble(1);
                else
                    throw new ObjectNotFoundException();
            } catch (SQLException sqe)
            {
                throw new EJBException(sqe);
            } finally
            {
                try
                {
                    if (ps != null) ps.close();
                    if (con != null) con.close();
                } catch (Exception e)
                {
                    System.out.println("Error closing JDBC resourcest: " +
e);
                    throw new EJBException(e);
                }
            }


            return pk;
        }


        public void ejbLoad()
        {
            Connection con = null;
            PreparedStatement ps = null;
            accountId = (String) ctx.getPrimaryKey();

            try
            {
                con = getConnection();
                ps = con.prepareStatement("select balance from Accounts
where
```

```
                                               id = ?");
            ps.setString(1, accountId);
            ps.executeQuery();
            ResultSet rs = ps.getResultSet();

            if (rs.next())
                balance = rs.getDouble(1);
            else
                throw new NoSuchEntityException();

        } catch (SQLException sqe)
        {

            throw new EJBException(sqe);
        } finally
        {
            try
            {
                if (ps != null) ps.close();
                if (con != null) con.close();
            } catch (Exception e)
            {
                System.out.println("Error closing JDBC resourcest: " +
e);
                throw new EJBException(e);
            }
        }
    }


    public void ejbPostCreate(String accountId, double initialBalance)
    {
    }


    public void ejbRemove()
    {

        Connection con = null;
        PreparedStatement ps = null;

        try
        {
            con = getConnection();
            accountId = (String) ctx.getPrimaryKey();

            ps = con.prepareStatement("delete from Accounts where id =
                                ?");
            ps.setString(1, accountId);

            if (!(ps.executeUpdate() > 0))
```

```
                {
                    throw new NoSuchEntityException();
                }
            } catch (SQLException e)
            {
                throw new EJBException(e);
            }


        }


    public void ejbStore()
    {
        Connection con = null;
        PreparedStatement ps = null;

        try
        {
            con = getConnection();
            ps = con.prepareStatement("update Accounts set balance = ?
                                    where id = ?");
            ps.setDouble(1, balance);
            ps.setString(2, accountId);
            if (!(ps.executeUpdate() > 0))
                throw new NoSuchEntityException();
        } catch (SQLException sqe)
        {
            throw new EJBException(sqe);
        } finally
        {
            try
            {
                if (ps != null) ps.close();
                if (con != null) con.close();
            } catch (Exception e)
            {
                System.out.println("Error closing JDBC resourcest: " +
e);

                throw new EJBException(e);
            }
        }
    }


    private Connection getConnection() throws SQLException
    {
        InitialContext ctx = null;
        try
        {
            ctx = new InitialContext();
            DataSource ds = (javax.sql.DataSource)
```

```
                        ctx.lookup("ejbPool");
                    return ds.getConnection();
                } catch (NamingException e)
                {
                    throw new EJBException(e);
                }
            }


        }
```

Processing Error Exception

```
package examples.dualpersistent;

public class ProcessingErrorException extends Exception {

  public ProcessingErrorException() {}
  public ProcessingErrorException(String message) {super(message);
}
```

EJB Home Factory

Here we present an example of an EJB Home Factory.

Simple EJB Home Factory

```
package com.portal.util;

import javax.ejb.*;
import java.rmi.*;
import javax.rmi.*;
import java.util.*;
import javax.naming.*;

/**
 * EJB Home Factory, maintains a simple hashmap cache of EJBHomes
 * For a production implementations, exceptions such as NamingException
 * can be wrapped with a factory exception to futher simplify
 * the client.
 */
public class EJBHomeFactory
{

    private Map ejbHomes;
    private static EJBHomeFactory aFactorySingleton;

    Context ctx;
```

```
    /**
     * EJBHomeFactory private constructor.
     */
    private EJBHomeFactory() throws NamingException
    {
        ctx = new InitialContext();
        this.ejbHomes = Collections.synchronizedMap(new HashMap());
    }


    /*
     * Returns the singleton instance of the EJBHomeFactory
     * The sychronized keyword is intentionally left out the
     * as I don't think the potential to intialize the singleton
     * twice at startup time (which is not a destructive event)
     * is worth creating a sychronization bottleneck on this
     * VERY frequently used class, for the lifetime of the
     * client application.
     *
     * Alternatively, you can sychronize this method, OR you can
     * simply Intialize the hashMap and factory using static
Intializers.
     */
    public static EJBHomeFactory getFactory() throws
HomeFactoryException
    {

        try
        {
            if ( EJBHomeFactory.aFactorySingleton == null )
            {
                EJBHomeFactory.aFactorySingleton = new EJBHomeFactory();
            }

        } catch (NamingException e)
        {
            throw new HomeFactoryException(e);
        }

        return EJBHomeFactory.aFactorySingleton;
    }


    /**
     * Lookup and cache an EJBHome object using a home class.
     * Assumes that the JNDI name of the EJB Home being looked for
     * is the same as the fully qualified class name of the
     * same EJB Home.
     * If EJB-REF tags are being used externally, then the classname
     * of the EJB Home can be mapped to the actual JNDI name of the
     * deployed bean transaprently at deployment time.
     * If EJB-REF tags are not used, then the EJB's must be deployed
     * with JNDI names equal to their fully qualified home interfaces.
```

```
                */
               public EJBHome lookUpHome(Class homeClass)
               throws HomeFactoryException
               {

                    EJBHome anEJBHome;
                    anEJBHome = (EJBHome) this.ejbHomes.get(homeClass);

                  try
                  {
                     if(anEJBHome == null)
                     {
                         anEJBHome = (EJBHome) PortableRemoteObject.narrow
                                      (ctx.lookup (homeClass.getName()),
homeClass);
                         this.ejbHomes.put(homeClass, anEJBHome);
                     }
                  }
                  catch (ClassCastException e)
                  {
                      throw new HomeFactoryException(e);
                  }
                  catch (NamingException e)
                  {
                      throw new HomeFactoryException(e);
                  }

                  return anEJBHome;

               }


               /**
                 * Lookup and cache an EJBHome object.
                 * This 'alternate' implementation delegates JNDI name knowledge
                 * to the client. It is included here for example only.
                 */
               public EJBHome lookUpHome(Class homeClass, String jndiName)
               throws HomeFactoryException
               {

                    EJBHome anEJBHome;

                    anEJBHome = (EJBHome) this.ejbHomes.get(homeClass);

                  try
                  {
                     if(anEJBHome == null)
                     {
                         System.out.println("finding HOME for first time");
                         anEJBHome = (EJBHome) PortableRemoteObject.narrow
                                      ( ctx.lookup (jndiName), homeClass);
```

```
                        this.ejbHomes.put(homeClass, anEJBHome);
                }
        }
        catch (ClassCastException e)
        {
            throw new HomeFactoryException(e);
        }
        catch (NamingException e)
        {
            throw new HomeFactoryException(e);
        }


            return anEJBHome;

    }


}
```

Business Delegate

Included here is an implementation of a business delegate made to wrap a stateful session bean. These business delegates are slightly more complex than the ones that wrap stateless session beans, as these guys need to use a handle for an EJBObject in order to survive serialization by a servlet engine that may passivate its HTTPSession cache, or perhaps attempt to serialize copies of its HTTPSession to support session replication across a cluster.

The changed/extra code (over the stateless delegate example in Chapter 8) is highlighted in **bold**. The only major change in the SFSB version of the Business Delegate is the use of a getEJB() method before every invocation of a business method on an EJB. This is done to ensure that the EJBObject still exists (was not lost in serialization), in order to recreate it from the handle in case of serialization. Also, clients must remember to call *remove* on the delegate when they are done with it, so that the SFSB can be removed.

```
public class ForumServicesDelegate implements Serializable
{

    private transient ForumServices sb;
    private Handle remoteHandle;

    public ForumServicesDelegate() throws DelegateException
    {
        try
        {
            ForumServicesHome home = (ForumServicesHome)
                EJBHomeFactory.getFactory().lookUpHome
                            (ForumServicesHome.class);
```

```
        this.sb = home.create();

        //store a handle incase we get serialized
        this.remoteHandle = sb.getHandle();

    }
    catch(Exception e)
    {
        throw new DelegateException();
    }
}


//business method
public long addForum(long categoryPK, String forumTitle,
                    String summary)
    throws NoSuchCategoryException,DelegateException
{

    try
    {
        return getEJB().sb.addForum
                    (categoryPK, forumTitle, summary);
    }
    catch(CreateException e)
    {
        throw new DelegateException();
        //log errors, etc
    } catch(RemoteException e)
    {
        throw new DelegateException();
        //log errors, etc
    }
}

private ForumServices getEJB() throws DelegateException
{
    //test if the delegate was serialized
    try
    {
        if (sb == null)
        {
            //if so, recreate session bean reference
            sb = (ForumServices) PortableRemoteObject.narrow
            (remoteHandle.getEJBObject(),ForumServices.class);
        }
    }
    catch (ClassCastException e)
    {
        throw new DelegateException();
    }
```

```
         catch (RemoteException e)
         {
             throw new DelegateException();
         }
         return sb;
    }

    public void remove() throws DelegateException
    {
        //once the client is done with the
        //stateful delegate, allow client to call
        //remove, so we can tell the EJB server to
        //remove the SFSB
        try
        {
            getEJB().remove();
        }
        catch (RemoteException e)
        {
            throw new DelegateException();
        }
        catch (RemoveException e)
        {
            throw new DelegateException();
        }

    }

}
```

Sequence Blocks

Included is a complete implementation of the Sequence Block pattern, based on a submission by Jonathan Weedon from Borland Corporation. The Sequence entity bean exposes only local interfaces (it is only called by the Sequence Session Bean). The Sequence Session Bean exposes both local and remote interfaces (should be called by local interfaces in production; remote is provided for testing purposes). Ejb-jar.xml descriptors are also included.

Sequence Entity Bean Local Interface

```
package examples.sequencegenerator;
public interface Sequence extends javax.ejb.EJBLocalObject
{
  public int getNextKeyAfterIncrementingBy(int blockSize);
}
```

Sequence Entity Bean Local Home Interface

```
package examples.sequencegenerator;

public interface SequenceLocalHome extends javax.ejb.EJBLocalHome
{
  Sequence create(String name) throws  javax.ejb.CreateException;
  Sequence findByPrimaryKey(String name) throws
javax.ejb.FinderException;
}
```

Sequence Entity Bean Code

```
package examples.sequencegenerator;
import javax.ejb.*;

abstract public class SequenceBean implements EntityBean
{

    public int getNextKeyAfterIncrementingBy(int blockSize)
    {
        this.setIndex(this.getIndex()+ blockSize);
        return this.getIndex();
    }

    public String ejbCreate(String name)
    {
        this.setName(name);
        this.setIndex(0);
        return name;
    }


    abstract public int getIndex();
    abstract public String getName();
    abstract public void setIndex(int newIndex);
    abstract public void setName(java.lang.String newName);

    public void ejbActivate() {}
    public void ejbLoad() {}
    public void ejbPassivate() {}
    public void ejbPostCreate(String name) {}
    public void ejbRemove() {}
    public void ejbStore() {}

    public void setEntityContext(EntityContext unused) {}
    public void unsetEntityContext() {}


}
```

Sequence Session Remote Interface

```
package examples.sequencegenerator;
import java.rmi.*;

public interface SequenceSession extends javax.ejb.EJBObject {
  public int getNextNumberInSequence(String name) throws
RemoteException;
}
```

Sequence Session Home Interface

```
package examples.sequencegenerator;
import javax.ejb.*;
import java.rmi.*;
public interface SequenceSessionHome extends javax.ejb.EJBHome {
  SequenceSession create() throws CreateException, RemoteException;
}
```

Sequence Session Local Interface

```
package examples.sequencegenerator;

public interface SequenceSessionLocal extends javax.ejb.EJBLocalObject {
  public int getNextNumberInSequence(String name);
}
```

Sequence Session Local Home Interface

```
package examples.sequencegenerator;
import javax.ejb.*;
import javax.naming.*;

public interface SequenceSessionLocalHome extends javax.ejb.EJBLocalHome
{
  SequenceSessionLocal create() throws CreateException;
}
```

Sequence Session Bean Implementation

```
package examples.sequencegenerator;
import javax.ejb.*;
import javax.naming.*;

public class SequenceSessionBean implements   javax.ejb.SessionBean {
```

```java
    private class Entry {
      Sequence sequence;
      int last;
    };

    private java.util.Hashtable _entries = new java.util.Hashtable();
    private int _blockSize;
    private int _retryCount;
    private SequenceLocalHome _sequenceHome;

public int getNextNumberInSequence(String name)
{

    try
    {
        Entry entry = (Entry) _entries.get(name);

        if (entry == null)
        {
            // add an entry to the sequence table
            entry = new Entry();
            try
            {
                entry.sequence = _sequenceHome.findByPrimaryKey(name);
            }
            catch (javax.ejb.FinderException e)
            {
                // if we couldn't find it, then create it...
                entry.sequence = _sequenceHome.create(name);
            }
            _entries.put(name, entry);
        }
        if (entry.last % _blockSize == 0)
        {
            for (int retry = 0; true; retry++)
            {
                try
                {
                    entry.last =
                entry.sequence.getNextKeyAfterIncrementingBy(_blockSize);
                    break;
                }
                catch (javax.ejb.TransactionRolledbackLocalException e)
                {
                    if (retry < _retryCount)
                    {
                        // we hit a concurrency exception, so
                        //try again...
                        continue;
                    }
```

```
            else
            {
                // we tried too many times, so fail...
                throw new javax.ejb.EJBException(e);
            }
        }
    }
}

        return entry.last++;
    }
    catch (javax.ejb.CreateException e)
    {
        throw new javax.ejb.EJBException(e);
    }
}
}
 public void setSessionContext( javax.ejb.SessionContext sessionContext)
{
    try {
      Context namingContext = new InitialContext();
      _blockSize = ((Integer)namingContext.lookup
                  ("java:comp/env/blockSize")).intValue();
      _retryCount = ((Integer) namingContext.lookup
                  ("java:comp/env/retryCount")).intValue();

      _sequenceHome = (SequenceLocalHome) namingContext.lookup
                  ("SequenceLocalHome");
    }
    catch(NamingException e) {
      throw new EJBException(e);
    }
  }

  public void ejbActivate() {}
  public void ejbCreate() {}
  public void ejbPassivate() {}
  public void ejbRemove() {}


}
```

Sequence Session and Entity EJB-JAR.xml

```
<?xml version="1.0"?>
<!DOCTYPE ejb-jar PUBLIC '-//Sun Microsystems,
 Inc.//DTD Enterprise JavaBeans 2.0//EN'
'http://java.sun.com/dtd/ejb-jar_2_0.dtd'>

<ejb-jar>
```

```xml
<enterprise-beans>
<entity>
     <ejb-name>Sequence</ejb-name>
     <local-home>examples.sequencegenerator.SequenceLocalHome</local-
home>
     <local>examples.sequencegenerator.Sequence</local>
     <ejb-class>examples.sequencegenerator.SequenceBean</ejb-class>
     <persistence-type>Container</persistence-type>
     <prim-key-class>java.lang.String</prim-key-class>
     <reentrant>False</reentrant>
     <cmp-version>2.x</cmp-version>
     <abstract-schema-name>SequenceBean</abstract-schema-name>
     <cmp-field>
          <field-name>index</field-name>
     </cmp-field>
     <cmp-field>
          <field-name>name</field-name>
     </cmp-field>
     <primkey-field>name</primkey-field>
     <env-entry>
          <env-entry-name>datasourceName</env-entry-name>
          <env-entry-type>java.lang.String</env-entry-type>
          <env-entry-value>bookPool</env-entry-value>
     </env-entry>
     <resource-ref>
     <res-ref-name>jdbc/bookPool</res-ref-name>
          <res-type>javax.sql.DataSource</res-type>
          <res-auth>Container</res-auth>
     </resource-ref>
</entity>

<session>
     <ejb-name>SequenceSession</ejb-name>
     <home>examples.sequencegenerator.SequenceSessionHome</home>
     <remote>examples.sequencegenerator.SequenceSession</remote>
     <local-
home>examples.sequencegenerator.SequenceSessionLocalHome</local-home>
     <local>examples.sequencegenerator.SequenceSessionLocal</local>
     <ejb-class>examples.sequencegenerator.SequenceSessionBean</ejb-
class>
     <session-type>Stateless</session-type>
     <transaction-type>Container</transaction-type>
     <env-entry>
          <description />
          <env-entry-name>retryCount</env-entry-name>
          <env-entry-type>java.lang.Integer</env-entry-type>
          <env-entry-value>5</env-entry-value>
     </env-entry>
     <env-entry>
          <description />
          <env-entry-name>blockSize</env-entry-name>
```

```
        <env-entry-type>java.lang.Integer</env-entry-type>
        <env-entry-value>10</env-entry-value>
    </env-entry>
</session>
</enterprise-beans>

<assembly-descriptor>
<container-transaction>
    <method>
        <ejb-name>Sequence</ejb-name>
        <method-name>getNextKeyAfterIncrementingBy</method-name>
    </method>
    <trans-attribute>RequiresNew</trans-attribute>
</container-transaction>
<container-transaction>
    <method>
        <ejb-name>SequenceSession</ejb-name>
        <method-name>*</method-name>
    </method>
    <trans-attribute>Required</trans-attribute>
</container-transaction>
</assembly-descriptor>
</ejb-jar>
```

Stored Procedures for Auto-Generated Keys

Here we have an example of a stored procedure that will insert a row into the database and return the auto-generated primary key field within the same database call. The primary key is needed to return from *ejbCreate,* as mandated by the spec. The stored procedure uses an Oracle *sequence* named accountID to generate primary keys.

InsertAccount Stored Procedure for Oracle

```
create or replace procedure insertAccount
    (owner IN varchar,
     bal IN integer,
     newid OUT integer)
AS
BEGIN
    insert into accounts (id, ownername, balance)
                 values (accountID.nextval, owner, bal)
                 returning id into newid;

END;
```

References

Web Sites

MartinFowler.com. "Information Systems Architecture." Available at: www.
martinfowler.com/j2ee/blueprints/index.html.
Sun Microsystems. "J2EEBlueprints." Available at: http://java.sun.com/j2ee/
blueprints/index.html.
TheServerSide.com. "Patterns Repository." Available at: www.theserverside.com/
patterns.

Books and Articles

Alexander, Christopher, Sara Ishikawa, and Murray Silverstein. 1977. *A Pattern
Language: Towns, Buildings, Construction*. Oxford University Press.
Alur, D., J. Crupi, and D. Malks. 2001. *Core J2EE Patterns*. Prentice-Hall.
Brown, K. January 26, 2000. "Limit Parameters for EJB Creates." *Portland Pattern
Repository*. Available at: www.c2.com/cgi/wiki?LimitParametersForEjbCreates.
Brown, K. May 5, 2001. "What's a Controller Anyway?" *Portland Pattern Repository*.
Available at: www.c2.com/cgi/wiki?WhatsaControllerAnyway.
Brown, K., and B. Whitenack. 1995. "Crossing Chasms: A Pattern Language for
Object-RDBMS Integration." *Pattern Languages of Program Design 2*, Vlissedes,
Coplien, and Kerth, eds. Addison-Wesley.

Carey, J., B. Carlson, and T. Graser. 2000. *San Francisco Design Patterns*. Addison-Wesley.

Coad, P. 1990. *Object-Oriented Analysis*. Yourdon Press.

Cockburn, A. 1995. "Prioritizing Forces in Software Design." *Pattern Languages of Program Design 2*, Vlissedes, Coplien, and Kerth, eds. Addison-Wesley.

Cockburn, A. 2000. *Writing Effective Use Cases*. Addison-Wesley.

"Exception Patterns." *Portland Pattern Repository*. August 19, 2001. (Multiple contributors). Available at: www.c2.com/cgi/wiki?ExceptionPatterns.

Fowler, M. 1999. *Refactoring: Improving the Design of Existing Code*. Addison-Wesley.

Fowler, M., and R. Mee. 2001. *2001 J2EE Summit*. Crested Butte, CO.

Fowler, M., with K. Scott. 1997. *UML Distilled*. Addison-Wesley.

Gamma, E., R. Helm, R. Johnson, and J. Vlissides. 1995. *Design Patterns: Elements of Reusable Object-Oriented Software*. Addison-Wesley.

Gamma, E., et al. 1994. *Design Patterns: Elements of Reusable Object-Oriented Software*. Addison-Wesley.

Hunt, A., and D. Thomas. 1999. *The Pragmatic Programmer*. Addison-Wesley.

Jeffries, R., et al. 2000. *Extreme Programming Installed*. Addison-Wesley.

Johnston, J. 2000. *The Complete Idiot's Guide to Psychology*. Alpha Books.

Kassem, N. 2000. *Designing Enterprise Applications with the Java 2 Platform, Enterprise Edition*. Addison-Wesley.

Maister, D. 1997. *True Professionalism*. Touchstone.

Matena, V., and B. Stearns. 2001. *Applying Enterprise Java Beans*. Addison-Wesley.

Roman, E. 2002. *Mastering EJB*. John Wiley & Sons.

Smith, D. August 8, 2001. "Technical Debt." *Portland Pattern Repository*. Available at: www.c2.com/cgi/wiki?TechnicalDebt.

Stafford, Randy. September 2, 2001. "Object Relational Impedance Mismatch." *Portland Pattern Repository*. Available at: www.c2.com/cgi/wiki?ObjectRelationalImpedanceMismatch.

Index